Financial Markets, Money and the
Real World

To Louise

*In grateful appreciation of a wonderfully productive relationship
for more than a half-century*

Financial Markets, Money and the Real World

Paul Davidson

Editor of the Journal of Post Keynesian Economics and Professor Emeritus at the University of Tennessee, USA

Edward Elgar
Cheltenham, UK • Northampton, MA, USA

Published by
Edward Elgar Publishing Limited
Glensanda House
Montpellier Parade
Cheltenham
Glos GL50 1UA
UK

Edward Elgar Publishing, Inc.
136 West Street
Suite 202
Northampton
Massachusetts 01060
USA

A catalogue record for this book
is available from the British Library

Library of Congress Cataloguing in Publication Data
Davidson, Paul, 1930–
    Financial markets, money, and the real world / Paul Davidson.
      p. cm.
    Includes index.
      1. Capital market. 2. International finance. 3. Liquidity (Economist).
4. Money. I. Title
HG4523.D38 2002
332–dc21   2002019549

ISBN 1 84064 740 X

Printed and bound in Great Britain by Biddles Ltd, *www.biddles.co.uk*

Contents

v

Contents

Figures and tables

FIGURES

TABLES

1. Keynes, you should be alive today!

> Keynes's fundamental insight was that we do not know – cannot calculate – what
> the future will bring. In such a world, money offers psychological security
> against uncertainty. When savers become pessimistic about future prospects,
> they can decide to hoard their savings [in liquid assets] rather than invest them
> in business. Thus there is no guarantee that all income earned will be spent. This
> amounts to saying that there is no natural tendency for all available resources to
> be employed (Lord Skidelsky[1])

The Englishman, John Maynard Keynes, was unquestionably the most
important economist of the twentieth century. The policies he proposed to
fight the Great Depression as well as those he worked on to develop a new
postwar international monetary system helped save the entrepreneurial
directed, market-oriented economies of the world from collapse.

Keynes's biographer, Lord Skidelsky suggests that the task Keynes 'set
for himself was to reconstruct the capitalist social order on the basis of
improved technical management'.[2] As a strong proponent of an improved
capitalist system, Keynes did not criticize the existing system 'on the
grounds that it unfairly or unjustly distributed life-chances; rather, that the
laissez-faire system did not protect economic and social "norms". Injustice
became a matter of uncertainty, justice a matter of contractual pre-
dictability'. (We shall see that the concepts of uncertainty, contracts and
money were at the heart of Keynes's revolutionary vision of the economy
in which we live.)

1.1 POSTWAR ECONOMIC PERFORMANCE

For almost a quarter of a century after the Second World War, governments actively pursued the types of economic policies that Keynes had
advocated in the 1930s and 1940s. The result was that per capita economic
growth in the capitalist world proceeded at a rate that has never been
reached in the past or matched since (see Table 1.1). Adelman[3] has characterized this postwar 'Keynesian' era of unsurpassed economic global prosperity as a 'Golden Age of Economic Development . . . an era of
unprecedented sustained economic growth in both developed and developing countries'. The *average* annual per capita economic growth rate of

OECD (Organization for Economic Cooperation and Development) nations from 1950 to 1973 was 'almost precisely double the previous *peak* growth rate of the industrial revolution period. Productivity growth in OECD countries was more than triple (3.75 times) that of the industrial revolution era'.[4]

Table 1.1   Real GDP (annualized growth rate)

Years	Real GDP per capita %		
	World	OECD Nations	Developing nations*
1700–1820	na	0.2	na
1820–1913	na	1.2	na
1919–1940	na	1.9	na
1950–1973	na	4.9	3.3
1973–1981	na	1.3	na
1981–1990	1.2	2.2	1.2
1991–1993	−0.4	0.6	2.6
1993–2002*	2.7	2.0	3.0

Years	Total real GDP %		
	World	Industrial nations	Developing nations**
1950–1973	na	5.9	5.5
1966–1973	5.1	4.8	6.9
1974–1980	3.4	2.9	5.0
1981–1990	2.8	2.9	2.4
1991–1997	2.2	1.9	5.0
1993–2002*	3.5	2.7	5.1

Notes:
 * Includes estimates for 2001 and 2002 assuming no recession in these years.
** Excluding Eastern and Central Europe and Former Soviet Union.

Sources: I. Adelman, 'Long Term Economic Development', Working Paper No. 589, California Agricultural Experiment Station, Berkeley, CA, March 1991; International Monetary Fund, *World Economic Outlook*, IMF, Washington, DC, 1999, 2001.

The resulting prosperity of the industrialized world was transmitted to the less-developed nations through world trade, aid and direct foreign investment. As Table 1.1 indicates, from 1950 to 1973, average per capita economic growth for all less-developed countries (LDCs) was 3.3 per cent, almost triple the average growth rate experienced by the industrializing nations during the industrial revolution. Aggregate economic growth of the LDCs increased at almost the same rate as that of the developed nations, 5.5 per cent and 5.9 per cent, respectively. The higher population growth of the LDCs caused the lower per capita income growth.

By 1973, however, Keynes's analytical vision of how to improve the operation of a market-oriented, entrepreneurial system had been lost by politicians, their economic advisors and most academic economists. As a result, Keynes's policy prescriptions fell from grace. As Table 1.1 demonstrates, since 1973, the economic performance of capitalist economies is much more dismal than it was during the quarter century following the Second World War. The annual growth rate in investment in plant and equipment in OECD nations fell from 6 per cent (before 1973) to less than 3 per cent (since 1973). Less investment growth means a slower economic growth rate in OECD nations (from 5.9 per cent to 2.7 per cent) while labor productivity growth declined even more dramatically (from 4.6 per cent to 1.6 per cent).

Keynes, once offered a toast 'to economists who are the trustees, not of civilization, but the possibilities of civilization'.[5] With the building of proper economic institutions to guide the operations of a market-oriented economic system, nations could foster full employment and rapid economic growth that would improve, on average, the economic well-being of all members of society. With persistent full employment and rapid economic growth the pressure of economic problems on society could easily disappear within a few generations. Then society could devote more of its efforts into producing a more civilized society where we shall 'value ends above means and prefer the good to the useful. We shall honour those who can teach us how to pluck the hour and the day virtuously and well'.[6]

In the twenty-first century, most nations (even those who still proclaim themselves communist) show a preference for productive economic activities to be directed by entrepreneurs – and not socialist technocrats. It is therefore worth asking whether the vision of the economy propagated by today's mainstream economists has helped (or hindered) the reconstruction of the capitalist system that promotes the possibilities for civilization. For as Keynes correctly noted:

> The ideas of economists and political philosophers, both when they are right and when they are wrong, are more powerful than is commonly understood. Indeed the world is ruled by little else. Practical men, who believe themselves quite exempt from intellectual influences, are usually the slaves of some . . . economist . . . [Ultimately] it is ideas . . . which are dangerous for good or evil.[7]

This volume is dedicated to resurrecting Keynes's analytical vision as an aid for developing twenty-first century policies that will reinstate a golden age of rapid economic growth that is the prerequisite for creating a civilized society for our global community.

1.2   KEYNES'S REVOLUTION

In 1936, Keynes published his *General Theory of Employment, Interest and Money*. This 'general theory' was advanced to promote civilized solutions to the 'outstanding faults of the economic society in which we live . . . its failure to provide full employment and its arbitrary and inequitable distribution of wealth and incomes'.[8]

As several scholars have noted,[9] the first three words of the title of Keynes's book mimics those of Albert Einstein's famous contribution to physics, *The General Theory of Relativity*. This is not just a coincidence, for just as Einstein's 'General Theory' overthrew the dominance of classical Newtonian theory and led physicists to a revolutionary way of thinking about the physical world, so Keynes believed his 'General Theory' would depose classical economic theory from the minds of economists and revolutionize the way we think about our economic world.

On New Year's Day in 1935, Keynes wrote a letter to George Bernard Shaw. In this letter Keynes stated:

> To understand my new state of mind, however, you have to know that I believe myself to be writing a book on economic theory which will largely revolutionize not I suppose at once but in the course of the next ten years the way the world thinks about economic problems. When my new theory has been duly assimilated and mixed with politics and feelings and passions, I cannot predict what the final upshot will be in its effect on actions and affairs, but there will be a great change and in particular the Ricardian Foundations of Marxism will be knocked away.
>
> I can't expect you or anyone else to believe this at the present stage, but for myself I don't merely hope what I say. In my own mind I am quite sure.[10]

Classical economic theory had dominated academic discussions for more than a century before Keynes developed his general theory to explain why the classical analysis was not applicable to the economic problems of a money-using, market-oriented entrepreneurial economy. Classical theory subverts the possibilities of developing a civilized society in a capitalist economic system because it presumes that the problems of dealing with uncertainty and the resulting demand for liquidity are irrelevant for determining unemployment, production and the price level. Yet when households and entrepreneurs become pessimistic regarding the uncertain economic future in the world in which we live, their resulting liquidity demands can significantly disrupt the stability of a nation's economy.

During the Second World War, Keynes applied his revolutionary analysis to propose the creation of new international financial institutions and an innovative international payments system for the postwar world. Keynes argued that a global economic system with free international trade and unfettered international financial markets was incompatible with the existence of global full employment and global prosperity. The need for international institutions to provide technical management of the global economy was paramount. Keynes's proposals for an international clearing union and an international money were not acceptable to the US delegation at the 1944 Bretton Woods conference. Nevertheless most of his important proposals, in a modified form, initially were incorporated in such international institutions as the International Monetary Fund (IMF), the World Bank, and the US policy known as the Marshall Plan. As a result, for more than a quarter century after Keynes's death in 1946, the non-Communist world of industrial nations and LDCs developed into a more productive and civilized society than ever before existed in the history of mankind. With the resurrection of classical economic theory in academia in the 1950s and 1960s, university-trained economic policy advisors began providing classical advice to government decision makers facing important economic problems. The result was the dismantling of Keynes's innovative proposals and a regression toward the barbaric policies of the classical system where unemployment is the main weapon against inflation and available resources are rarely used to their full potential.

Keynes's vision produced innovative thinking in policy discussions. Keynes's revolutionary theoretical framework, however, was not understood by most academic economists at America's prestigious universities, not even by many who identified themselves as 'Keynesians'. Since these academic economists failed to adopt the logically consistent, innovative theoretical analysis laid down by Keynes, what developed in mainstream professional writings and popular economics textbooks after the Second World War was a modernized version of the pre-Keynesian classical system. Prominent academic economists at the Massachusetts Institute of Technology (MIT), Harvard and Yale universities attempted to graft Keynes's macro-policy suggestions for solving the unemployment problem onto the axiomatic foundations of classical microeconomic theory. The resulting Neoclassical Synthesis Keynesianism (or Old Keynesianism) as espoused by Nobel Laureates Paul Samuelson, Robert Solow and James Tobin conquered mainstream academic discussions as completely as the Holy Inquisition conquered Spain (to paraphrase one of Keynes's more colorful expressions). The theoretical ideas generated by these self-proclaimed Neoclassical Synthesis Keynesians, however, are based on classical axioms that are logically incompatible with the portion of Keynes's 'general theory' that is applicable to our entrepreneurial economy.

1.3   THE ACADEMIC RESURRECTION OF CLASSICAL ECONOMICS

The resulting logical inconsistencies between these Old Keynesians's classical microfoundations and their Neoclassical Synthesis Keynesian macropolicies provided an opportunity for logically consistent classical theorists to launch a successful theoretical counter revolution against all 'Keynesians'. The result was the 1960s revivification of the classical theory (and the promotion of classical policies) that began to dominate academic discourse. By the mid-1970s, many economic textbooks declared Keynes's theoretical revolution dead. The winners of the academic debate were the old classical economists, especially the 'Monetarists', led by Milton Friedman.

By the 1980s, however, the New Classical economists replaced the Monetarists as king of the academic hill. The New Classical economists, like the Monetarists before them, denied the validity and relevance of Keynes's general theory and its policy implications. Old and New Classical economists insist that governmental policies cannot affect the long-run 'natural' rate of unemployment that is assumed to be predetermined and preprogrammed by Mother Nature into the economic system.

Also in the 1980s, a younger generation of 'New Keynesians' arose to challenge the New Classical theorists. Unfortunately, these New Keynesians accepted the basic microfoundation logic of the classical model, while their common sense suggested that the capitalist system did not work as efficiently as the classical model suggests. Accordingly, these New Keynesians invented all sorts of *ad hoc* constraints on the efficient functioning of the classical model to show that unemployment is a temporary problem due to rigidities in the price system that will disappear in the long run. Since the New Keynesians are too impatient to let the market restore full employment in the long run, they advocate policies to speed up the hypothesized market actions to achieve the long-run path. But these New Keynesians never deal with the fundamental problems of uncertainty, contracts, liquidity and money that Keynes identified as the source of the major faults of the real economy in which we live.

The models of the Old Classical Monetarists, the New Classical economists, and even the New Keynesians provided the rationale and fig-leaf political cover for many of the uncivilized economic policies that were adopted by government policy makers and central bankers in the last quarter of the twentieth century. The result has been a significant decline in the rate of economic growth and persistent high rates of unemployment around the globe. And for some groups in the industrial nations as well as some of the nations struggling to become more economically developed there has been a regression in terms of economic progress compared to the post-Second World War golden age of economic development.

1.4 DIFFERING VIEWS ON THE ROLE OF FINANCIAL MARKETS

One of the main theoretical differences between the classical vision of how an economy operates and Keynes's general theory involves the role of financial markets and their impact on the 'real economy' of production and employment opportunities. For the classical scheme, free financial markets are the efficient allocator of capital goods that promotes the economic progress of society. In Keynes's scheme of things, real world financial markets provide liquidity and not necessarily efficiency. In good times the liquidity of financial markets encourages capital accumulation and rapid economic growth. In bad times, however, this appearance of liquidity in financial markets is capable of producing persistent high rates of unemployment, excess idle capacity, slow economic growth and even depression. When fears of an uncertain future rise, 'Money, or what Keynes called liquidity, emerges, above all, as a strategy for calming the nerves'[11] but at what can be a terrible cost to the real economy.

In stark contrast to the emphasis that Keynes places on money and liquidity for causing persistent unemployment, the fundamental classical presupposition that dominates today's academic economics profession thought is that money, the demand for liquidity and financial market activity *cannot* affect the secular, long-run equilibrium real growth path of the economy and the 'natural rate of unemployment'. In other words, monetary events have no impact on the long-run trend of the real economy; the real and monetary sectors are independent of each other.

This fundamental classical belief in the independence of the real economy from monetary and financial influences is labeled the *neutral money axiom*.[12] By imposing this neutral money axiom as a fundamental building block of 'scientific economics', today's orthodox economists are assuming that in the long run there is a natural rate of unemployment and real future production flow that are already predetermined and cannot be improved by any deliberate actions of governments. Since all mainstream economists accept the neutrality of money as a fundamental article of faith, it is no wonder that logically consistent 'talking heads' economists proclaim that fiscal policies aimed at increasing demand can only make things worse in the long run. What they do not tell the public is that their promotion of a *laissez-faire* government fiscal and regulatory orientation ✓ as a socially desirable policy is an assumption rather than a conclusion of their 'scientific' studies of the economic system in which we live.

Given their axiomatic foundation, classical theory can attribute systemic short-run unemployment problems only to the existence of temporary monopolies producing rigid prices and/or irrational government interference in the market. Consequently, the only socially desirable goal of government policy is to assure completely 'liberalized' (that is, unfettered) free financial, product and labor markets so that the preordained long-run outcome occurs closer in time to the present.

The classical neutral money axiom is similar in its policy implication to the assumption of an unchanging gravitational constant in classical Newtonian physics. In the latter, from the moment of the creation of our solar system until its end in the far distant future, the immutable law of gravity determines the path of the planets around the sun. Newton's heavenly clockwork mechanism implies that any attempt by government to repeal the law of gravity in order to affect the path of the planets is bound to fail. By analogy, economists who build their economic models of the world on the neutral money axiom are logically constrained to argue that government interference in the marketplace to change the path of the economic system is useless – or worse.

In a moment of surprising candor, Professor Oliver Blanchard, a New Keynesian member of the economics faculty of the Massachusetts Institute of Technology and the prestigious National Bureau of Economic Research, has characterized all the macroeconomic models widely used by mainstream economists as follows: 'All the models we have seen impose the neutrality of money as a maintained assumption. This is very much a matter of faith, based on theoretical considerations rather than on empirical evidence'.[13] In other words, there is no empirical evidence underlying the fundamental classical presumption of neutral money. Rather this belief in neutral money is merely the dogma of mainstream economists that permits them to claim that only the absence of governmental interference to regulate markets can permit the economy to achieve its goal of efficiency in our time. Mainstream economists are, in other words, assuming what they pretend to be proving.

The first and second world wars, the stock market crash of 1929 and the ensuing Great Depression had a strong influence on Keynes and others who questioned the reasonableness of applying the neutral money axiom to the world of experience while trying to explain the persistence of large-scale unemployment in the capitalist system. In developing the applicability of his general theory to a market-oriented economy, Keynes specifically argued that the neutral money axiom must be rejected in both the short run and the long run.[14] It was the rejection of this and two other restrictive and unrealistic classical axioms that permitted Keynes to develop his analytical vision – a vision that generated successful postwar policy solutions to the unemployment problem and the international monetary payments problems. The result was 'the golden age of economic development' that ended in 1973 with the abandonment of Keynes's policies by governments of the free world.

The financial market crises of the 1990s, cumulating in the 1997 East Asian currency crisis and the Russian debt default of 1998, induced a seizing up of global financial markets in the fall of 1998 that almost precipitated a global market crash (while causing great economic suffering in the real economy of many nations). The global economy still struggles with the aftermath of these crises and the possibility that volatile financial market episodes in the future will have real impacts of whole industries and national economic systems. It is time once again to question the use of the neutral money presumption and other restrictive classical axioms to develop economic models that rationalize economic policies such as those promoting liberalization of financial and labor markets, dismantling the social safety nets for workers and so on and the resulting movement toward a complete *laissez-faire* capitalist system.

1.5   FIVE KEY POINTS

There are five key points underlying Keynes's analytical vision of the pros and cons of the entrepreneurial economic system in which we actually live. Comprehending the validity of these points can help governments design institutions and policies that will promote economic prosperity and a global civilized society for all in the twenty-first century.

These five points are:

1. The outstanding faults of an entrepreneurial society are its failure to provide sustained full employment and its arbitrary and inequitable distribution of income and wealth.
2. The failure to provide sustainable full employment is *not* due to supply-side market imperfections such as monopolies or rigid money (or real) wages. Hence policies designed (a) to increase wage-price and exchange rate flexibility and (b) to liberalize financial markets will not solve *per se*, and may well exacerbate, the unemployment problem.[15]

3. Government's responsibility is to 'exercise a guiding influence' on private spending decisions to assure that there is never a persistent lack of effective demand for the products of industry. Government-operating budgets should be balanced. If private spending fails to produce full employment, then government should run a capital account deficit to employ resources to produce, with the cooperation of private initiative, additional productive facilities.[16]

4. Persistent unemployed workers and excessive idle capacity create an intolerable 'public scandal of wasted resources'.[17] The ultimate cause of such a scandal is nested in the human weakness of speculation and an obsession with liquidity. Consequently, a necessary condition for solving the unemployment problem involves (a) dampening destabilizing financial speculation by assuring orderly financial markets and (b) providing all the liquidity that entrepreneurs can use for 'bank credit is the pavement along which production travels, and the bankers if they knew their duty, would provide the transport facilities to just the extent that is required in order that the productive powers of the community can be employed to their full capacity'.[18]

5. Liquidity is a double-edged sword. The good cutting edge provides an orderly, well-organized market where financial assets can be readily resold for cash. Liquid financial markets encourage savers to provide funding to entrepreneurs for durable investments that savers would not be willing to furnish if their investment was illiquid. Liquid markets encourage financial asset holders to believe they have a fast exit strategy to liquidate their position the moment they are dissatisfied with the way matters are developing. Without liquidity, the risk of funding investments as a minority owner would be intolerable.

    The 'bad' edge of the sword appears when a strong bearish view develops in financial markets. The resulting demand for liquidity impedes the production of new investments even when real resources are idle and available to be employed. The basic message of Keynes's *General Theory* is that too great a demand for liquidity can prevent 'saved' (that is, unutilized or involuntarily unemployed) real resources from being employed to expand the economy's productive facilities.

This volume is dedicated to explaining these five points and indicating how once their applicability is understood, economists can help to promote the possibilities of a civilized society.

1.6   KEYNES, THE POET OF MONEY

Keynes's criticism of classical economic theory 'consisted not so much in finding logical flaws in its analysis, as in pointing out that its tacit assumptions are seldom or never satisfied, with the result that it cannot solve the economic problems of the actual world'.[19] The discussion in this volume is similarly oriented – not as an investigation of the intricate logical flaws in the structure of Old and New Classical, or Old and New Keynesian theories (though at times such flaws will be noted in passing).

Following Keynes, our analysis will be developed around some important characteristics of the economic system in which we live, namely:

1. The future outcomes of crucial economic decisions are uncertain in the sense that these outcomes cannot be reliably predicted on the basis of past or current market data. As Nobel Laureate John Hicks noted, for economic models to reflect the world in which we live they must incorporate the idea that decision makers 'know' that they do not know what will 'happen'.[20] Crucial economic decisions are made in the light of an unalterable past, while moving toward an uncertain, perfidious future.
2. Production takes time and therefore if long-duration productive processes are to be undertaken by entrepreneurs, they must make money contractual commitments in the present involving performance and payments at specified dates in the uncertain future,

In contrast to these fundamental characteristics of the economy in which we live, classical theory presumes:

1. Decision makers on average 'know', if not with perfect certainty at least in the sense of statistically significant (reliable) forecasts, all the possible future outcomes for all possible decisions that can be taken today. In other words, decision makers are presumed to have 'rational expectations' regarding all possible future outcomes and therefore cannot make persistent mistakes. If one assumes people can on average reliably predict the future, then it follows that bureaucrats in government, the IMF, or the World Bank, cannot make better decisions than individuals do in a liberalized market environment.
2. If any contracts are entered into at market prices other than those determined by the assumed to exist preprogrammed long-run real outcomes of the economic system, parties to such 'false trade' contracts can recontract their commitments *without a penalty* in order to reach the 'correct' equilibrium price. In other words, it is assumed that any errors made by people in free markets can be corrected by recontracting

without costs to themselves or to society. Classical theory implicitly assumes that it is always possible to costlessly correct any individual errors of foresight, thereby reinforcing the notion that there is no need for government to try to correct economic problems as they arise.

3.   When the economy is on its equilibrium growth path, decision makers are making choices that are completely consistent with the economy's long-run (presumed to exist) most efficient preprogrammed path.

It is only when we remove classical restrictive axioms underlying how 'rational' decision makers operate in a market-oriented, money-using, entrepreneurial economy that we can analyse the role of financial markets and money in the real world. For as Keynes wrote:

> *For the importance of money essentially flows from its being a link between the present and the future.* We can consider what distribution of resources between different uses will be consistent with equilibrium under the normal economic motives in which our views concerning the future are fixed and reliable in all respects; – with a further division, perhaps, between an economy which is changing and one subject to change, but where all things are foreseen from the beginning [that is, a world of rational expectations[21]]. Or we can pass from this simplified propaedeutic to the problems of the real world in which our previous expectations are liable to disappointment and expectations concerning the future affect what we do today. *It is when we have made this transition that the peculiar properties of money as a link between the present and the future must enter into our calculations* . . . we cannot even begin to discuss the effect of changing expectations on current activities except in monetary terms.[22]

Mainstream economists assume that booms and slumps are merely random shock-induced episodes superimposed on the preprogrammed long-run steady-state equilibrium growth path. Today's Post Keynesian[23] followers of Keynes, on the other hand, argue that the actual historical path of real world economies is not one which can be decomposed logically into independent secular trend and short-run trade-cycle aspects. Such a dichotomous construction is merely the handiwork of the classical economist's imagination, and if accompanied by empirical analysis of the historical record it is likely to be the artistic creation of the econometrician misapplying the basic tools of the statistician.

It is only in a world where the future is uncertain that the importance of money, contractual arrangements, and financial market activity becomes predominant in determining future real world outcomes. Lord Skidelsky, Keynes's biographer, insisted that the basic theme of Keynes's *General Theory* was that 'monetary forces were not temporary disturbances . . . they entered fundamentally into the determination of equilibrium states. All economic values were monetary values, which meant that the theory of money and the theory of production could not be separated'.[24] It was Keynes's liquidity preference theory of money and financial markets that was the revolutionary aspect of Keynes's analysis.

For putting forth this view of the revolutionary aspect of Keynes's *General Theory*, Skidelsky notes that 'Don Patinkin has reproached me [Skidelsky] with having adopted a "post-Keynesian" interpretation of Keynes's economics'.[25] And Skidelsky's response to Patinkin's reprimand is 'If I am guilty of this fallacy, I can say only that this is how Keynes's economics appeared to me'.

If the biographer of Keynes is to be believed, it is the Keynes-Post Keynesian view that the essential properties of money and the reasons why savers demand money (and other liquid assets) to hold as a store of wealth rather than using their savings to buy and hold durable real capital goods produced by industry that is the foundation upon which the Keynes's principle of effective demand is based (this principle will be explained in the next chapter). As Skidelsky pointed out:

> Keynes is the poet of money. The struggle between consumption and . . . investment . . . is fought with the weapons of goods and money, and it is money, ultimately – in chapters 15 and 17 [of *The General Theory*] – which controls the outcome . . . [money] is first and foremost a store of value, an alternative to consumption and investment, a 'subtle device' through which the fear of the future takes its revenge on the hopes of the present.[26]

1.7   A BRIEF OUTLINE OF THIS MONOGRAPH

To understand this 'poet of money' argument we shall have to first develop the analytical tools and concepts that were the basis of Keynes's general theory and then explain their relevance for entrepreneurial hiring and production decisions in a money-using, market-oriented, contractual economy.

Chapter 2 develops the analytical concepts that are the basis for Keynes's poetry of money. As such, the chapter is full of technical apparatus and professional jargon. It will be of most interest to professional economists but it may put off the more general reader. I therefore suggest that the general reader, who is not interested in the theoretical apparatus underlying the general theory will lose little by omitting initially Sections 2.3–2.5 and Appendix 2A2 of this chapter.

Chapter 3 discusses how the various schools of economic thought have attempted to explain economic reality where the economic future cannot be reliably predicted while the success or failure of today's crucial economic decisions depends on outcomes that will only be known when the future becomes the immediate past. Three restrictive classical axioms that Keynes argued are inapplicable to a market economy are discussed and the implications that this overthrowing of classical axioms has for a money-using economy.

Chapter 4 draws a distinction between the concept of investment as the purchasing of newly produced capital goods and investment as the purchase of financial assets on an organized market. Chapters 5 and 6 then delve into the question of why people want to be liquid and how that affects the bull and bear behavior in financial markets. The role of the banks and nonbank financial intermediaries in promoting investment and providing liquid assets for savers is discussed. Chapter 7 explains how savers' decisions regarding what liquid financial assets to use as a store of value can create instability in economic growth rates even when planned savings exactly equals planned investment.

The discussion in these early chapters is restricted to what economists call a 'closed economy', that is, an economic system where there is no trade with foreigners and the same currency is used to denominate all contractual transactions. Chapter 8 introduces into the analysis the complications of an 'open economy' with foreign trade, and international contracts and payments made with different currencies. Chapter 9 discusses how imbalances between the value of exports and the value of imports affect payments between nations and impacts the real economic growth that any one nation can maintain in a global economic system.

Chapter 10 discusses the problem of liquidity in an international setting where the exchange rates between different currencies can be either fixed or variable. Chapter 11 answers the question as to why, if international financial markets are as efficient as mainstream economists claim, there has been so much volatility in these markets in the last decades of the twentieth century. Chapter 12 examines the flaw in the Tobin tax proposal that has been presented as the policy for reducing volatility in both domestic and international financial markets. Chapter 13 raises the question as to whether the recurring international currency crises can be fixed by patching up the existing international payments system to prevent liquidity leaks (the plumbing solution) or whether an entire new international payments system (a new financial architecture) is required. The flaws in the publicly discussed plumbing prescriptions are explained. Chapter 14 provides a new financial architectural plan for international payments based on Keynes's 'poetry of money'. This proposal is then compared with two more classical architectural proposals that have been developed by John Williamson and Ronald McKinnon respectively. As this book manuscript was being completed, the terrorist attack of September 11, 2001 took place. The attack augmented the uncertainty and fear of the future already existing as the global economy teetered on a worldwide recession. Chapter 15 raises the question as to whether the global financial community will try to muddle through the resulting economic dislocations, or will nations recognize the positive role that governments can play in rebuilding a strong financial capitalist system.

NOTES

1. R. Skidelsky, *Keynes*, Oxford University Press, Oxford, 1995, p. 1.
2. Ibid., p. 21.
3. I. Adelman, 'Long Term Economic Development', Working Paper No. 589, California Agricultural Experiment Station, Berkeley, March 1991.
4. Ibid., p. 15.
5. R. Skidelsky, *John Maynard Keynes Fighting for Britain*, Macmillan, London, 2000, p. 168.
6. J.M. Keynes, 'Economic Possibilities for our Grandchildren', *Nation and Atheneum*, October 1930, reprinted in *The Collected Writings of John Maynard Keynes*, vol. 9, edited by D. Moggridge, Macmillan, London, 1972, p. 331.
7. J.M. Keynes, *The General Theory of Employment, Interest and Money*, Harcourt, Brace, New York, 1936, pp. 383–4.
8. Ibid., p. 372.
9. R. Skidelsky, *John Maynard Keynes, The Economist As Savior, 1920–1937*, Macmillan, London, 1992, pp. 487–8, J.K. Galbraith, 'Keynes, Einstein and Scientific Revolution', in *Keynes, Money and the Open Economy*, edited by P. Arestis, Cheltenham: Edward Elgar, 1996, pp. 14–25.
10. *The Collected Writings*, vol. 13, 1973, pp. 492–3.
11. Skidelsky, 1995, p. 90.
12. An axiom is defined as a statement that needs no proof because it is accepted as a fundamental and universal truth.
13. O. Blanchard, 'Why does money affect output', in *Handbook of Monetary Economics*, vol. 2, edited by B.M. Friedman and F.H. Hahn, North-Holland, New York, 1990, p. 828.
14. *The Collected Writings*, vol. 13, pp. 408–11.
15. Keynes, *The General Theory*, Ch. 19.
16. Ibid., p. 378.
17. Ibid., p. 381.
18. J.M. Keynes, *A Treatise on Money*, vol. 2, Macmillan, London, 1930, p. 220.
19. Keynes, *The General Theory*, p. 378.
20. J.R. Hicks, *Economic Perspectives*, Oxford University Press, Oxford, 1977 p. vii.
21. One of the founding fathers of the rational expectations school, Sargent has noted that rational expectations 'imputes to the people inside the model much *more* knowledge about the system they are operating in than is available to the economist or econometrician who is using the model to try to understand their behavior . . . in particular . . . laws of motion that the agents in the model are assumed to know' (T.J. Sargent, *Bounded Rationality in Macroeconomics*, Clarendon Press, Oxford, 1993, p. 21). In other words, agents with rational expectations possess 'views concerning the future [that] are fixed and reliable in all respects'.
    Furthermore, in models where there is the possibility of 'regime changes', that is, where possible future changes can occur, then, according to Sargent, 'Under rational expectations . . . the agents in the model should have been given the opportunity to take this possibility into account . . . [the regime change] option should be described and the initial equilibrium recomputed under a set of beliefs for private agents about how likely it is that government will choose that option' (p. 27). In other words, regime

change–rational expectations models presume an economy which is subject to change, but where things (possible regime changes) are foreseen from the beginning.

22. Keynes, *The General Theory*, pp. 293–4, second emphasis added.
23. In discussing Keynes's legacy, Skidelsky notes that the 'Post Keynesian school has continued to emphasize Keynes's stress on the importance of time and uncertainty, the use of money as a store of value, and the "animal spirits" theory of investment'. (Skidelsky, 1995, p. 127).
24. Skidelsky, 1992, p. 442.
25. Ibid., p. 442. In conversation with me, Skidelsky indicated that Patinkin accused Skidelsky of 'swallowing the Post Keynesian argument hook, line and sinker'.
26. Ibid., p. 543.

2. Keynes's principle of effective demand

Keynes's general theory demonstrated that even a competitive economy with instantaneously flexible wages and prices can suffer from persistent high levels of unemployment. To understand why this can occur, it is necessary to discuss the major aspects of Keynes's analytical framework. Some rather technical matters are discussed in Sections 2.3–2.5 and Appendix 2A2 of this chapter. Those general readers not interested in these analytical intricacies can skip these portions of the current chapter.

2.1 IS LACK OF COMPETITION THE FUNDAMENTAL CAUSE OF UNEMPLOYMENT? LIQUIDITY VERSUS SAY'S LAW

Long before Keynes developed the principle of effective demand in his general theory, classical economists 'explained' that unemployment was the result of short-run 'imperfections' or monopoly elements on the supply side of the market system. These imperfections took the form of rigidities in the money wage rate (and/or product prices) due to noncompetitive labor and product markets.[1] If the government did not interfere during this temporary period of unemployment, then the resulting weak markets would induce increased competition that would weed out these imperfections leaving a stronger, more powerful economy to carry on. In the long run, the causes of these imperfections would always be liquidated by market forces and full employment of resources would be restored. If, on the other hand, the government intervened in economic matters during these temporary periods of unemployment, then the economic situation could only deteriorate and the economy would take a longer time to right itself.

In true Social Darwinian fashion, classical theory asserted that episodes of unemployment and depression were merely symptoms of nature's law of the jungle where the market environment killed off the weak and inefficient and thereby assured the 'survival of the fittest'. When the economic system purged itself of all its inefficient elements, it would generate full employment and prosperity for all the efficient survivors.

A wonderful example of this classical prescription is revealed in the memoirs of Herbert Hoover, the President of the United States during the onset of the Great Depression. Whenever the President wanted to take positive action to end the depression, his Treasury Secretary, Andrew Mellon, always cautioned against government action and offered the same advice. 'Mr. Mellon had only one formula. Liquidate labor, liquidate stocks, liquidate the farmer, liquidate real estate. It will purge the rottenness out of the system . . . People will work harder, lead a more moral life'.[2]

Keynes, on the other hand, argued that the fundamental cause of unemployment was not any imperfections such as monopoly elements, or wage rigidities in labor markets. Rather the cause was nested in the peculiar properties possessed by money and liquid assets which, in bad times, encouraged people to try to liquidate assets. A lack of effective demand could not be automatically cured by weak market forces 'purging the rottenness [monopoly elements] out of the system'. Keynes noted that it is the non-neutrality of money (due to the attributes of any assets that possess liquidity) in both the short and long runs, and not to any degree of monopoly or other imperfection on the supply side of product or labor markets, that is the fundamental cause of persistent unemployment in the entrepreneurial economy in which we live.

In the very first paragraph of *The General Theory* Keynes challenged the classical explanation for unemployment and its proposed remedies when he wrote:

> I have called this book the *General Theory of Employment, Interest and Money*, placing the emphasis on the prefix *general*. The object of such a title is to contrast the character of my arguments and conclusions with those of the classical theory of the subject . . . which dominates economic thought, both practical and theoretical of the governing and academic classes of this generation, as it has for a hundred years past . . . I shall argue that the postulates of the classical theory are applicable to a special case only and not the general case . . . . The characteristics of the special case assumed by the classical theory happen not to be those of the economic society in which we actually live, with the result that its teaching is misleading and disastrous if we attempt to apply it to the facts of experience.[3]

The nineteenth-century economic proposition known as Say's Law is the foundation of the classical argument that a free market system inevitably generates full employment. Keynes was convinced that weaker classical economists did injury to their logical consistency when they espoused Say's Law of markets while simultaneously making less than perfectly flexible wages and prices *the* necessary condition for explaining unemployment.

Say's Law evolved from the writings of a French economist, Jean Baptiste Say, who in 1803 claimed that 'products always exchange for products'. In

1808, the English economist, James Mill, translated Say's French language dictum into 'supply creates its own demand'. Mill's phraseology has since been established in economics as Say's Law. It was this economic law that Keynes railed against in his *General Theory*.

2.2 SAY'S LAW

A simplified explanation of Say's Law is as follows: the sole rational explanation of why people work to produce, that is supply, things for the market, is to earn income. Engaging in income-earning productive activities is presumed to be disagreeable. The more hours one works the more disagreeable or unpleasant is the work, that is, in the jargon of economists, the marginal disutility of working increases with hours per week worked.

On the other hand, only the products of industry provide utility or happiness for people. The best things in life are not free. Accordingly, people are willing to work as long as the income they earn permits them to purchase goods and services that provide sufficient utility to compensate for the unpleasantness of engaging in their income-earning activity. If people are rational utility maximizers, then all income earned in the market by the selling of goods and services should be spent to buy (demand) things produced by others. The very act of production generates enough income, and therefore the demand for utility-generating goods and services, to purchase everything produced. Business people seeking profits will always be able to find sufficient demand for any output produced by the workers they hire. There is, in a Say's Law world, never any obstacle to full employment since everything produced by workers can always be bought by the income earned in the production process.

Under Say's Law, goods always exchange for goods. Money is only a 'veil' behind which the real economy operates unhampered by financial considerations. The notion that money is merely used as an intermediary in the exchange of goods for goods is encompassed, in the lexicon of economists, by the classical neutral money axiom. If money is neutral, then there is no inherent obstacle in a competitive economic system to prevent output and employment from being at the maximum flow possible given the size of the population and the technology available to producers.

If unemployment is observed, classical economists argued, it is because idle workers refuse to accept a job at a wage rate low enough to equate the demand for labor with the available supply of labor. In other words it is the truculence of labor resisting job offers at a market equilibrium wage that creates the perception of large numbers of unemployed. The logic of classical theory implies that unemployed workers are not to be pitied (as bleeding heart liberals would like us to believe) for it is the workers' market-defiant behavior of refusing to accept lower wages that cause them to remain idle. Classical theory provides the rational for Andrew Mellon's advice to President Hoover. When the unemployed workers have starved long enough, they will be less truculent and 'will work harder, lead a more moral life'.

The only full employment policy that government should undertake is to make sure financial markets and labor markets are free of government interference so that wages and other fringe benefits fall rapidly in periods of unemployment. Legislation that reduces the power of labor unions as well as repeals minimum wage laws are desirable, for these laws would remove supply-side rigidities from the determination of the wage rate. Hardheaded classical theorists would also suggest that unemployment compensation laws and other laws providing a social safety net (for example, welfare payments to the poor) merely increase workers' bellicose behavior and permit workers to refuse to accept reduced market wages for their labor. The repeal of such legislation would therefore be socially desirable; workers would become more docile and ready to accept lower wages, thereby making them employable.

Keynes, on the other hand, stated that the classical economists' claim that curing unemployment required cutting wages is an *'ignoratio elenchi'*.[4] In other words, in blaming workers' refusal to accept lower wages, classical theorists are engaged in offering a 'proof' that is irrelevant to the question: 'What causes unemployment in the entrepreneurial economy in which we live?'. Keynes compared this *'ignoratio elenchi'* of classical economists to an explanation that might be given by Euclidean geometers in a nonEuclidean world

> who, discovering that in experience straight lines apparently parallel often meet, rebuke the lines for not keeping straight – as the only remedy for the unfortunate collisions which are occurring. Yet in truth, there is no remedy except to throw over the axiom of parallels and to work out a non-Euclidean geometry. Something similar is today required in economics. We need to throw over the . . . postulate[s] of the classical doctrine and to work out the behaviour of a system in which involuntary unemployment in the strict sense is possible.[5]

By throwing over three fundamental classical axioms (see Chapter 3), Keynes was able to develop his principle of effective demand in *The General Theory* as the analogue of a 'nonEuclidean' economics explanation of the existence of persistent unemployment in the real world. Keynes demonstrated that the classical assumptions of the existence of wage and price rigidities and monopoly elements are neither a necessary nor a sufficient condition to explain unemployment, recessions and sluggish economic growth. Nor will cutting wage rates, *ceteris paribus*, increase the number of workers hired in a money-using, entrepreneurial economy.[6]

2.3 CLASSIFICATION AND THE PRINCIPLE OF EFFECTIVE DEMAND

In his biography of Keynes, Roy Harrod wrote: 'Classification in economics, as in biology, is crucial to scientific structure . . . It was Keynes's extraordinarily powerful intuitive sense of what was important that convinced him that the old classification was inadequate. It was his highly developed logical capacity that enabled him to consider a new classification of his own'.[7]

In order to explain why Say's Law 'is not the true law relating the aggregate demand and supply function',[8] Keynes developed a new classification scheme for handling demand factors compared to the way demand is categorized in classical economics. Say's Law specifies that the total of all expenditures on the products of industry (aggregate demand) is always exactly equal to the total costs (including gross profits) of aggregate production (aggregate supply). Moreover, the more workers employed, the greater the total costs of production and *pari passu* total spending. Letting D^w symbolize aggregate demand and Z^w aggregate supply (both measured in wage units, that is, nominal values deflated by the money-wage rate), then one can specify:

$$D^w = f_d(N) \tag{2.1}$$

and

$$Z^w = f_z(N). \tag{2.2}$$

Say's Law asserts that

$$f_d(N) = f_z(N) \tag{2.3}$$

'for *all* values of N, i.e., for all values of output and employment'.[9] In an economy subject to Say's Law, the total costs (including profits and rents) of the aggregate production of firms (whether in pure competition or not) are recouped by the sale of output. There is never a lack of effective demand. The aggregate demand and aggregate supply curves as expressed in equations (2.1) and (2.2) coincide (see Figure 2.1). In a Say's Law economy, there is never an obstacle to full employment, no matter what the degree of price flexibility in this system.

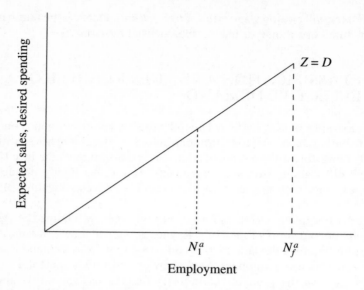

Figure 2.1   Say's Law version of aggregate supply and demand

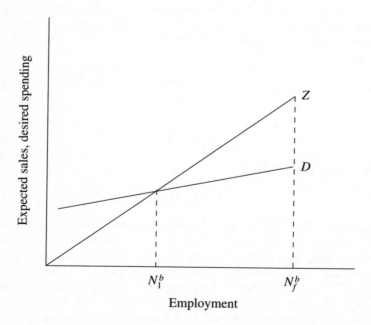

Figure 2.2   A general theory of aggregate supply and demand

To develop the 'true law' relating the aggregate demand and aggregate supply in a money-using, market-oriented, entrepreneurial economy, Keynes indicated that the aggregate demand and aggregate supply functions, $f_d(N)$ and $f_z(N)$, need not be coincident (see Figure 2.2). Keynes developed a logical argument of why, as a general case, there is no necessity for the determinants of the aggregate demand function to be identical with the determinants of aggregate supply. Instead these aggregate demand and supply functions, like Marshallian micro demand and supply curves, tended to be equal to each other only at a single point of intersection. This intersection Keynes called the point of 'effective demand'.[10]

As equation (2.1) suggests, classical theory fitted all expenditures into a single category of aggregate demand, D^w (where D^w is determined entirely by the same determinants as aggregate supply). Keynes taxonomically differentiated his theory from classical economics by dividing all expenditures into two demand classes, that is,

$$D^w = D^w_1 + D^w_2 = f_d(N). \tag{2.4}$$

D^w_1 was defined as representing *all* expenditures which 'depend on the level of [current] aggregate income and, therefore, on the level of employment N':[11]

$$D^w_1 = f_1(N). \tag{2.5}$$

In other words, the first expenditure class, D^w_1, is determined by all the factors that determine aggregate supply. Nevertheless, there is a second class of expenditures, D^w_2, that represents *all* expenditures *not* related to current income and employment and therefore determined by different determinants than those of the aggregate supply function, that is,

$$D^w_2 \neq f(N). \tag{2.6}$$

To demonstrate that his dichotomous demand classification scheme was a general analysis that could lead to unemployment equilibrium, Keynes had to explain why his second expenditure category, D^w_2, is not related to current income and employment by being equal to 'planned' saving (where the latter is defined as $f_z(N) - f_1(N)$).

If, as classical theory assumes, D^w_2 spending is always equal to planned savings out of any level of current income, then

$$D^w_2 = f_z(N) - f_1(N) \tag{2.6}$$

and

$$D^w = D^w_1 + D^w_2 = f_1(N) + f_z(N) - f_1(N) = f_z(N). \tag{2.7}$$

Comparing equation (2.7) and equation (2.2), shows that, if planned savings is assumed to be equal to planned investment,[12] then aggregate demand and supply are identical and therefore Say's Law is applicable.

To assure that equations (2.6) and (2.7) are not a general case, Keynes asserted that those future outcomes associated with today's crucial investment decisions are uncertain in the sense that the future cannot be either perfectly foreknown or statistically predicted by analysing past and current market price signals.[13]

In an uncertain environment, expected future profits, the basis for current D^w_2 investment spending in a simple two-sector model, can be neither reliably forecasted from existing market information, nor endogenously determined from today's 'planned' savings function $(f_z(N) - f_1(N))$.[14] Rather, investment expenditures depend on the exogenous expectations of entrepreneurs about future profitability, or what Keynes called 'animal spirits'. Thus investment spending is not related to aggregate supply (income) and employment, that is,

$$D^w_2 \neq f(N) \tag{2.8}$$

in either the short or long runs.

Explicit recognition of the possibility of two distinct and independent classes of current demand expenditures for producible goods and services required Keynes to throw over the aforementioned classical axioms. The resulting smaller axiomatic foundation underlies Keynes's claim that his enunciation of the principle of effective demand provides a more general theory of employment equilibrium than classical theory. The expanded axiomatic base of classical theory indicates that the latter is 'a special case only and not . . . the general case' where the category of 'all expenditures *not* related to current employment' will never contain any spending items. In terms of equation (2.4) classical theory states:

$$D^w_2 = 0 \tag{2.9}$$

and therefore

$$D^w_1 = f_1(N) = f_z(N) = Z \tag{2.10}$$

for *all* values of N.

After demonstrating that the classical theory is a special case of a general theory, the next logical task is to explain why 'the characteristics of the special case assumed by classical theory happen not to be those of the economic society in which we actually live'.[15] Keynes had to demonstrate that even if $D^w{}_2 = 0$, the $D^w{}_1$ function would not be coincident with his macro analogue of the age-old supply function.[16] To do this Keynes jettisoned the classical axioms of neutral money (where the possession of money *per se* provides no utility) and the axiom of gross substitution. If the possession of money and other liquid assets is deemed to provide security against an uncertain future in a way that the products of industry cannot, then a *utility-maximizing* person will want to withhold some income from the purchase of producible goods and use this portion of one's income to purchase liquid assets as resting places for savings – especially as one's income increases. Consequently, in an entrepreneurial, money-using economy, there is a fundamental psychological law where the marginal propensity to spend income on the products of industry is less than unity,[17] that is, people will save a portion of their income in the form of liquid assets rather than the products of industry. It therefore follows that the general statement for the behavioral aggregate $D^w{}_1$ function underlying Keynes's principle of effective demand in a money-using, entrepreneurial economy is:

$$D^w{}_1 = f_1(N) \neq f_z(N). \qquad (2.11)$$

Planned savings $(f_2(N) - f_1(N))$ is equal to the amount out of current income that utility-maximizing agents plan not to spend on the products of industry. The decision to save today means 'a decision not to have dinner today. But it does not necessitate a decision to have dinner or to buy a pair of boots a week hence or a year hence or to consume any specified thing at any specified date'.[18]

By proclaiming a 'fundamental psychological law' associated with 'the detailed facts of experience' where the marginal propensity to spend out of current income on the products of industry is always less than unity, Keynes finessed the possibility that classical theory's equation (2.10) is ever applicable to the world in which we live. If the marginal propensity to spend is always less than unity, then $f_1(N)$ would never coincide with $f_z(N)$, even if $D^w{}_2 = 0$.

The basic message of Keynes's principle of effective demand is that (for a given level of entrepreneurial investment spending) too great a demand for savings in the form of liquid assets can prevent 'saved' (that is, unutilized or involuntarily unemployed) real resources from being employed to expand the economy's stock of productive facilities.[19] The unemployment problem is basically always a liquidity problem.

2.4   WHY FLEXIBLE WAGES DO NOT ASSURE FULL EMPLOYMENT

We have now developed the tools and concepts necessary to explain why persistent unemployment can exist even in a purely competitive economy that possesses completely flexible prices and money-wages. We can demonstrate that classical economists are assuming, rather than proving, that flexible wages and prices assure full employment when they assert that

1. rigidity of wages and prices *per se* is the only necessary and sufficient condition for the existence of an involuntary unemployment equilibrium, and therefore
2. reducing the wage rate will automatically increase employment until full employment is obtained.

In Figure 2.3, assume a discrete one-time exogenous decline in the aggregate demand function from D'_w to D_w. If nothing else occurred, employment would fall from N_f to N_a as the point of effective demand declines from point F to point A. Even if money wages and product prices instantaneously fall, however, the aggregate supply function, Z_w in Figure 2.3, will be unchanged, since aggregate supply is measured in terms of monetary sums deflated by the appropriate money-wage rate. If wages and prices are instantaneously flexible, then when the money-wage declines, the money aggregate sales proceeds (Z) declines proportionately, but there is no change in the monetary aggregate supply proceeds deflated by the money-wage rate at any level of employment. Having fixed the position of the aggregate supply function measured in terms of the money-wage unit by construction, Keynes can insist that for classical economists to demonstrate that completely flexible wages and prices will restore full employment

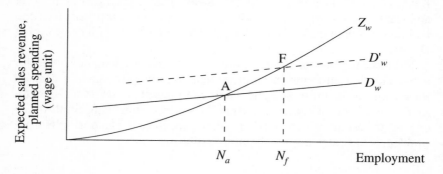

Figure 2.3   Flexible wage rate and aggregate supply and demand

after an exogenous decline in the aggregate demand function, they must demonstrate what the effects of the assumed instantaneous decline in all wages and prices have on the two components ($D^w{}_1$ and $D^w{}_2$) of the aggregate demand function. In other words, by deflating aggregate supply by the money-wage, Keynes has fixed one blade of the aggregate demand – aggregate supply scissor (to use Marshall's scissor analogy) so that any change (cutting of the employment cloth) must be explained by movements in the aggregate demand blade of the scissor.

As Keynes put it: 'the precise question at issue is whether the reduction in money-wages will or will not be accompanied by . . . an aggregate demand . . . which is somewhat greater measured in wage units'.[20] Classical analysis, however, has no answer to this precise question. Keynes's analysis,[21] on the other hand, involved tracing how a change in money-wages and prices affects both the $D^w{}_1$ and $D^w{}_2$ components of the aggregate demand function when both are measured in wage units.

Keynes's parameterization of the money-wage forces the classical analyst to evaluate how any hypothesized change in the money-wage works through the $D^w{}_1$ and $D^w{}_2$ components of aggregate demand. If the classical theorist's claim that a too high wage causes unemployment and a sufficient decline in the wage (that is, flexible wages) *per se* will always cure the unemployment problem is to be proven, then the classicist must demonstrate that a fall in the wage rate will increase some component of aggregate demand measured in terms of the wage unit.[22]

2.5   SOME FURTHER CLARIFICATIONS

Since Keynes's aggregate supply and demand curves are behavioral functions and since only the aggregate demand function is fully developed in detail in *The General Theory*, some economists have suggested that Keynes's analysis of the aggregate supply function remains incomplete. When his colleague Dennis Robertson raised the same issue in 1935, Keynes explained he was quite willing to accept the classical theory's explanation of the behavior of profit-maximizing sellers as the basis of his aggregate supply analysis. Hence there was no need to spend much time on the aggregate supply function. Moreover, by fixing the position of the aggregate supply function (by constructing it in terms of the wage unit), the degree of competition between sellers underlying the aggregate supply curve is not important. Fixing the position of the aggregate supply function lays all the emphasis on changes in the aggregate demand function for explaining the cause of change in the level of employment hiring.

Keynes specifically denied that his aggregate supply function required imperfect competition to explain the persistence of involuntary unemployment, in his 1939 rebuttal of Lorie Tarshis's and John Dunlop's claim that imperfectly competitive supply-side market conditions are a necessary condition for involuntary unemployment. Keynes responded that he readily accepted 'the prevailing generalization at the time I was writing my *General Theory* . . . for a closed system as a whole. In a competitive system prices are governed by marginal costs'.[23] but even then involuntary unemployment equilibrium can be shown to exist. In response to Tarshis's criticism, Keynes indicated that his willingness 'to concede a little to the other view' of pure competition was for the purpose of showing that the principle of effective demand does not assure a full employment output even if a purely competitive flexible price system exists[24].

The revolutionary aspect of Keynes's analysis lies in his liquidity preference theory of money. In a money-using, entrepreneurial economy, liquidity is essential to meet contractual liabilities as they come due. What Keynes's principle of effective demand demonstrates is that the unemployment problem is nested in three words 'liquidity, liquidity, liquidity'.

APPENDIX 2A1   A SIMPLE ILLUSTRATION OF THE PRINCIPLE OF EFFECTIVE DEMAND

Keynes's aggregate supply function represents the relationship between entrepreneurs' expected sales revenues tomorrow and the amount of labor hiring today that the entrepreneur requires to produce sufficient output to meet tomorrow's expected demand. In Figure 2A1.1, the aggregate supply curve (Z) emanates from the origin to indicate that if entrepreneurs expect zero sales revenue tomorrow they will hire zero workers today. If, on the other hand, they expect to sell z_1 worth of goods in the future, they will hire n_1 workers today. Alternatively, if they expect a greater profit-maximizing sales revenue of z_2 tomorrow (where $z_2 > z_1$), they will hire n_2 workers today, while if z_5 sales are expected then n_5 workers will be hired (where $z_5 > z_2 > z_1$). Accordingly, the aggregate supply curve is drawn (in Figure 2A1.1) as upward sloping to represent the common sense notion that if entrepreneurs expect to sell more, they will hire more workers.

The aggregate demand function (D) represents the desired expenditures of all buyers at any level of aggregate employment. In Figure 2A1.1, D is drawn as upward sloping, but independent of the aggregate supply function (Z). The positive slope of D represents the notion that if employment is larger, more income is earned, and therefore the demand for (spending on) goods and services will be larger.

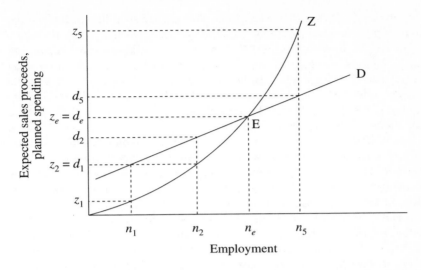

Figure 2A1.1   Illustration of the principle of effective demand

The curves in Figure 2A1.1 are drawn to illustrate why a less than full employment equilibrium situation can occur. For descriptive simplicity assume that the production of the economy can be represented as an aggregation of what happens on a single tomato farm. On Monday morning, our representative entrepreneur, Farmer Brown, has to decide on the number of workers to hire to harvest sufficient tomatoes to maximize profits at next Saturday's market. Assume (as in Figure 2A1.1) that Farmer Brown expects his profit-maximizing sales next Saturday to be z_1 dollars (say $1000) worth of tomatoes. According to this supply schedule he has calculated that hiring n_1 workers to produce q_1 tomatoes will bring in revenues of z_1 (where $z_1 = p_1 q_1$, and p_1 is the price Farmer Brown expects to be able to sell q_1 tomatoes). The resulting n_1 workers hired by Farmer Brown toil all week and receive their week's pay on Friday night from their employer.[25]

On Saturday morning, Farmer Brown takes his harvested tomatoes to market. At 8 a.m. the market opens and consumers (mainly, but not only, the employees of Farmer Brown and the other entrepreneurs in the system) come to market with the income they received the night before. Farmer Brown expects to sell the last tomato he has brought to market to the last customer expected to arrive a few seconds before closing time (5 p.m.). If his expectations regarding demand are met, then he correctly guessed the size of the market when he made his hiring decision last Monday morning.

From Figure 2A1.1, we can see that if in the aggregate, all entrepreneurs hire the equivalent of n_1 workers, then the planned spending of buyers that make up the level of aggregate demand will be equal to d_1 ($=p_1q_{1d}$, where $q_{1d}>q_1$). As drawn in Figure 2A1.1, planned spending exceeds the amount entrepreneurs expected to sell ($d_1>z_1$). Several hours before the market closes (say 3 p.m.) Farmer Brown (representing all entrepreneurs in the system) finds he has sold his last tomato. For the rest of the market day disappointed buyers arrive at Farmer Brown's counter trying to purchase tomatoes, but his shelves are bare.[26]

On the following Monday morning Farmer Brown must again choose the number of workers to hire based on this Monday's expectations of sales for the following Saturday. Assume that Farmer Brown kept a record of how many tomatoes last Saturday's disappointed buyers said they would have bought had he still had tomatoes for sale. Brown may adopt the d_1 potential expenditures of last Saturday as the best estimate of next Saturday's sales proceeds (z_2), that is, z_2 ($=p_2q_2$). According to Figure 2A1.1, Farmer Brown will therefore hire n_2 workers in the expectation of earning z_2 revenue. Again, the workers labor in the fields and are paid on Friday evening.

Farmer Brown arrives at Saturday's market with q_2 tomatoes that he expects to sell at a price of p_2. The market doors open at 8 a.m. and buyers keep arriving at Farmer Brown's counter during the market day. From Figure 2A1.1, we see that Farmer Brown has underestimated again this Saturday's demand for tomatoes which will be d_2 ($=p_2q_{2d}$ where $q_{2d}>q_2$). The presumed unforeseen increase in demand is the result of more workers being hired and therefore swelling the number of income earners who are tomato buyers).

As drawn in Figure 2A1.1, Farmer Brown's underestimate of market demand is less than it was last Saturday, that is,

$$(d_2-z_2) < (d_1-z_1).$$

Consequently, this Saturday Farmer Brown will not sell his last tomato until later in the day than last Saturday, say 4:15 p.m.

How many workers will representative Farmer Brown hire on the following Monday, and on each Monday after that? If this hypothesized process of adjusting expectations of next week's sales proceeds in the light of the past week's revenues plus evidence of disappointed buyers continues, then Farmer Brown's hiring decisions will tend to follow the dotted line in Figure 2A1.1 until Farmer Brown expects sales proceeds equal to z_e, when he hires n_e workers. Since $d_e=z_e$, on that Saturday Farmer Brown will sell his last tomato just as the clock strikes 5 p.m. and the market closes. There are no frustrated buyers. Farmer Brown (representing all entrepreneurs) realizes that his expectations of sales are just being met and there should be no further incentive to change employment plans.

Consequently, as long as the aggregate demand curves remain as drawn in Figure 2A1.1, then once entrepreneurs have hired the equilibrium level of employment (n_e), their expectations of sales are just being fulfilled by buyers' demands and there is no reason for them to alter their hiring plans.

This intersection of the aggregate supply and demand functions, point E in Figure 2A1.1, is designated *the effective demand* by Keynes.[27] The point of effective demand[28] can occur at any level of employment – even one where all workers who wish to work at the going real wage will not be employed.

APPENDIX 2A2 DERIVING KEYNES'S AGGREGATE SUPPLY AND DEMAND ANALYSIS FROM MARSHALLIAN MICRO DEMAND AND SUPPLY FUNCTIONS

Keynes argued that money value and employment are the two 'fundamental units of quantity'[29] to be used when dealing with macroeconomic relationships. The aggregate sales proceeds and intended demand purchases in Keynes's aggregate supply and demand functions are always measured either in money value terms or in a money value deflated by the money-wage. This deflator Keynes called the wage unit.

Keynes's aggregate supply function is derived from ordinary Marshallian micro flow- supply functions.[30] The aggregate supply function relates the aggregate number of workers (N) that profit-maximizing entrepreneurs would want to hire for each possible level of expected sales proceeds (Z) – given the money-wage rate, technology, the degree of competition (or monopoly), and the degree of integration of firms.

For any given degree of integration, gross domestic product (GDP) is directly related to total sales proceeds. If each firm is fully integrated from raw material production to finished product sales then aggregate sales proceeds equals GDP in monetary terms

The aggregate supply function in monetary terms is specified as:

$$Z = f_1(w, N) \tag{2A2.1}$$

or in money-wage unit terms as:

$$Z_w = f_2(N) \tag{2A2.2}$$

where Z is measured in money units and Z_w is in terms of wage units, while N is hiring in terms of employment units.

For purposes of simplicity and ease of comparability with the ordinary Marshallian micro supply function, only the form of equation (2A2.1) will be developed. Equational form (2A2.2) of the aggregate supply function can be derived by dividing all money sums expressed in equation (2A2.1) by the money-wage rate.

The Marshallian flow-supply curve for each firm indicates the profit-maximizing output possibilities for alternative market demand conditions facing the firm. The profit-maximization condition is

$$p(1-1/|E_{df}|) = MC_f \qquad (2A2.3)$$

where p is the market price, $|E_{df}|$ is the absolute value of the price elasticity of demand facing the firm for any given level of effective demand, $1/|E_{df}|$ is the firm's degree of monopoly (μ_f) and MC_f is the marginal cost schedule facing the firm. The supply schedule of any profit-maximizing firm (s_f) is related to its marginal cost and its degree of monopoly,

$$s_f = f_1(MC_f, \mu_f). \qquad (2A2.4)$$

Assuming labor is the only variable input in the production process, the firm's marginal cost equals the money-wage (w) divided by the firm's marginal productivity of labor (mp_f) where the latter is a function of hiring by the firm and the laws of returns involved in the technology of the firm, that is,

$$MC_f = w/mp_f. \qquad (2A2.5)$$

For any given 'law of returns' facing the firm, there will be a different marginal production cost structure. With diminishing returns, marginal production costs increase with increasing output. With constant returns to labor, marginal production costs are constant. With increasing returns, marginal costs decline with increases in output and employment.[31]

For a perfectly competitive firm, $|E_{df}| = \infty$, the firm has no monopoly power ($\mu_f = 0$). In this case, the marginal cost schedule of the firm is its flow-supply curve. For conditions of less than perfect competition, the degree of monopoly will vary between zero and one as $1 > |E_d| < \infty$. Whenever $0 > \mu_f < 1$ both marginal costs and monopoly power affect the firm's supply curve offerings at alternative market prices.[32] If the firm has some degree of monopoly power, the supply function would be the marginal cost schedule multiplied by some scalar equal to $[1/\mu_f]$.

The Marshallian industry flow-supply schedule(s) is simply obtained by the usual lateral summation of the individual firm's supply curves. The industry supply schedule is, therefore, related to the average industry mark-up or 'average' degree of monopoly (μ) *and* the industry's marginal cost schedule (MC), that is,

$$s = \Sigma s_f = f_4(MC, \mu). \qquad (2A2.6)$$

Given (a) each firm's production technology, (b) the money-wage, and (c) average degree of monopoly based on specified market conditions for any given potential output and employment level, a unique industry supply function can be derived. Output across firms in the same industry may be homogeneous and therefore can be aggregated to obtain the industry supply schedule.

Keynes rejected this homogeneity of output assumption as the basis for summing across industries to obtain the aggregate supply function.[33] It is necessary to convert the Marshallian industry supply function, s, which relates prices (p) and quantities (q) to a function (that we may call Keynes's industry supply function) whose units can be aggregated across industries to obtain an aggregate supply function. Keynes's industry supply function relates total industry sales proceeds in money terms (z) with total industry employment hiring (n), that is,

$$z = f_2(n). \qquad (2A2.7)$$

Given productivity, the money-wage, and the degree of monopoly, every point on the Marshallian industry supply function is associated with a unique profit-maximizing price–quantity combination whose product equals total expected sales proceeds (that is, $p \times q = z$). Every industry output level (q) can be associated with a unique industry hiring level, that is, $q = f(n)$. Given industry A's supply curve, if entrepreneurs of that industry expect a price of p_1^a, they will produce q_1^a and expect a total sales revenue of z_1^a ($= $ to $p_1^a q_1^a$). To produce q_1^a output, n_1^a workers will have to be hired in the A industry. Consequently, z_1^a and n_1^a describe the coordinates of one point on Keynes's industry supply function.

In a similar manner, every point of the Marshallian industry supply function in the p versus q quadrant can be transformed to a point on the Keynes industry supply curve in z ($= pq$) versus n space. For every industry where a traditional Marshallian flow-supply function can be formulated, a Keynes industry supply function can also be uniquely specified. All of Keynes's industry supply functions can then be aggregated together to obtain the aggregate supply function of Figure 2A1.1 in terms of aggregate money proceeds (Z) and the aggregate quantity of employment units (N), provided one reasonably assumes that corresponding to any given point of aggregate supply there is a unique distribution and employment between the different industries in the economy.[34]

If all firms in each industry are fully integrated, then the aggregate expected sales proceeds is equal to the GDP of the economy.[35] The distribution of GDP between workers and capitalists will reflect the average distribution of the total revenue of each of the firms in the economy. The distribution for each firm can be obtained if we combine equations (2.8) and (2A2.5) to obtain

$$p\,(1-1/|E_{df}|)=w/MP_f. \tag{2A2.8}$$

Rearranging terms

$$w/p=(MP_f)(1-1/|E_{df}|). \tag{2A2.9}$$

The fraction of the total revenue of the firm paid to wage earners is called the wage share. The wage share for each firm is the total wages bill of the firm (wn_f) divided by total sales proceeds (pq). It is (wn_f)/(pq_n). The average product of labor (ap_f) in the firm is equal to q/n_f. If both sides of equation (2A2.9) are multiplied by the reciprocal of the average product of labor (n_f/q),

$$(w/p)(n_f/q)=(MP_f)(1-1/|E_{df}|)(n_f/q)$$

then the wage share is obtained as

$$(wn_f/pq)=[(MP_f)/(AP_f)](1-1/|E_{df}|) \tag{2A2.10}$$

If all firms in the economy are fully integrated, then the wage share in GDP, at any level of employment, is

$$W/Z=(MP/AP)(1-M) \tag{2A2.11}$$

where W is the aggregate wage bill, Z is GDP, MP is the aggregate marginal product of labor, AP is the average product of labor, and M is the average degree of monopoly in the economy. In a purely competitive economy, $M=0$, and the aggregate wage share is equal to the economy's MP/AP ratio.

The aggregate wage bill (W) is total money-wages (wN) paid to workers at any level of aggregate employment. Given a money-wage rate of w_1, the aggregate wage bill line, W_1 ($= w_1 N$) will be a straight line emanating from the origin. The slope of this wage bill line is w_1. Given the MP/AP ratio as determined by productivity relations, and the economy wide average degree of monopoly, the distribution of income for any given level of employment can be derived. The vertical distance between the wage bill line and the aggregate supply curve at each employment level depends on the economy-wide MP/AP ratio and degree of monopoly. (In a purely competitive economy, the vertical distance between the Z curve and the wage bill line depends only on the MP/AP ratio.) If the MP/AP is a constant at each level of employment,[36] then the aggregate supply curve is a straight line emanating from the origin. If the MP/AP ratio declines (due to diminishing returns), then the Z curve will be convex to the wage bill line.

Given our discussion of the aggregate demand categories D_1 and D_2, for any given money-wage is w_1, the slope of the aggregate demand curve will depend on the marginal propensities to consume of the various income recipients.[37] The point of effective demand, E, is given by the intersection of the aggregate demand curve and the aggregate supply curve.

Unlike the upward-sloping aggregate demand curve, the Marshallian micro demand curve facing an industry is normally downward sloping. Despite these different slopes, the aggregate demand curve can be derived from a Marshallian micro demand and supply analysis.

At an expected price of p_1, entrepreneurs in industry A will produce q_1 output, will hire n_1 workers, and expect a total revenue of z_1 ($= p_1 q_1$). A Marshallian demand curve is based on the assumptions of given tastes, given other industry demand and supply conditions, and *given the aggregate demand schedule*. The demand schedule for an industry 'can only be constructed on some fixed assumption as to the nature of demand and supply in other industries and as to the amount of the aggregate effective demand'.[38] If entrepreneurs in industry a expect p_1 choose to produce q_1 there must be implied concomitant prices and outputs of all other industries that will generate a level of aggregate income such that there will be a specific Marshallian downward-sloping demand curve facing industry A.

At an alternative expected supply price of p_2, entrepreneurs in representative industry A expect to sell q_2 output for a total revenue of z_2 ($= p_2 q_2$) and will hire n_2 workers. This increased output and employment in representative industry A will be associated with similar increases in all other industries. The result will be larger factor incomes throughout the economy associated with supply price p_2 compared to supply price p_1. The larger aggregate factor payments imply a new, outward-shifted Marshallian demand curve facing industry A.

Implicit in this analysis is the recognition that if employment and output increase in each industry, then aggregate factor incomes rise and the quantity of aggregate demand increases. Every movement up the given aggregate demand curve associated with an alternative higher level of employment and output generates a higher member of a Marshallian family of industry demand curves.

NOTES

1. 'For the Classical Theory has been accustomed to rest the self adjusting character of the economic system on an assumed fluidity of money-wages; and, when there is rigidity, to lay on this rigidity the blame for maladjustment' (J.M. Keynes, *The General Theory of Employment, Interest and Money*, Harcourt, Brace, New York, 1936, p. 257).
2. H. Hoover, *The Memoirs of Herbert Hoover; The Great Depression 1929–1941*, Macmillan, New York, 1952, p. 30.
3. Keynes, *The General Theory*, p. 3.
4. Ibid., p. 259.
5. Ibid., pp. 16–17.
6. During the Great Depression, classical theorists argued that unemployment would end when the market would self-correct this supply imperfection. In the long run, market forces would cause wages and prices to fall sufficiently to restore full employment. Keynes, on the other hand, in a September 1935 broadcast for the BBC, argued: 'We must not regard the conditions of supply . . . as the fundamental sources of our troubles . . . [I]t is in the conditions of demand which our diagnosis must search and probe for an explanation'.
7. R.F. Harrod, *The Life of John Maynard Keynes*, Macmillan, London, 1951, pp. 463–4.
8. Keynes, *The General Theory*, p. 26.
9. Ibid., pp. 25–6.
10. Ibid., p. 25.
11. Ibid., p. 28.
12. Planned saving would automatically equal planned investment if savers voluntarily decided to store all their savings directly in the form of real capital goods. Chapters 4 through 6 explain why savers do not want to store their savings in real capital goods.
13. As explained in Chapter 3, the ergodic axiom of classical economics assumes that the future can be reliably predicted from past and current market price data. Hence, although, in the 1930s, neither the classical theorists nor Keynes knew the term ergodic, Keynes's concept of uncertainty overthrows this classical postulate (which was implicitly rather than explicitly stated in classical theory).
14. Keynes, *The General Theory*, p. 210.
15. Ibid., p. 3.
16. Even if D_2 were to be defined in some way as related to aggregate income, that is,

$$D_2 = f_2(N) \qquad\qquad (2.7')$$

so long as

$$f_1(N) + f_2(N) \neq f_z(N) \qquad\qquad (2.8')$$

for *all* values of N, then Say's Law is not applicable. Hence, even if D_2 is defined as related to employment, neoclassical theory is still a special case where $f_1(N) + f_2(N) = f_z(N)$ for all values of N.
17. Keynes argues that there is a fundamental psychological law that as income increases (decreases), the amount that people spend via D_1 will increase (decrease) by some lesser amount. Hence the marginal propensity to spend on D_1 is less than unity.

18. Keynes, *The General Theory*, p. 210.
19. In essence we can catagorize 'saving' into two kinds – saving type-A and saving type-B. The more familiar economists's concept of saving – what I have labeled type-A – is derived from the national income and product accounts (NIPA). Basil Moore has correctly indicated that this type-A saving is that form of 'saving [that] is the accounting record of investment' (B.J. Moore, 'Savings and investment: the theoretical case for lower interest rates', in P. Davidson (ed) *A Post Keynesian Perspective on 21st Century Economic Problems*, Cheltenham: Edward Elgar, 2002. pp. 140ff). Since NIPA is nothing more than double entry bookkeeping, the accounting definition of saving is all currently produced goods that are not categorized as consumption.

    Saving type-B, on the other hand, has been ignored by most economists even though it conforms to the more usual, colloquial concept where things that are 'saved' are *not* used in this accounting period. Given this latter conceptualization, all idle resources (whether they be labor, capital or land) not used today are saving type-B. In other words, whenever saving type-B is greater than zero, resources that are available to be employed in today's production process at the going (real) market price, are involuntarily unemployed.
20. Keynes, *The General Theory*, pp. 259–60.
21. Ibid., p. 257.
22. Harrod's argument regarding the importance of Keynes's new classification scheme is right on the mark. The classical taxonomy of supply and demand deflected attention away from the necessity of studying the components of aggregate demand to explain involuntary unemployment, whether money-wages (and prices) are flexible or not.
23. *The Collected Writings of John Maynard Keynes*, vol. 13, edited by D. Moggridge, Macmillan, London, 1973, pp. 399–400.
24. Ibid., p. 411.
25. The payroll will probably be financed by a working capital loan from Farmer Brown's banker.
26. Out of the z_1 sales revenue received, Farmer Brown pays off his working capital loan from the banker that financed his payroll. Whatever remains is his gross profit.
27. Keynes, *The General Theory*, pp. 25, 55.
28. The reader can see that a similar process of movement towards the point of effective demand can be described even if Farmer Brown started with over optimistic sales proceeds expectations of z_5 and hence hired n_5 workers. At the end of the first Saturday, in this case, Farmer Brown would find himself holding an unwanted inventory of unsold, but perishable tomatoes when the market doors closed at 5 p.m. Accordingly he would reduce his hiring level, but sales would then fall off further until the point of effective demand was reach.
29. Keynes, *The General Theory*, p. 41.
30. Ibid., pp. 44–5. The following derivation of the aggregate supply function has its origins in Keynes's *General Theory* (1936) as elucidated by S. Weintraub, *An Approach to the Theory of Income Distribution*, Philadelphia, Chilton, 1957 and further developed by P. Davidson, 'More on the aggregate supply function' *Economic Journal*, **72**, 1962 as reprinted in L. Davidson (ed.), *Money and Employment, the Collected Writings of Paul Davidson*, Vol. 1, London: Macmillan, 1990, pp. 467–72, and P. Davidson and E. Smolensky, *Aggregate Supply and Demand Analysis*, New York, Harper & Row, 1964.
31. The last two cases are incompatible with perfect competition; they require some degree of monopoly and hence some positive mark-up, $k > 0$ over marginal costs, so that market price covers average unit costs. If marginal user costs (MUC) are not negligible, then $MC_f = w/MP + MUC$.
32. In the simplest case when aggregate demand changes, the demand curve facing the firm shifts without altering the degree of monopoly of the firm. For example, for the purely competitive case, shifts in the firm's demand curve does not alter the competitive market conditions. In more complex cases the degree of monopoly may vary as aggregate demand changes and the firm's demand curve shifts, that is $\mu_f = f_2(N)$.
33. Keynes, *The General Theory*, Ch. 4.

34.   Ibid., p. 282.
35.   Implicit in this statement is the assumption that all production firms are organized by profit-making entrepreneurs in the private sector, that is, there are no charitable or government organized firms.
36.   Assuming diminishing returns, the *MP/AP* ratio will be a constant at each level of employment, if the marginal product and average product decline at the same rate. This would occur, for example, in a Cobb–Douglas production function of the form $q = \alpha n^\beta$. Otherwise it will cause the aggregate supply function to be convex relative to the wage bill line. For a further explanation of the shape of the aggregate supply function, see P. Davidson and E. Smolensky, *Aggregate Supply and Demand Analysis*, Harper & Row, New York, 1964, pp. 126–8.
37.   A fuller derivation is given in Davidson and Smolensky, ibid., Ch. 10.
38.   Keynes, *The General Theory*, p. 259.

3. Uncertainty and reality in economic models

3.1 A PARABLE: THE FABLE OF THE P'S, OR WHAT MORTALS THESE P'S FOOL!

Many years ago in the never-never land of Chicago where the busy P's of economic theory often flourish, there dwelt a wise and famous Knight (Frank H.) who recognized the sterility of using a classical economic theory that presumed the economic future could be reliably predicted by the use of probability theory. This Knight attempted to redirect the economics profession toward the study of relevant economic problems where the future was uncertain and therefore incapable of being reliably forecasted. If the future is merely risky, this Knight maintained, then these risks are measurable and by using probability theory the economic future is actuarially knowable. An uncertain economic future, however, is incapable of any measurement. Hence the term uncertainty must be restricted to 'non-quantitative' views about the future and it is this 'true' uncertainty, and not risk, the Knight insisted, that forms the basis of economic decision making.[1]

At about the same time, in a distant land across the seas, the brave and intelligent warrior, Keynes, who had also labored in the field of probability and nonmeasurable uncertainty, took up the cudgel and attempted to produce a revolution in economic thinking by developing a taxonomic structure that differentiated an uncertain future from a probabilistic risky one.

Now it came to pass that with the upheaval of the Great Depression and the Second World War, politicians were open to Keynes's proposals for policies to cure the outstanding faults of the capitalist system and for several decades there were continuing progress and growth. But after a time, in the land of Chicago, new leaders appeared who desired to resurrect the classical structure; and one, who was a most exalted classical savant of the day, mounted a balcony and said to his followers:

Oh Students, Scholars, wherefore art thou Scientists? Deny thy forefather (F.H. Knight) and refuse his conceptual distinctions between

probabilistic risk and uncertainty. If thou wilt but do this we can recon-
quer the free world with the elegance of mathematics and the scientific
laws of probability.

What's in a name? That which we call uncertainty can be more easily
handled when dealt with 'as if' it had another name. So uncertainty, was
it but called risk, would obtain that dear perfection without which scientific quantification and probability analysis is inapplicable.

If you, the next generation of classicists has but the will to do, and the
soul to dare, then we will win out. Today Chicago and then MIT, tomorrow the free world!

And this modern generation of students was taken by these words and they
said of their new scientific leader: 'He speaks the kindest words, and looks
such things, Vows with so much passion, swears with so much grace. That
'tis a kind of heaven to be deluded by him'.[2] And thus it was that classical
economists recaptured the academic heaven and earth and the dark ages
descended once more upon the economic community.

Moral: Those who insist on quantifying nonquantifiable concepts can
only provide a regressive form of analysis.

As this parable suggests, economists are split into two irreconcilable
theoretical camps about the meaning of uncertainty regarding future outcomes and consequently what decision makers can know about the future
and how this affects choices made. These two camps provide very different
explanations of the cause of unemployment, inflation and financial market
volatility. Understanding the difference in these two concepts of uncertainty is essential to understanding the philosophical differences between
economists who see no active role for government in the economy and those
who urge positive actions to cure the faults of the capitalist system while
preserving the good attributes of capitalism that can produce a global
golden age of economic development and prosperity

3.2   AXIOMS AND MODEL BUILDING

The best way to evaluate any economic model is to consider the model
builder as if he/she is a magician. Model builders rarely make logical
errors in moving from axioms to conclusions, any more than professional
prestidigitators drop the deck of cards while performing a card trick.
Economic model builders are proficient at creating the illusion of pulling
policy conclusion rabbits out of their black hat model. The more surpris-

ing the policy rabbits pulled from the hat, the greater the audience enjoyment and applause.

A careful examination of the rabbits the magician put into the hat backstage is required to evaluate the relevance of the policy rabbits pulled from the black hat on stage. The policy rabbits pulled from the classical economists' hat cannot be criticized if the axiomatic rabbits being put into the hat have been accepted, often unwittingly, by the audience. In other words, before accepting the conclusions of any economist's model as applicable to the real world, the careful student should always examine and be prepared to criticize the applicability of the fundamental postulates of the model; for, in the absence of any mistake in logic, the axioms of the model determine its conclusions.

Neutral money was a fundamental axiom of nineteenth-century classical theory. By the early twentieth century, this neutrality of money presumption became one of the basic axioms of the prevailing orthodoxy in economics textbooks. An axiom is defined as 'a statement universally accepted as true . . . a statement that needs no proof because its truth is obvious'. For those who are trained in classical economic theory, the neutrality of money is an article of faith, requiring no proof or justification (as the cited quotation from Oliver Blanchard in Chapter 1 revealed).

A religious person who accepts as a fundamental truth the Bible's story of creation where a Divine Being created humans and all the animals in six days must reject any 'scientific' evolutionary evidence that purports to demonstrate that humans evolved from lower life forms over thousands of years. Similarly, a true believer in the axiomatic foundations of classical theory will deny that money can be shown to be ultimately nonneutral in the long run. This is not to deny that some members of the 'New Keynesian' school and even some Old Classical school Monetarists accept the notion that money may be nonneutral in the short run, because of some 'temporary' supply-side failure of the free market. Nevertheless all mainstream economists believe that in the long run, money is neutral.

In 1933 Keynes explicitly indicated that the 'monetary theory of production' that he was developing explicitly rejected the classical neutrality of money assumption as applicable in either the short run or the long run. Keynes's resulting analytical system required fewer restrictive axioms than classical theory. By definition, therefore, Keynes provided a more general theory of employment. Once the neutrality of money is rejected as a necessary axiomatic building block, then Say's Law is not applicable as the organizing principle for studying a market system where money is used as a means of settling contractual obligations and liquidity plays an essential role. Keynes noted:

An economy which uses money but uses it merely as a *neutral* link between trans-actions in real things and real assets and does not allow it to enter into motives or decisions, might be called – for want of a better name – a *real-exchange economy*. The theory which I desiderate would deal, in contradistinction to this, with an economy in which money plays a part of its own and affects motives and decisions and is, in short, one of the operative factors in the situation, so that the course of events cannot be predicted either in the long period or in the short, without a knowledge of the behavior of money between the first state and the last. And it is this which we ought to mean when we speak of *a monetary economy* . . .

Booms and depressions are peculiar to an economy in which . . . money is not neutral. I believe that the next task is to work out in some detail such a mone-tary theory of production. That is the task on which I am now occupying myself in some confidence that I am not wasting my time.[3]

Here, in Keynes's own words, is his claim that a theory of production for a money-using economy must reject what classical theorists have always believed is a 'universal truth', the neutrality of money. But this neutrality axiom had been the foundation of classical economic theory for 125 years before Keynes, ever since James Mill introduced Say's Law into English economics. No wonder Keynes's *General Theory* was considered heretical by most of his professional colleagues who were wedded to the classical analysis. Keynes was delivering a mortal blow to the very foundation of classical faith. No wonder Keynes's original analysis and the further elab-oration and evolution of Keynes's system by Post Keynesian economists in recent decades has not been understood by the majority of economists who, as Professor Blanchard has expressly noted, are ideologically bonded to either the old or new classical tradition of neutral money.

To accept Keynes's logic and its Post Keynesian development threatens the Panglossian conclusion that, in the long run, all is for the best in this best of all possible worlds where an unfettered market economy assures full employment for all those who want to work. The less-restrictive axiomatic foundation of Keynes's general theory allows for the possibility that an entrepreneurial system might possess some inherent faults such as its 'failure to provide for full employment'.[4] This fundamental flaw in the capi-talist system can be ameliorated by developing corrective policies and insti-tutions for our financial markets. *There can be a permanent role for government to correct systemic economic faults.* The Keynes-Post Keynesian logic is just as antithetical to the classical Social Darwinistic classical eco-nomics as the view on the origin of human life as asserted by the 'scientific theory of evolution' is to the 'scientific creationism' biblical view of some fundamentalist Christian religions.

3.3   CLASSICAL AXIOMS AND MONEY'S ELASTICITY PROPERTIES

By invoking three additional axioms, classical theory thus becomes a special case of Keynes's general analytical system. These three restrictive axioms assure that the aggregate demand function is the same as the aggregate supply function. This is a Say's Law world where there is no obstacle to reaching full employment. These three necessary additional classical postulates underlying Say's Law are:

1.   *neutral money*,
2.   *the gross substitution axiom*, and
3.   *the ergodic axiom*.

The axiom of gross substitution asserts that everything is a substitute for everything else. Gross substitution means that when relative prices change, agents will buy more of the relatively cheaper item and less of the now more expensive one while spending the same amount of income. This axiom therefore assures that if all market prices are perfectly flexible, then all markets, including the labor market, clear instantaneously (and even with less than perfect flexibility of current prices all markets clear at least in the long run). And a cleared labor market is one where everyone who wants to work has a job; there is no unemployment. Arrow and Hahn[5] have demonstrated, however, that if gross substitution is removed as a universal assumption, then all existence proofs of general equilibrium (that is, proofs that there exists a price vector that will clear all markets simultaneously) are jeopardized. In other words, if the axiom of gross substitution is not initially imposed, then it cannot be demonstrated that even with instantaneous flexible prices all markets will clear simultaneously; full employment of all resources cannot be shown to be an automatic outcome of free markets.

The ergodic axiom asserts that the future can always be statistically reliably calculated from past and present market data.[6] In nineteenth-century Old Classical theory ergodicity was usually implicitly assumed under the claim that decision makers possessed perfectly reliable foreknowledge of the future. In New Classical theory, ergodicity is a necessary condition for agents to form rational expectations about a presumed statistically reliable predictable future.[7]

While Keynes was developing his principle of effective demand in the early 1930s, the modern classical axiomatic theory of value had not yet been developed. Consequently, Keynes could not explicitly label all the axiomatic equivalents of the 'axiom of parallels' that he claimed had to be 'overthrown' to produce a general theory of employment, interest and money. As the earlier quotation indicated, Keynes specifically noted that in his new 'monetary theory of production' the neutral money axiom was not applicable to the operation of a monetary, entrepreneurial economy in either the short run or the long run. Nevertheless, the gross substitution axiom and the ergodic axiom are not specifically identified in *The General Theory* as axioms to be rejected in a general theory. But the gross substitution axiom is incompatible with Keynes's emphasis on the essential elasticity properties of liquid assets (in Chapter 17 of *The General Theory*) and the ergodic axiom is not consistent with Keynes's concept of uncertainty regarding future outcomes of today's decisions (in Chapters 11 and 12).

Once these three classical axioms are jettisoned, Keynes's concept of liquidity and the importance of money in the real economy comes to the foreground of the analysis. Keynes noted that money and all other liquid assets must possess two essential elasticity properties.[8] These intrinsic properties are:

1. The elasticity of production of all liquid assets (including money) is zero. This elasticity property means that money and liquid assets in general are not producible by the use of labor in the private sector. In essence, *money does not grow on trees*. Entrepreneurs cannot hire the otherwise unemployed workers to harvest money trees whenever people demand to hold additional liquid assets as a store of value instead of using the money earned as income to buy the products of industry.
2. The elasticity of substitution between all (nonproducible) liquid assets and the producible goods and services of industry is zero. Any increase in demand for liquidity (that is, a demand for nonproducible liquid financial assets to be held as a store of value), and the resulting changes in relative prices between nonproducible liquid assets and the products of industry, will not divert this increase in demand for nonproducible liquid assets into a demand for producible goods and/or services.

The 'attribute of "liquidity" is by no means independent of these two [elasticity] characteristics'.[9] Thus, as long as wealth owners demand any liquid asset that has 'low elasticities of production and substitution and low carrying costs'[10] as a resting place (store of value) for their savings out of current income, then involuntary unemployment equilibrium is possible even in the long run. In a money-using, entrepreneurial economy, earned income is saved in the form of nonproducible financial assets rather than spent on the products of industry.

Classical theory, on the other hand, assumes that *only* producible goods and services provide utility. Why then would any rational human being engage in unpleasant income-earning activities only to store that portion of their income that they save in the form of nonproducible liquid assets which classical theorists insist provides no utility to the saver? In the classical long run, only an irrational lunatic would behave this way and make a fetish over the liquidity of one's portfolio. Yet, in the world of experience, sensible people do store their savings in the form of currency, bank deposits and a plethora of other financial assets traded on well-organized, orderly financial markets.

In a world where the ergodic axiom is not applicable, people recognize that they do not 'know' the future in a statistically reliable sense. Decision makers' may fear a future that they 'know' that they cannot know. It is sensible for decision makers to store some portion of their income in money and other nonproducible liquid assets that can be readily converted into money as long as future liabilities can be expected to be legally discharged by the tendering of money. Sensible behavior of savers then implies that they do not use all their earned claims on industry's products and resources today. He who hesitates to buy the products of industry today is saved to make a purchase decision another day. The more liquid the asset used to store savings today, the more readily it can be used another day to command resources in the future.

If decision makers fear an uncertain, unpredictable future then the possession of nonproducible liquid assets is a security blanket providing the holder with considerable utility in a way that producibles cannot, for the latter require using up one's claim on resources today.

One of the most erudite classical scholars, Frank Hahn, demonstrated that involuntary unemployment equilibrium can occur in any market system including a competitive economy with perfectly flexible relative prices, whenever 'there are in this economy *resting places* for savings other than reproducible assets'.[11] Hahn explains that the existence of 'any nonreproducible asset allows for a choice between employment-inducing and non-employment inducing demand'.[12] Nonreproducible assets must, by definition, have an elasticity of production of zero. If the price of nonproducibles (used as saving vehicles) rises relative to producibles in this economy, then, as long as the gross elasticity of substitution between producibles and nonproducibles is zero, savings will continue to 'rest' in nonproducibles that represent a 'non-employment inducing demand'.

Hahn's 'resting place' analogy, therefore, implies a zero elasticity of substitution between nonproducible assets used as savings and the producible goods or industry. Thus decades after Keynes spelled out the essential elasticity properties of all liquid assets in his *General Theory*, Hahn mathematically demonstrated that the specific elasticity properties Keynes attributed to liquid assets are necessary and sufficient conditions for the possible existence of involuntary unemployment even in a purely competitive economic system with ubiquitous instantaneously flexible prices.

If one incorporates ergodicity, gross substitution and neutral money into the microfoundations of theory as classical economists do, then these axioms assure that all income is always spent on the products of industry.[13] In the simplest classical case, all current expenditures are equal to current income as utility maximizers are constrained by their income (budget-line constraint) in their choice among producible good A and good B (which represents all other producibles). To spend less than one's income on the products of industry (that is, to use nonreproducibles as vehicles for saving out of current income) is to reveal a preference for a position below the budget line and thereby to engage in nonutility-maximizing behavior.

The backstage rabbits of classical utility-maximizing micro theory require all income earned to be spent only on producible goods. If this utility-maximizing behavior is unquestioningly accepted as *the* microfoundation of macroeconomics, then the aggregation of all market micro demand (for producibles) must be classified under the $D^w{}_1$ expenditure category (as described in Chapter 2). There can be no market demands for Keynes's $D^w{}_2$ category where expenditures are not related to current income. Since any additional supply of the products of industry must increase people's income *pari passu* (the micro equivalent is an upward shift in budget-constraint lines), therefore, every increase in supply creates an exact equivalent additional total demand for the products of industry[14] in classical theory. Consequently, in either the short run or the long run, classical economic theory assumes that the aggregate supply and demand functions are identical. Say's Law prevails and Figure 2.1 (of Chapter 2) is the logically consistent relationship between the aggregate demand and supply functions.

3.4   TWO CONCEPTS OF ECONOMIC REALITY

The two fundamentally different concepts of uncertainty in economics are the classical theory concept where an uncertain future is actuarially certain and the Keynes concept where the future is unknown and unknowable. The explanation of how economic agents make decisions under uncertainty conditions in various classical and Keynes-type models depend on (a) the analyst's conception of the cause of uncertainty in the external economic reality in which decision makers operate, and (b) the ability of agents to understand that reality.

All classical models are based on the presupposition that the external economic reality is immutable and therefore the future path of the economy, like the movement of the planets in Newton's classical theory, depends on fundamental parameters that are unalterable by any human (government) action. In some classical models, however, the model builder assumes that decision makers already 'know' the immutable future path of the economy, that is, agents either have perfect foreknowledge of the future or have formed 'rational expectations' about future outcomes. In other classical models there is some limitation on humans' ability to foresee the immutable future path of the economy. Some agents can make persistent errors in the short run. These persistent error-making economic agents are 'killed off' by competitive market forces. In the long run, the survival of the fittest, nonerror-making agents push the economy toward its long-run immutable equilibrium path.

In contradistinction to the classical model, in Keynes's model crucial future outcomes are uncertain and hence are not statistically predictable. The economic future is conceived as being transmutable and can be created by human actions today. In such a world, decision makers know that they do not know just what will happen on any given future date.

The role of money, liquidity and monopolistic imperfections in market forces for determining the volume of involuntary unemployment is different in models that utilize the classical concept of uncertainty *vis-à-vis* those that are based on Keynes's concept. In the next section we shall indicate how orthodox economists in the nineteenth and twentieth centuries handled the problem of what people knew about the future when they made decisions. This will require that we distinguish between the classical and Keynes concepts of uncertainty in a precise technical sense. With this background, the reader will be better able to understand why mainstream economists recommend liberalizing markets rather than direct government action to improve the economy. Post Keynesian followers of Keynes's *General Theory*, on the other hand, argue that there is a need for government to build new institutions to cure the major economic faults of a market-oriented entrepreneurial system.

3.5   A BRIEF EXCURSION INTO THE HISTORY OF ECONOMIC THOUGHT

The economy is a process in historical time. Time is a device that prevents everything from happening at once. The production of commodities takes time and the consumption of goods, especially durables, takes considerable time. Economics is the study of how households and firms make decisions regarding today's production and consumption expenditures when the outcome (payoff) of these decisions occurs at a significantly later calendar date. Any study of the behavior of economic decision makers, therefore, requires the analyst to make an assumption regarding what today's decision makers 'know' about future outcomes.

David Ricardo, one of the forefathers of classical economics, and his nineteenth-century followers, assumed a world of perfect certainty. All households and entrepreneurs possessed complete knowledge of a pre-sumed-to-exist preprogrammed external economic reality that governed all past, present and future economic outcomes. The external economic environment was assumed *immutable* in the sense that it was not susceptible to change induced by human action. The path of the economy was determined by timeless natural laws. Economic decision makers had complete knowledge of the market outcomes determined by these immutable laws. Households and firms never made errors in optimizing their economic choices. They always spent everything they earned on things with the highest 'known' future payout in terms of utility for households and profits for businesses. Accordingly, there could never be a lack of demand for the products of industry or for workers who wanted to work to produce the things that people valued most highly. The assumption of perfect fore-knowledge of the future permitted nineteenth-century classical economists to justify a *laissez-faire* philosophy for the economic system. Government policy actions could never provide a higher payout for the use of resources today than that obtained by individuals making fully informed decisions in a free market system.

In the early twentieth century, classical economists tended to substitute the notion of probabilistic risk premiums and 'certainty equivalents' for the perfect foreknowledge presumption of earlier Ricardian classical theory. Risk premiums provided uncertainty allowances where the latter referred to the difference between the estimated value of a future event, held with an objective (frequency distribution) probability of less than unity and the value of a perfectly certain event (that is, an event associated with a prob-ability equal to unity) that evokes the same behavior. The future was assumed to be *actuarially certain*. It was this actuarially certain classical model that Frank Knight was reacting against.

While rejecting Ricardo's nineteenth-century perfect foreknowledge model, today's mainstream economists follow the dictum of Old Keynesians and Robert Lucas that if economists are to be hardheaded sci-entists, then they must accept, as a universal truth, the presumption of an existence of a predetermined, preprogrammed, immutable economic reality that can be fully described by unchanging objective conditional probability functions.[15] This does not preclude an economy that is moving or changing over time. It does mean that all future movements and changes are already predetermined by the fundamental real parameters of the system. Whereas in the nineteenth-century classical economics assumed that economic decision makers already knew all future outcomes, late twentieth century classical theory required that if agents are to make optimal decisions, then they must form probabilistic expectations that mimic the objective probability programmed reality that it presumed governed future outcomes.

This classical probabilistic analysis evolved into what economists call the New Classical Theory of 'rational expectations' where individuals make decisions regarding future outcomes based on their subjectively formed probability distributions as they learn from experience. If these expectations are rational then it is presumed that the subjective probability distributions of decision makers are identical to the presumed-to-exist immutable objective probability distributions that govern the future path of the external reality that the decision makers live in.

Today's mainstream economists, whether they call themselves New Classical or New Keynesian, define the uncertainty concept in economics as involving immutable objective probabilistic distributions that govern past and present events as well as future outcomes.[16] Since economic agents in New Keynesian and New Classical models are presumed to be rational, then (by definition) people in these models are assumed to form rational expectations. In a world of rational expectations no one makes persistent errors. The future is already known in an actuarial sense by the market. These rational expectations models assume away the problem facing most of us in the real world, namely how do we make crucial decisions regarding a future that cannot be accurately forecast by the use of statistical probabilities.

The new classical presumption that statistically reliable estimates of probabilistic risks is the measure of an actuarially knowable uncertain future permits today's mainstream economists to preserve intact most of the analysis and conclusions that had been developed under the nineteenth-century classical Ricardian perfect certainty presumption. Unlike the perfect certainty model, however, conflating the concept of uncertainty with the probabilistic risk permits each individual decision maker to make an occasional random erroneous choice (in the short run) just as a single sample mean can differ from the true universe value. The assumption that people with rational expectations already 'know' the objective probabilities assures correct choices on average for those 'fittest' decision makers who survived in the Darwinian world of free markets. The *laissez-faire* approach to resolving economic problems is justified *by assumption*.

3.6   UNCERTAINTY AND ERGODIC STOCHASTIC PROCESSES

When mainstream economists measure uncertainty in terms of a probability distribution function, then logical consistency requires them to assert that existing market data are part of a time-series realization generated by an ergodic stochastic process. Paul Samuelson made the acceptance of the ergodic axiom the *sine qua non* of the scientific method in economics.

To make a 'scientific' statistical statement regarding the characteristics of any statistical universe requires the analyst to draw a sample from that universe. An arithmetic mean and standard deviation is calculated from the sample observations to achieve a statistically reliable estimate of the parameters of the universe. It therefore follows that if one wants to make reliable forecasts about the universe of events on a particular future date, today's decision makers should obtain and analyse sample data from that future universe. Since it is impossible to draw a sample from a future statistical universe, mainstream economists invoke the assumption of an economic reality system governed by ergodic stochastic economic processes. This ergodic axiom asserts, as a universal truth, that drawing a sample using past time-series and/or current cross-sectional market data is equivalent to drawing a sample from the universe of future market data. In an ergodic environment, the stochastic process generates immutable objective probabilities that govern all past, present and future data. Invoking the ergodic axiom means that the outcome at any future date is merely the statistical shadow of events that have already occurred; the future is written in today's historical 'evidence'. To fully comprehend why this is so, we must delve into some technical statistical jargon regarding stochastic processes, that is, processes that generate probability distributions, and the necessary and sufficient conditions for a stochastic system to be either ergodic or nonergodic.

A historical record of the magnitude of some economic variable collected over a period of calendar time is called a time-series realization of a stochastic process. A realization is defined as a series of sample values of a multidimensional variable over a period of time. A stochastic process makes up a statistical universe of such time series. The term *time statistics* refers to statistical averages (for example, the mean, standard deviation, and so on) calculated from a single realization over any period of calendar time. *Space statistics*, on the other hand, are the statistical averages calculated from data generated at a single fixed point of calendar time and are formed (calculated) over the universe of realizations existing at that specific calendar date (that is, space statistics are averages obtained from cross-sectional data).

If, and only if, the stochastic process is ergodic, then time and space statistics coincide except for random errors. These time and space statistics will tend to converge (with the probability of unity) as the number of observations increases. If, therefore, ergodicity is assumed, then statistics calculated from past time-series or cross-sectional data are statistically reliable estimates of the space statistics that will occur at any specific future date. Accordingly, the ergodic presumption assures that outcomes on any specific future date can be reliably predicted by a statistical analysis of existing past and current market data. Presuming ergodic conditions, therefore reduces the modeler's problem to explaining how and at what cost agents obtain and process existing historical and/or current market data (in the form of market 'price signals') to form statistically reliable probabilistic estimates (rational expectations) about the future.

All rational expectations models require the ergodic axiom as a fundamental logical foundation. This presupposition imposes the logical condition that all economic relationships are 'natural' laws of motion that have been preprogrammed into the system at the initial instant of the system's creation.[17] These natural laws cannot be changed by human action. Rational decision makers recognize that future outcomes of any decision made each day are already determined by the preprogrammed external reality. Historical market data provides 'information' for calculating probability (or decision weights)[18] that can be used to produce a statistically reliable forecast of the future outcome of any decision choice made today. This presumption reduces the modeler's analyst's problem to either (a) assuming that people in their model have already processed the necessary information and therefore 'know' the future, or (b) explaining how and at what cost agents obtain and process existing market data to form reliable estimates about future outcomes. The New Keynesian theory of asymmetric information suggests that if it is costly to extract the information from existing market data, then one can assume that some agents obtain reliable forecasts before others.

Old Classical theorists assumed that the people in their model have *perfect* foreknowledge of the deterministic future.[19] New Classical theorists do not claim that decision makers have perfect foreknowledge of the external reality. Rational expectations models only assume that people have already processed past information and current market signals to calculate subjective probabilities that are presumed to be identical with the objective probability functions describing the external reality that governs future events.

Such an assumption cannot be a correct description of the reality in which we live, as even one of the leaders of the rational expectations school, Thomas Sargent, has admitted. Sargent wrote that a rational expectations model imputes to the people inside the model much *more* knowledge about the system they are operating in than is available to the economist or econometrician who is using the model to try to understand their behavior. In particular, an econometrician faces the problem of *estimating* probability distributions and laws of motion that the agents in the model are assumed to know.[20]

Despite the patently false axiomatic foundation of rational expectations models, it is widely used because it permits the analyst to reach the same *laissez-faire* conclusions that would be forthcoming in a perfectly certain Ricardian world.

Knight's 1921 seminal work (*Risk, Uncertainty and Profit*) drew a distinction between 'true' uncertainty and probabilistic risk, where the latter is calculable based on probability distributions generated by ergodic processes and is, therefore, conceptually insurable. True uncertainty is neither calculable nor insurable. In Keynes's analysis of an entrepreneurial economy, whenever the full consequences of many of today's important economic decisions occur far in the future, true uncertainty would prevail and economic behavior could not be described as an 'outcome of a weighted average of quantitative benefits multiplied by quantitative probabilities'.[21]

Keynes implicitly rejected the classical ergodic axiom[22] as applicable to an entrepreneurial economy. With the later development of the theory of ergodic stochastic process analysis, it is possible now to interpret Keynes's uncertainty concept in terms of this stochastic concept. In Keynes's model, decision makers recognize that the external reality in which they operate is in some, but not necessarily all, economic dimensions uncertain. Consequently, decision makers 'know' they cannot reliably predict the future on the basis of any statistical analysis of past market data.[23] This nonergodic concept of uncertainty implies that the future is *transmutable* or *creative* in the sense that future economic outcomes may be permanently changed in nature and substance by today's actions of individuals, groups (for example, unions, cartels and/or governments), often in ways not even perceived by the creators of change.[24]

This nonergodic view of modeling uncertainty has been described by Sir John Hicks as a situation where people in the model 'do not know what is going to happen and know that they do not know what is going to happen. As in history!'.[25] In support of this nonergodic view, Hicks declared that 'I am bold enough to conclude from these considerations that the usefulness of "statistical" or "stochastic" methods in economics is a good deal less than is now conventionally supposed'.[26] And in a letter (dated 12 February 1983) Hicks wrote to me:

> I have now read your RE [rational expectations] paper . . . I do like it very much. I have never been through the RE literature . . . but I had just enough of it to be

put off by the smell of it. You have now *rationalized* my suspicions, and have shown me that I missed a chance of labeling my own point of view as *nonergodic*. One needs a name like that to ram a point home.

Partly in reaction to the obviously unrealistic conditions necessary for accepting the rational expectations hypothesis, in recent years some mainstream economists have raised questions regarding the use of ergodic stochastic concepts to define uncertainty as probabilistic risk. For example, Robert Solow stated: 'economics is a social science . . . much of what we observe cannot be treated as the realization of a stationary stochastic process without straining credulity'.[27]

A stationary stochastic process[28] is a necessary but not sufficient condition for ergodicity. Nonstationary processes must be nonergodic systems. If, as Solow suggests, time-series data are generated by nonstationary (and therefore nonergodic) processes, then Solow is implying that only idiots would ever believe that most important macroeconomic processes are ergodic. Yet all mainstream academic economists who crave to be thought of as 'hardheaded' scientists – including Robert Solow – accept Samuelson's creed that economics can be a science only if it presumes the ergodic axiom. If Solow is to be believed, then the 'best and the brightest' in the mainstream of modern-day economics have been duped by what Phillip Mirowski once called 'physics envy' into accepting the ergodic axiom as an article of faith.

3.7   IMMUTABLE VERSUS TRANSMUTABLE THEORIES OF REALITY

If the external economic reality is ergodic (and therefore immutable), then society cannot enact laws (policies) to alter the inevitable predetermined future outcomes any more than a legislature can overturn either Nature's 'law of gravity' or the probability distribution associated with a fair game of roulette. In this conception, humans have no freedom to alter their long-run economic future. Moreover the state cannot have any more 'information' about the future than individuals in a free market can obtain. This view results in the Ronald Reagan-type rhetorical question: 'How can bureaucrats in Washington know better how to spend your money than you do?'

The only issues for immutable reality theorists are: (a) how, and at what cost, do humans obtain reliable information regarding the future from existing market data and (b) if each agent's computing ability is not sufficient to obtain statistically reliable conditional probabilities (or decision weights), that is, each agent faces an epistemologically uncertain future, then does a nonhuman *deus ex machina* exist that can provide the relevant probabilities and predictions that are, in principle, computable in an ergodic system?

In responding to these queries, orthodox economists have developed a number of variants of two basic types of immutable reality models. In Table 3.1, type 1 immutable reality models are distinguished from type 2 immutable reality models by a fundamental epistemological assumption regarding how much, if any, reliable information about the immutable reality can be obtained and processed by agents in the short run.

Table 3.1   Concepts of external economic reality

Concept	Examples of theories using this postulate
A. *Immutable reality* (an ergodic system) Type 1 in the short run, the future is predetermined and known to the people in the model	1. Classical perfect certainty models 2. Actuarial certainty equivalents, e.g., rational expectations models 3. New Classical models 4. Some New Keynesian theories
Type 2 in the short run, the future is predetermined but is not completely known to all people in the model due to some limitation in the cost of human information processing and computing power	1. Savage's expected utility theory 2. Some Austrian theories 3. Some New Keynesian models e.g., asymmetric information and coordination failure theories) 4. Chaos, sunspot and bubble theories
B. *Transmutable or creative reality* (a nonergodic system) Some aspects of the economic future will be created by human action today and/or in the future	1. Keynes's *General Theory* 2. Post Keynesian monetary theory 3. Post-1974 writings of Sir John Hicks 4. G.L.S. Shackle's crucial experiment analysis 5. Old Institutionalist theories

Type 1 immutable reality models presume that at the initial instant agents already reliably 'know' the preprogrammed future path of the external reality. Type 1 models include Old Classical perfect certainty models, New Classical and all New Keynesian models that assume that agents already possess rational expectations, as well as any other models where in the short run, agents 'know' actuarial certainty equivalents.

Type 2 immutable reality models assume that, in the short run, agents' knowledge regarding reality is severely incomplete or even completely unknown as some limitation on human ability (that is, some constraint on humans' computing power) or costs of analysis prevent agents from using (collecting and analysing) historical time-series and/or cross-sectional data to obtain short-run, statistically reliable knowledge regarding future economic variables. Epistemological human ignorance about some aspect(s) of the immutable economic reality is the hallmark of type 2 immutable reality models.

In mainstream economics, the long run is conventionally defined as that point of time when all agents' plans are being met and no forecasting errors occur.[29] In the long run, all type 1 and type 2 immutable reality models presume that the external predetermined reality is somehow revealed to all successful market participants, or, at least, successful agents behave 'as if' they know this reality. According to Mankiw:

> Most [economists] accept the natural-rate hypothesis which interpreted broadly states that classical economics is right in the long run. Moreover, economists today are more interested in long-run equilibrium. The long run is not so far away that one can cavalierly claim, as Keynes did, that 'in the long run we're all dead'.[30]

Some mainstream economists even conceptualize the long-run equilibrium position as a 'center of gravity' toward which the system is reverting, even if the system never reaches this long-run equilibrium position in any given period of calendar time.[31] As a logical construct, however, the long run ultimately must be realized unless either (a) the analyst postulates continuous additional exogenous 'shocks' to the system, or (b) the analyst deals only with an open-ended model where the long run is never reached within strict time limits placed on the model's future time horizon.[32] In the latter case, no matter how many calendar time periods are covered by open-ended models they are, by construction, short run.

Except for the perfect certainty case, immutable reality models typically employ a subjectivist orientation. Agents form subjective expectations (usually, but not necessarily in the form of Bayesian subjective probabilities). In type 1 models these subjective probabilities are assumed to be the same as the underlying objective probabilities. In type 2 immutable models, short-run subjective probabilities need not coincide with the presumed immutable objective probabilities. Today's decision makers can make short-run errors regarding the uncertain (that is, risky) future for they do not possess sufficient mental processing power (even if past and present market data ('information') exist) to reliably 'know' the objective probabilities that govern future outcomes. By definition of the conventional long run, however, agents 'learn' so that subjective probabilities or decision weights tend to converge onto an accurate description of the programmed external reality in the long run.

Grandmont and Malgrange have characterized this learning process as follows:

> 'Individual traders are bound to make significant forecasting errors . . . while they are learning the dynamical laws of their environment, during the period of transition of the economy toward an hypothetical long-run equilibrium – if it ever reaches one along which all forecasting errors vanish eventually.'[33]

Those agents whose subjective probabilities do not converge on the objective probabilities that govern the external reality will make persistent systematic forecasting errors. The market is typically seen as embodying some form of a Darwinian process of natural selection that weeds out these persistent error makers who make inefficient choices until, in the long run, only agents who do not make systematic errors remain.

Theories that claim that free markets are efficient are usually based on some variant of this Darwinian theme where the long-run intrinsic real values of all economic assets are determined by the programmed real parameters of production and exchange that cannot be changed by any deliberate human action. In the long run, rational agents make efficient choices as subjective expectations adapt to the predetermined and immutable reality.[34]

3.8   UNCERTAINTY AND 'IRRATIONAL' BEHAVIOR

For Keynes and the Post Keynesians, long-run uncertainty is an attribute of a transmutable reality concept. A fundamental tenet of Keynes's revolution is that probabilistic risks, conceptually knowable on the basis of past and present market signals, must be distinguished from those aspects of the future that are uncertain and cannot be known today.

Probabilistic risk characterizes routine, repeatable economic decisions where it is reasonable to presume an unchanging reality (that is, an ergodic system). Keynes, however, rejected the ergodic axiom as applicable to all economic expectations when he insisted that the 'state of long term expectations' involving nonroutine matters that are 'very uncertain' form the basis for important economic decisions involving investment, the accumulation of wealth, finance and funding.[35] In these areas, agents 'know' they are dealing with an uncertain, nonprobabilistic creative economic external reality.[36]

As a matter of logic, rational expectations are rational in a hypothetical ergodic world. Rational expectations are irrational when agents 'know' that the system is not ergodic. Under nonergodic economic conditions, it is sensible for decision makers to make choices that would be seen as 'irrational' in an immutable ergodic system. For example, to mainstream theorists, the fact that income recipients may decide over their entire life never to spend (to save) some current income on any products of industry may seem 'irrational'. In the real world, these 'irrational' income recipients save in the form of money and other liquid assets as a permanent hedge against a permanently uncertain future.

For example, analysing a sample of more than 9000 households, investigators from the Poverty Institute at the University of Wisconsin found that 'the elderly spend less than the nonelderly at the same level of income and the oldest of the elderly have the lowest average propensity to consume'.[37] Instead of exhibiting a spending pattern over their life cycle as rational utility maximizers would in an ergodic world where people save for their retirement years and then spend down their wealth as they age, the elderly in the Wisconsin study who 'face a complex problem of uncertainty about their health, life expectancy, and ability to maintain independent households . . . respond by reducing their consumption' and increase their savings propensity out of every level of income during retirement.[38] In so doing, these households would be irrational if they lived in the ergodic world of New Classical models, but they are being perfectly sensible in the nonergodic reality in which we live.

3.9   CRUCIAL DECISIONS AND SCHUMPETERIAN ENTREPRENEURS

Shackle has developed the concept of crucial choice, that is, a situation where a decision is made that changes forever the economic environment so that the identical decision conditions can 'never to be repeated'.[39] The future is transmutable in that it can be created by crucial choice decisions[40] although the future that is created is often not precisely what anyone intended. In Shackle's crucial choice models the future is not discovered through the Bayes–LaPlace theorem regarding relative frequencies or via any error-learning model. This principle of cruciality ties Shackle's Austrian background with Schumpeter's theory of creative destruction where an entrepreneur who introduces innovative changes creatively destroys forever the existing economic environment.

If entrepreneurs have any important function in the real world, it is to make crucial decisions. Entrepreneurship, which is but one facet of human creativity, by its very nature, involves crucialities in a nonergodic setting. To restrict entrepreneurship to robot decision making through ergodic calculations in a stochastic world, as Lucas and Sargent do,[41] ignores the role of the Schumpeterian entrepreneur – the creator of technological revolutions that bring about future changes that are often inconceivable even to the innovative entrepreneur. Exogenous expectations in a transmutable environment are a necessary condition for assuming the human free will that creative entrepreneurs exhibit.

Ergodic probability models are a beguiling representation of decision making only in a world where routine decisions are made by Lucas and Sargent's 'robot decision maker' entrepreneur.[42] In a Lucas and Sargent New Classical model, an electronic computer can make all the entrepreneurial decisions. Since crucial decisions are never made by entrepreneurs in Lucas and Sargent's world, these models cannot explain the essential creative function of entrepreneurial behavior in a Keynes–Schumpeter world where the reality is transmutable.

The possible existence of crucial decisions has implicitly been recognized and summarily rejected by mainstream theorists in their desire to be seen as 'hardheaded' scientists obeying Samuelson's canon that invoking the ergodic hypothesis is necessary to do scientific economics. For example, Lucas and Sargent indicate that they desire to draw conditional inferences about human behavior from observed economic times series:

> [W]e observe an agent, or a collection of agents behaving through time; we wish to use these observations to infer how this behavior *would have* differed had the agent's environment been altered in some specified way. Stated so generally, it is clear that some inferences of this type will be impossible to draw. (How would one's life have been different had one married someone else?) The belief in the possibility of a non-experimental empirical economics is, however, equivalent to the belief that inferences of this kind can be made, under *some* circumstances.[43]

Unlike Shackle, whose principle of cruciality defines a sufficient condition for the existence of nonergodic worlds, Lucas and Sargent provide neither necessary nor sufficient conditions when '*some* circumstances' will prevail. If Lucas and Sargent are correct and only in 'some circumstances' can statistical inferences based on a realization be drawn, then an immutable (ergodic) reality where rational expectations can exist cannot be ubiquitous in economics. Necessarily there must be *other* circumstances where nonergodic circumstances pertain, and in such instances probability theory and the rational expectation hypothesis can be a seriously misleading analogy.[44]

If the relatively innocuous (and replicative?) choice of spouse is admitted by Lucas and Sargent to be so crucial that despite the large number of marriages recorded over time, statistical inferences about conditional probabilities regarding happy marriages cannot be drawn, then should not decisions 'marrying' entrepreneurs to plant and equipment, or to production runs, or even decisions marrying the economy to money supply policies, or to specific banking institutions, and so on, also be classified as crucial choices?

Crucial choices are more common than one might expect. Where there are transaction costs, no decision is fully reversible.[45] Mainstream micro as well as macro theorists ignore this element of cruciality. Orthodox theorists avoid Shackle's crucial decision concept by assuming the ability to recontract without costs if one does not initially trade at the general equilibrium prices that embody the objective reality governed by the real parameters of a predetermined economic system. Because of the substantial transactions costs involved in investment, production, and (at least) big ticket consumption decisions, in these areas, agents are necessarily married to their choices. Decisions in these areas are normally crucial and nonergodic conditions prevail.

In the real world, some economic processes may appear to be ergodic, at least for short subperiods of calendar time, while others are not. The epistemological problem facing every economic decision maker is to determine whether (a) the phenomena involved are currently governed by probabilities that can be presumed ergodic – at least for the relevant future, or (b) nonergodic circumstances are involved. It is only in the later case that entrepreneurship, money, liquidity and contracts have important and essential roles to play.[46] It is only the latter case where important policy decisions need to be made.

Arrow and Hahn have written:

> [T]he terms in which contracts are made matter. In particular, if money is the good in terms of which contracts are made, then the prices of goods in terms of money are of special significance. This is not the case if we consider an economy without a past or a future . . . If a serious monetary theory comes to be written, the fact that contracts are made in terms of money will be of considerable importance.[47]

A nonergodic (uncertain) environment provides an analytical rationale for the existence of fixed money contracts and nonneutral money. The Post Keynesian emphasis on a nonergodic external reality provides the basis for a 'serious monetary theory' that Arrow and Hahn have called for.

Finally, as Arrow and Hahn demonstrated, all general (full employment) equilibrium existence proofs are jeopardized in a world with fixed money contracts over time, that is, it cannot be demonstrated that a freely competitive market system will automatically generate full employment.[48] In other words, if transactors in the real world enter into monetary contracts, mainstream economic models are not relevant. Only a nonergodic setting provides the analytical basis for the use of fixed money contracts and therefore provides for the possibility of the existence of long-period unemployment equilibrium – and the possibility of the nonexistence of a general equilibrium in the absence of deliberate government policy to assure there is never a lack of aggregate effective demand.

APPENDIX 3A   ARE PROBABILITIES KNOWABLE BUT UNKNOWN BECAUSE OF LIMITED HUMAN COMPUTING POWER?

In this appendix we explain why Knight's 'uncertainty' model, as well as the expected utility model of Savage, and the recent fads of chaos theory, sunspot theory and bubble theory models all fail to break out of the classical axiomatic foundation. Those not interested in these aspects of the history of economic thought can skip this appendix without loss.

Frank Knight

Knight explicitly distinguished between quantifiable risks and uncertainties. Knight wrote:

> [T]he practical difference between the two categories, risk and uncertainty, is that in the former the distribution of the outcome in a group of instances is known (either through calculation *a priori* or from the statistics of past experience), while in the case of uncertainty, this is not true, the reason being in general that it is impossible to form a group of instances, because the situation dealt with is in a high degree unique.[49]

In an ergodic universe, any single event can appear to be unique to the observer only if he/she does not have a sufficient knowledge of reality to properly classify this event (by a priori reasoning if not from the frequency distribution of past occurrences) with a group of similar conditional events. Knight explains that uncertainty involving 'unique events' occurs because agents possess only 'partial knowledge' of the cosmos.[50]

Knight's reflections on the immutability of the economic cosmos are ambiguous. He appears to argue that uncertainty is an epistemological factor in an ontological immutable reality when he writes that the 'universe may not be knowable . . . [but] objective phenomenon [reality] . . . is certainly knowable to a degree so far beyond our actual powers . . . [and therefore] any limitation of knowledge due to lack of real consistency in the cosmos may be ignored'.[51]

In other words, Knight suggests that any lack of knowledge about external reality that might be attributed to a lack of real consistency over time in the cosmos is insignificant and may be ignored when compared to humans' cognitive failures to identify the predetermined external reality. Knight suggests, rather than dogmatically claims, that it 'is *conceivable* that all changes might take place in accordance with known laws'.[52] Though Knight left the theoretical door slightly ajar, it does appear that his analysis is primarily based on the concept of a predetermined immutable cosmos.

The primary difference between risk and uncertainty for Knight is that uncertainty exists only because of the failure of humans' actual powers to process the information 'knowable' about the programmed economic cosmos.

Since probabilistic risks can be quantified by human computing power, Knight correctly argued that the future is insurable against risky occurrences. The cost of insurance, or self-insurance, will be taken into account in all entrepreneurial marginal cost calculations (or by contingency contracts in a complete Arrow Debreu system). This insurance process permits entrepreneurs to make rational profit-maximizing production and investment choices. The existence of what appears to be a 'unique' and therefore an uncertain event in Knight's scheme, on the other hand, seems to arise only because humans do not have sufficient cognitive powers to group correctly uncertain outcomes by their common characteristics. For Knight all agents cannot capture the insurance costs of these 'uncertain' events in their marginal cost computations.

If we accept Knight's position that humans' inability to 'know' areas of the consistent, that is, immutable, cosmic reality in which we live is so large that it permits us to 'ignore' (for analytical purposes) the possibility of a transmutable reality, then the probabilities associated with 'uncertain' events are already programmed into the 'consistency in the cosmos'.[53]

Leonard Savage

Savage's expected utility theory presumes that a decision maker examines all possible future outcomes of any action taken today. Savage characterizes this examination process as 'Look before you leap'.[54] The first postulate underlying Savage's 'look before you leap' expected utility theory framework is the ordering axiom, that is, the presumption that there exists a finite set of acts and outcomes and that each agent can make a complete and transitive preference ordering of all possible alternative choices.[55]

Savage recognizes that his ordering axiom-based 'Look before you leap' analysis is not a general theory of decision making for it fails to explicitly deal with uncertainty *per se*. Savage admits that 'a person may not know [all] the consequences of the acts open to him in each state of the world. He might be . . . ignorant'[56] and hence might want to leave his options open. This leaving options open, which Savage characterized as 'You can cross that bridge when you come to it' is, Savage admits, often a more accurate description of human behavior. In fact, the 'look before you leap' approach '[c]arried to its logical extreme . . . is utterly ridiculous . . . because the task implied is not even remotely resembled by human possibility . . . the "look before you leap" principle is preposterous if carried to extremes'.[57]

   Savage is careful to call attention to the fact that there is a 'practical necessity of confining attention to, or isolating, relatively simple situations in almost all applications of the theory of decision [expected utility theory] developed in this book'.[58] The ordering axiom implies that the expected utility explanation of decision making is useful only when one 'attack[s] relatively simple problems of decision by artificially confining attention to so small a world that the "Look before you leap" principle can be applied'.[59] Expected utility theory is 'practical [only] in suitably limited domains . . . At the same time, the behavior of people is often at variance with the theory. The departure is sometimes flagrant'.[60]

   If in some areas of economic activity the ability of humans to form a complete preference ordering regarding all potential consequences of all possible actions is beyond human computing power, then expected utility theory cannot provide a useful explanation of the behavior of decision makers in these areas. These areas include decisions involving investment and savings in liquid assets.

   If people recognize that they are ignorant of all possible current acts and all future consequences, they may wish to defer making the 'rational' decisions of expected utility theory. Agents can recognize that they are unable to 'look before they leap'. Decision makers may prefer to leave their options open ('Cross that bridge when they come to it') when either (a) the decision maker 'knows' he/she is unable to specify and/or order a complete list of prospects regarding all possible choices, even if the future is predetermined,[61] or (b) the future is transmutable so that agents 'know' it is impossible to possess today a complete list of prospects for any specific future date.

   Whenever Savage's ordering axiom is violated, expected utility theory is not applicable. Hicks associates violations of Savage's 'ordering axiom' with Keynes' long-term 'liquidity' concept.[62] Accordingly, Keynes's emphasis of nonprobabilistic uncertainty and liquidity preference implies that expected utility theory is not logically applicable to Keynes's general analysis of the determination of employment in an entrepreneurial economy.

Chaos Theory

The short-run emphasis on the limitations of human computing power of type 2 theories may explain the recent popularity of complex mathematical models such as chaos theory or complexity theory models to analyse economic fluctuations – especially those in the financial markets. 'Chaos theory shows that a simple relationship that is *deterministic* but *nonlinear* can yield a complex time path . . . When chaos occurs economic forecasting becomes extremely difficult . . . basic forecasting devices become questionable'.[63]

This determinate theory of chaos claims that the fluttering of a butterfly's wings[64] in China will, through a complex but determinate system of nonlinear difference equations 'cause' a hurricane in the Atlantic Ocean. For an omnipotent Mother Nature, there is no uncertainty about butterfly-induced hurricanes in a structure described by such a programmed nonlinear equational system. The problem is that the structure is so complex that unless humans already know it or have some *deus ex machina* to describe it, it is extremely difficult to discover the future before the hurricane hits. In the long run, those who survive hurricanes act as if they knew the complex structure of these nonlinear models.

Austrian Theory

Modern-day Austrian economists such as O'Driscoll and Rizzo[65] believe in an economic world where there is an immutable external reality similar to the way nineteenth-century physicists viewed the working of the physical world. In their emphasis on uncertainty, however, Austrians often differ from mainstream Old and New Classical theorists. Many Austrians believe that the external reality may be predetermined by Mother Nature but this reality is too complicated for any single human being ever to process the information being sent out by market signals. The free market is the Austrians' *deus ex machina* that provides the (in principle calculable) relevant probabilities and predictions to coordinate plans and outcomes via a Darwinian process[66] in a world of epistemological uncertainty and a programmed external reality.

Sunspot Theory

Modern sunspot theorists, who often suggest compatibility 'to earlier Keynesian macromodels' involving 'animal spirits',[67] are attempting to marry the rational expectations hypothesis with the view that the subjective probability distributions need not, in the short run, match the objective (and assumed ergodic) probability functions governing real production and exchange processes.[68] In such systems, only in the 'hypothetical long run' will 'forecasting errors vanish'.

Such models of 'self-fulfilling' forecasts seem to permit mainstream economists to salvage a more sophisticated longer-run form of what Samuelson has called the 'ergodic hypothesis' (and thus meet Samuelson's criterion for economist-cum-hard scientists) while providing models that possess, at least in the long short run, a real world business cycle due to the errors of decision makers.

For sunspot theorists, 'sunspots' represent extrinsic uncertainty, that is a random phenomenon that does not affect 'tastes, endowments, or production possibilities . . . [t]he basic parameters defining an economy . . . the fundamentals of that economy'.[69] These fundamental forces of tastes, endowments and productive technology predetermine the economic reality environment and produce the predetermined long-run center of gravity or long-run equilibrium toward which the endogenous forces in the economy are always pushing. Only continuous demand and/or supply shocks[70] creating new exogenous 'extrinsic' uncertainty can prevent the system from settling down to this long-run equilibrium position.

The extrinsic or 'extraneous uncertainty', however, always 'disappears in the long run – or in a stationary state, or when enough contingent claims markets exist to cover all probabilities'.[71] that is, when probabilities associated with the presumed immutable reality are calculated by a *deus ex machina* marketplace.

Sunspot theorists only permit 'temporary' departures from the long-run equilibrium determined by immutable real economic 'fundamentals' in the system. In the long run, though we may all be dead, the ergodic economic process involving the real 'basic parameters' defining the economic system will persist and determine the final solution to the economic problem.

Despite claims of comparability to Keynes by demonstrating the possibility of short-run 'Keynes-type' unemployment, sunspot models are *not* compatible with Keynes's 'animal spirits' analysis where (a) money is non-neutral in both the short and the long runs, and (b) *crucial decisions* by humans (under uncertainty) alter the fundamental real forces of the economic system as decision makers create (and therefore affect) the future.

Bubble Theory

Speculative bubble theory attempts to explain the 'excessive' financial spot market price volatility often observed in the real world within the context of a predetermined external reality that imparts 'intrinsic' or fundamental values to all real economic assets. If the bubble is 'rational' in the orthodox theory sense, decision makers believe that there is a probability *p* of a positive deviation from the 'intrinsic' value (that is, the 'real' value inherent in an asset derived from the programmed immutable real parameters [fundamentals]) in the next period's financial spot market price. This probability will not only already be expressed in today's spot price, but it will also represent the prospect of an even larger deviation in each future period *ad infinitum*.

As long as the system is open-ended, the deviation of market values from intrinsic values can increase without limit. Although this 'bubble' analysis appears to utilize a rational expectations equilibrium framework it is fundamentally inconsistent with the logical foundation of rational expectations where subjective evaluations (in probability terms) equal the intrinsic objective valuation, that is, today's spot market price reliably reflects the intrinsic value (objective reality) of each asset. Moreover, in rational expectations equilibrium, current expectations are backward (rather than forward) looking in the sense that past data provide the reliable information upon which today's expectations are based. Nevertheless, the term 'bubble' suggests that sooner or later the bubble valuations will burst, that is, the deviation from the intrinsic value will not go on to infinity.[72]

Glickman has argued that the attempt to obtain theoretical consistency in the bubble literature leaves this bubble theory devoid of any explanation of 'why future deviations occur or why agents should expect that they will do so . . . the argument is therefore no more than a neoclassical abstraction which shuffles off into a mysterious and indefinite remote future the problem of what is happening today'.[73] Speculative bubble theory permits exuberant but false forecasts of intrinsic value to persist indefinitely only by postponing the long-run day of reckoning to the infinite horizon.[74]

Unlike the sunspot or speculative bubble theorists, Keynes reminded his readers that 'we must not conclude from this that everything depends on waves of irrational psychology . . . We are merely reminding ourselves that human decisions affecting the future, whether personal or economic, cannot depend on strict mathematical expectation, since the basis for making such calculations does not exist'.[75]

NOTES

1. F.H. Knight, *Risk, Uncertainty and Profits*, 1937 edition, University of Chicago Press, ✓ Chicago, pp. 19–21.
2. N. Lee, *The Rival Queens*, Gain & Bently, London, 1684, Act I.
3. J.M. Keynes, 'A monetary theory of production' (1933), reprinted in *The Collected Writings of John Maynard Keynes*, vol. 13, edited by D. Moggridge, Macmillan, London, 1973, p. 409.
4. J.M. Keynes, *The General Theory of Employment, Interest and Money*, Harcourt, Brace, New York, 1936, p. 372.
5. See K.J. Arrow and F.J. Hahn, *General Competitive Equilibrium*, Holden-Day, San Francisco, 1971, pp. 15, 127, 215, 305.
6. Classical theory deals with a system in which 'relevant facts were known more or less for certain . . . facts and expectations were assumed to be given in a definite and calculable form; and risks, of which, though admitted, not much notice was taken, were supposed to be capable of an exact actuarial computation. The calculus of probabilities, though mention of it was kept in the background, was supposed to be capable of reducing uncertainty to the same calculable status as that of certainty itself . . . [whereas] the fact that our knowledge of the future is fluctuating, vague and uncertain, renders wealth a peculiarly unsuitable subject for the methods of the classical economic theory . . . By "uncertain" let me explain I do not mean merely to distinguish what is known for certain from what is probable . . . About these matters there is no scientific basis to form any

calculable probability whatever. We simply do not know' [J.M. Keynes, 'The general theory of employment', *Quarterly Journal of Economics* (1937) reprinted in *The Collected Writings*, vol. 14, 1973, pp. 112–14.

7. In deterministic (that is, nonprobabilistic) classical models, the ordering axiom plays the same role that the ergodic axiom plays in stochastic models. The ordering axiom presumes that each economic agent 'knows' the outcome for every possible decision and can order these outcomes in terms of relative desirabilities In most of the exposition that follows only the ergodic axiom will be emphasized.

8. Keynes, *The General Theory*, pp. 230–31.

9. Ibid., p. 241.

10. Ibid., p. 238.

11. F.H. Hahn, 'Keynesian economics and general equilibrium theory' in *The Microfoundations of Macroeconomics*, edited by G.C. Harcourt, Macmillan, London, 1977, p. 31, italics added.

12. Ibid., p. 39.

13. Classical microfoundations assume that the earning of income always involves disutility, while the products of industry are the *only* scarce things which generate utility. It therefore follows that if future outcomes are knowable (that is, ergodic), then utility maximizers will bear the irksomeness of engaging in income producing activities only to the point where the marginal disutility of earning income equals the expected marginal utility of the products of industry that utility maximizers 'know' they want to buy. All utility-maximizing agents are on their budget constraint line, allocating *all* their income on purchasing producible goods and services. A demand to hold a nonproducible money or other assets solely for liquidity purposes is irrational, given the special assumptions of the classical case. Money is therefore merely a neutral veil.

14. In an intertemporal setting with gross substitutability over time, agents plan to spend lifetime income on the products of industry over their life cycle. The long-run marginal propensity to spend is unity.

15. P.A. Samuelson ('Classical and neoclassical theory', in *Monetary Theory*, edited by R.W. Clower, Penguin, London, 1969, pp. 104–5) and R. Lucas and T. Sargent (*Rational Expectations and Econometric Practices*, University of Minnesota Press, Minneapolis, 1981, p. xii) have made the assumption of a predetermined reality a necessary condition for scientific methodology in economics.

16. Lucas and Sargent, *op cit*.

17. It is as if the future economic history has already been written, and all market participants are merely actors who are reading the lines already written for them by the great Shakespeare author in the sky.

18. Milton Friedman would argue that even if agents do not calculate probabilities they act 'as if' they did.

19. As we shall explain in the appendix to this chapter, modern-day classical economists who utilize the deterministic *expected utility theory* as the microfoundation for decision making also presume agents have correct foreknowledge of future outcomes.

20. T. Sargent, *Bounded Rationality in Macroeconomics*, Clarendon Press, Oxford, 1993, p. 21.

21. Keynes, *The General Theory*, p. 161.

22. Unlike today's orthodox economists, Keynes did not write in the lexicon of stochastic processes in developing his concept of uncertainty. Nevertheless, in criticizing Tinbergen's use of econometric analysis, Keynes argued that Tinbergen's 'method' was not applicable to economic data because 'the economic environment is not homogeneous over a period of time', that is, economic time series are not stationary. Since nonstationarity is a sufficient condition for a nonergodic process, Keynes's criticism demonstrates his belief that important economic data are generated in a nonergodic environment.

23. The absence of ergodic conditions, therefore, is a sufficient condition for Keynes's concept of uncertainty. In a nonergodic environment, even if agents have the capacity to obtain and statistically analyse past and current market data, these calculations do not,

and cannot, provide a statistically reliable basis for forecasting the probability distributions, if any, that will govern outcomes at any specific date in the future.

24. It is also possible that changes that are not predetermined can occur even without any specific human action.

25. J.R. Hicks, *Economic Perspectives*, Oxford University Press, Oxford, 1977, p. vii.

26. J.R. Hicks, *Causality in Economics*, Basic Books, New York, 1979.

27. R.M. Solow 'Economic history and economics', *American Economic Review Papers and Proceedings*, **75**, 1985, p. 328.

28. A stationary stochastic process is a time-series realization where calculations of the time-series statistics are independent of the calendar time at which the data was collected.

29. Or as Friedman states: 'The long-run equilibrium in which, as I put it, "all anticipations are realized" and that is determined by "the earlier quantity theory plus the Walrasian equations of general equilibrium" . . . is a logical construct that defines the trend to which it [the actual world] is tending to return'. (M. Friedman, 'Comments on the critics' in *Milton Friedman's Monetary Framework*, edited by R.J. Gordon, University of Chicago Press, Chicago, 1974, p. 150).

30. N.G. Mankiw 'The resurrection of Keynesian economics', *European Economic Review,* **36**, 1992, p. 561.

31. Note the similarity to the physicists's conception of the equilibrium position of a swinging pendulum.

32. In contrast, in his general theory of an external nonergodic reality, Keynes provides for an explicitly logical explanation of why money is never neutral in either the short run or the long run.

33. J.M. Grandmont and P. Malgrange, 'nonlinear dynamics', *Journal of Economic Theory*, **40**, 1986, p. 9.

34. Even if, in the short run, successful agents do not 'know' they are making optimal choices.

35. Keynes, *The General Theory*, pp. 147–8.

36. It is here that Shackle's concept of a crucial decision is relevant. An agent engages in a crucial decision when 'the person concerned cannot exclude from his mind the possibility that the very act of performing the experiment may destroy forever the circumstances in which' choice is made. G.L. Shackle, *Uncertainty in Economics*, Cambridge University Press, Cambridge, 1955, p. 6.

37. S. Danziger, J. van der Gagg, E. Smolensky and M. Taussig, 'the life cycle hypothesis and the consumption behavior of the elderly', *Journal of Post Keynesian Economics*, **5**, 1982–83, p. 224.

38. Ibid., p. 226.

39. Shackle, *op cit.*, p. 7.

40. If important decisions regarding the accumulation of wealth, the possession of liquidity, the commitment to a production process with significant set-up costs and gestation period, and so on, are crucial, then the future 'waits, not for its contents to be discovered, but for that content to be *originated*' (G.L.S. Shackle, *Epistemics and Economics*, Cambridge University Press, Cambridge, 1980, p. 102).

41. Lucas and Sargent , op. cit., p. xii.

42. Ibid., p. xii.

43. Ibid., pp. xi–xii.

44. Any economic choice which once undertaken cannot be undone without significant (income or capital) costs must mean that the initial circumstances in all its relevant attributes cannot be replicated. Crucial decisions involve such costly actions which alter current probability structures, if they exist at all, in unpredictable ways; hence the ordering axiom is violated and no probability function can be defined. Rational expectations equilibrium models, on the other hand, presume given and unchanging subjective probability distributions. These models can be a useful analytical tool for studying noncrucial decision making involving small (that is, almost costless) differences in outcomes, for then choice can be easily replicated, for example, the choice of whether to purchase a Winesap or a Delicious apple based on rational expected utilities. In the view of Keynes,

Shackle and the Post Keynesians, it is very doubtful that choices between expensive and far-reaching commitments (for example, at the micro level the purchase of durables which cannot be resold without significant costs, or at the macro level choices between public policies) can be represented by such probabilistic analogies.

45. See J. Lesourne, *The Economics of Order and Disorder*, Clarendon Press, Oxford, 1992.
46. See P. Davidson, 'rational expectations: a fallacious foundation for studying crucial decision-making', *Journal of Post Keynesian Economics*, **5**, 1982–83 pp. 182–97, P. Davidson, 'Is probability theory relevant for uncertainty?', *Journal of Economic Perspectives*, **5**, 1991 pp. 129–43, P. Davidson, *Post Keynesian Macroeconomic Theory*, Edward Elgar, Cheltenham, 1994.
47. Arrow and Hahn, op. cit., pp. 356–7.
48. Ibid., p. 361.
49. Knight, op. cit., p. 233.
50. Ibid., p. 198. Proper classification can be, at least, conceptually discovered. A priori all observations should be lumped into the same class as long as the only difference in the value of each observation can be attributed solely to experimental error. When the difference in magnitudes among observations can be attributed to a systematic difference, then separate classes must be set up for observations that (a priori if not statistically) are known to be due to systematic differences. A truly unique occurrence, that is, the only conceptually possible occupancy in a class, can occur only if the analyst *knows the entire universe* of outcomes and therefore can dogmatically state that this observation is systematically different from *all* other possible conceivable observations obtainable from an infinity of realizations. For Knight, however, unique events are associated with 'partial knowledge' of the universe.
51. Ibid., p. 210.
52. Ibid., p. 198.
53. In the long run, those entrepreneurs who in their price–marginal cost calculations include these insurance costs 'as if' they knew the objective probabilities will make the efficient decision and will, in Knight's system, earn profits.
54. L. Savage, *The Foundation of Statistics*, John Wiley, New York, 1954, p. 16.
55. Ibid., pp. 16–19.
56. Ibid., p. 15.
57. Ibid., pp. 15–16.
58. Savage (ibid., pp. 82–4) admits that he finds 'it difficult to say with any completeness how such isolated situations are actually arrived at and justified' and he suggests 'tongue in cheek . . . that the fact that what are often thought of as consequences . . . in isolated decision situations are in reality highly uncertain . . . I therefore suggest that we must expect acts with actually highly uncertain consequences to play the role of sure consequences in typical isolated decision situations' where expected utility theory is applicable.
59. Savage, op. cit., p. 16.
60. Ibid., p. 20.
61. Some have argued that a complete ordering can always be obtained by defining a residual category, R, which covers all possible eventualities not conceived of by the agent. How can a rational agent transitively order the residual category R ('anything else not mentioned in occurrence A, B and C, where $A > B > C$')? Will this residual category always be less preferable to all listed occurrences, that is, $A > B > C > R$? Or is it possible that R may be preferable to one or more of the fully described listed categories, that is, $A > B > R > C$? Without knowing exactly what can happen in R how can an agent rationally evaluate and order R relative to other choices?
62. Hicks, *Causality in Economics*, p. 113.
63. W.J. Baumol and J. Benhabib, 'Chaos: significance, mechanism, and economic applications', *Journal of Economic Perspectives*, **3**, 1989, p. 79.
64. Does the butterfly have free will to decide if, and when, to flutter its wings, or is that also determined by some immutable nature law?

65. G.P. O'Driscoll and M.J. Rizzo, *The Economics of Time and Ignorance*, Blackwell, New York, 1985.
66. See O'Driscoll and Rizzo (ibid., pp. 38–40) for a description of a 'vague Darwinian process' operating in a free market economy.
67. Grandmont and Malgrange, op. cit., p. 10; D. Cass and K. Shell, 'Do sunspots matter?', *Journal of Political Economy*, **91**, 1983, p. 193.
68. Cass and Shell (op. cit., p. 194) state that they 'adopt the strong version of the rational expectations hypothesis: Consumers share the same beliefs about sunspot activity. This allows the interpretation that subjective probabilities are equal to objective probabilities'. I would have thought that the relevant objective probabilities involved the random variables depending on the unchanging economic parameters regarding tastes, endowments and production possibilities of *the immutable external economic reality* – what Cass and Shell (p. 196) call the 'basic parameters defining an economy', and not the objective probability of sunspot activity!
69. Ibid., pp. 194–6.
70. A 'shock' is defined as an exogenous force. If the shocked system has a tendency to return to its predetermined equilibrium position (or rate of growth), then the system is immutable.
71. C. Azariadis, 'Self-fulfilling prophecies', *Journal of Economic Theory*, **25**, 1981, p. 380.
72. The existence of a bubble which either deviates forever from intrinsic values, or a bubble that ultimately bursts are concepts that cannot exist, by definition, in a long-run rational expectations equilibrium in an ergodic system.
73. M. Glickman, 'The concept of information, intractable uncertainty, and the current state of efficient market theory', *Journal of Post Keynesian Economics*, **16**, 1994, pp. 325–50.
74. Modern bubble analysis is a bootstrap theory of financial price analysis. On judgment day, all rational bubble decision makers will be told by their creator that they made persistent errors regarding the true worth of assets. Hence they must spend eternity in the purgatory of irrational expectations since their subjective probabilities merely equaled future persistently erroneous distributions rather than the objective probability distribution of the real world.
75. Keynes, *The General Theory*, pp. 162–3.

4.   Investment: illiquid real capital versus liquid assets

Chapter 2 indicated that in *The General Theory*, Keynes identified two distinct classes of expenditures on the products and services of industry. The category D_1 spending is associated with all expenditures that are related to (and normally financed out of) current income. D_2 is defined as all expenditures not related to income. Consequently expenditures in this category are unlikely to be financed out of current income. D_1 and D_2 are precisely and unambiguously defined but in terms that were not easy to understand by the average person or politician. To make this classification more meaningful to the reader of *The General Theory*, Keynes indicated that consumption spending could be classified as D_1, while expenditure category D_2 was linked to the 'amount which it [the community] is expected to devote to new investment'.[1]

Once the vernacular terms of consumption and investment were introduced, the meanings of these spending categories become more equivocal. The term investment, for example, is often applied to different kinds of purchases in different contexts.[2] To avoid such ambiguities and sort out these different meanings of investment a strict technical set of definitions regarding investment expenditures, markets, real capital goods, financial assets and money will be developed in this chapter. A crisp taxonomy is, after all, the essential starting point in a meaningful discussion and analysis of economic problems.

4.1   TWO TYPES OF INVESTMENT

For the individual, investment spending denotes the purchase of some durable asset today that is expected to enhance future net cash inflows over the period that the purchaser holds the asset by an amount that exceeds the purchase price and yields a positive return. For the ordinary person the term investment is applied equally (a) to the purchase of equity, debt securities, or other financial assets traded on an organized financial market and (b) to the purchase of a real durable good to be used in production and exchange processes to generate a net cash inflow. Investment purchases fall into two broad classes of asset purchases:

1. *Financial assets* such as equities, debt instruments, derivatives, options, and so on. These securities may be newly issued or, if they are traded on an organized exchange, they may be purchased secondhand from current holders. Secondhand securities may have been issued many years earlier than the current accounting period. The selling of newly issued equity or debt securities (sometimes referred to as initial public offerings or IPOs) typically represents a seller's demand for liquidity for the purpose of funding the purchase of some long-lived real investment project.

2. *Real assets or capital goods* such as plant, equipment and inventory. These capital goods are durable produced commodities that are purchased primarily to be used in the production of goods and services for the purposes of yielding a net cash inflow for the enterprise. Real assets are either newly produced plant, equipment, or secondhand goods for inventory or goods produced in an earlier accounting period. Secondhand purchases when they occur are often part of bankruptcy or liquidation proceedings. Since, in the real world, there are very few organized markets for the purchase of secondhand capital goods, expenditures on such capital goods are a rather rare occurrence, generally associated with bankruptcy or liquidation proceedings.

In the lexicon derived from Keynes's *General Theory*, neither the purchase of newly issued securities nor expenditures on secondhand financial assets or secondhand real capital goods are categorized as a D_2 (investment) expenditure. In any macroeconomic analysis where Keynes's D_2 category is associated with the term investment, it is meant to apply only to the purchase of real capital goods produced during the current accounting period.

4.2 MARKETS, CONTRACTS, LIQUIDITY AND CHARTALIST MONEY[3]

In a money-using, market system, all economic transactions are made on either a spot market or a forward market. A *spot market* is any market where buyers and sellers contract for immediate payment and delivery at the moment of contractual agreement. A *forward* market is any market where the buyer and seller enter into a contractual agreement today for payment and delivery at specific dates in the future. A *contract* is a legal agreement between the parties to perform specific actions at a specified date. In an entrepreneurial system, contracts denominated in money terms are used ubiquitously to organize production and exchange transactions.

If either party to a legal contract reneges on its commitment, the aggrieved party can ask the state, under the civil law of contracts, to force the other party to honor its contractual commitments. The sanctity of contracts is the essence of an entrepreneurial system. Money is defined as that thing that will always discharge any and all legal contractual obligations. This view linking state enforcement of contracts with the definition of money is known as *chartalism*.

An *elemental contract* is one where the date of payment and date of delivery is the same specified date. There are only two types of elemental contracts; an elemental spot contract, when both (immediate) payment and delivery are specified to be carried out at the instant of contractual agreement and an elemental forward contract, when a specific future date is specified as the time where both delivery and payment will be made.

Actual real world contracts are often more complex than these elemental ones but any complex contract can always be analysed as a combination of elemental contracts. Thus, if deliveries (and/or payments) are to be made at a specified sequence of dates in a real world contract, this can be analysed as a series of elemental forward contracts each of which calls for delivery (and/or payment) at a different specified date. If the date of payment differs from the date of delivery, we can allow this difference by reckoning that the actual sales contract includes an elemental loan contract.

In an entrepreneurial system, all markets are organized on a spot money contract and/or a forward money contract basis. In mainstream economic textbooks, on the other hand, it is implicitly assumed that entrepreneurs typically only 'produce to (spot) market', that is, firms produce goods without any contractual orders from buyers on their order books. After production is complete, entrepreneurs bring the products to market to sell them at whatever spot market price clears the market.

This produce to spot market analysis is equivalent to Alfred Marshall's market period analysis of the 'fish market'. In the real world such entrepreneurial behavior is sometimes referred to as 'producing on speculation' since the seller is never sure as to what the spot market price that clears the market will be. Entrepreneurs in retail establishments typically 'produce to spot markets' by ordering goods from manufacturers before they have any orders to sell.[4] Nevertheless, if the product is durable, then the seller can always hold the product in inventory (at a cost)[5] if no buyer will pay today the seller's asking price.

Entrepreneurs may also 'produce to contract', that is, undertake the hiring of inputs and the supervision of the productive flow, only after they receive a contractual order from a buyer specifying quantity, a delivery date and a purchase price. In real world capitalist economies, entrepreneurs before the retail stage in the distribution chain typically 'produce to contract'.

The production period was defined by Keynes as the calendar 'time which elapses between the decision to employ labor in conjunction with capital equipment to produce output and output being "finished"'.[6] If a production period spans any significant length of calendar time, then it would be foolish for any entrepreneur to undertake the hiring of inputs and the organization of production unless the firm has some significant method of maintaining cost controls. These money cost controls are obtained by executing forward contracts with the suppliers of inputs. With the abolition of slavery the labor-hiring money-wage contract has become one of the most universally used forward contracts for production cost control purposes.

Spot purchases and delivery of all needed raw and intermediary materials at the initial start-up time of the production process would be cost inefficient, for it would involve incurring warehousing and other carrying costs for many material inputs that are not needed until well into the production period. If, on the other hand, the producer waited and entered a spot market for the purchase of material inputs on the actual day when the input was required in the production process, then from the very beginning the entrepreneur would have given up all control over material costs during the entire production process. Thus, the institution of forward money contracts is a *sine qua non* for cost-efficient entrepreneurial firms in production economies.[7] The success of the Toyota motor car company, for example, was associated with its innovative 'just in time' method of inventory control. In this method, forward contracting is used to make sure that suppliers' delivery is efficiently timed to Toyota's production schedule so that Toyota does not need to carry a large inventory of component parts.

In reality, of course, there are some products that may be sold on both spot and forward markets. For example, sales of the newspapers and magazines at the newsstand involve a spot market transaction, while subscriptions to such publications involve a forward contract for delivery in combination with a spot contract for payment – and, hence, an implicit interest-free loan from the buyer to the producer. In the newsstand spot market for newspapers and magazines, however, the publisher normally 'makes' the spot market price by being willing to credit the retail newsdealer for all unsold publications. This contractual repurchase agreement prevents a fall in the retail spot price to clear the market and thereby avoids 'spoiling the spot market' for tomorrow's newspaper and magazine.

In the single family housing market, a developer may build houses before they have a purchase contract from a buyer. The produce-to-market house is said to be built 'on speculation'. If, when the house is complete, the current spot market price will not provide a profit over the builder's costs of production, the builder may carry the house in inventory until he gets his price or is forced to sell by a lack of liquidity to maintain his operations.

Alternatively a developer may produce 'custom-built' houses, that is, houses produced to forward contract. In this case, no production occurs until the builder receives a legal contract assuring him that the buyer will pay him his contractually specified money (supply) price at the delivery ('closing') date. This supply price will permit the builder to recoup all the contractual cash outlays for land, labor and material inputs, as well as interest on any working capital loan obtained from his banker and still yield a sufficient profit to make it worthwhile for the builder–entrepreneur to exert the effort necessary to manage the production process.

That thing we call money is defined in terms of its primary function as the legal means of contractual settlement. The civil law of contracts specifies that all contractual obligations are enforceable only in terms of money. Liquidity is the ability to meet all one's money contractual liabilities as they come due. In an entrepreneur system where it is always possible that unforeseeable events may make it difficult to meet one's future contractual obligations, a primary consideration in the plans of all participants in the system is that before they put their plans into operation they need to possess sufficient liquidity to meet their existing and planned future contractual liabilities as well as to have ample liquidity to meet emergency future contractual commitments. This demand for the continuing ability to maintain one's liquidity would be unimportant if one lived in a cooperative economy where production is not organized on a money contract basis, or if one operated in an economy – the theoretical economy of mainstream economic theory – where spot money payments on all contracts were required even if delivery was specified for some date in the future.

In real world entrepreneur economies, workers and other resource owners as well as entrepreneurs willingly and freely enter into money contracts where the legal obligations for fulfilling one's commitments are spelled out in the civil law of contracts. As long as people in society are law-abiding, the civil law of contracts is the fundamental legal institutional basis for organizing production and exchange agreements in our society. The civil law of contracts requires the state to enforce performance or payment any time one party to a legal contract proves that the other party is unable or unwilling to fulfill its legal contractual obligations.

Legal tender is the thing that always discharges all public and private contractual liabilities. Acceptance of the civil law by the members of society means that whatever the state designates as legal tender must be money. Bank credit, while not being legal tender, can also function as a medium of contractual settlement as long as the holders of bank deposits believe that these bank liabilities can be immediately converted into legal tender at the option of the holder without significant costs. The institution of a Monetary Authority (that is, a central bank) that guarantees convertibility of specific deposit liabilities of banks into legal tender as long as the depository institutions have obeyed the regulatory rules of the central bank assures that private bank deposit liabilities that economists call demand deposits (that is, checking accounts) will be universally acceptable – in the eyes of the courts – in the discharge of contractual commitments. As long as residents have confidence in the legal system, the Monetary Authority of the state determines what it will permit to be the medium of contractual settlement – money.

In an entrepreneurial system, people expect production and exchange processes organized on a money contract basis to continue to operate into the indefinite future. Money is, therefore, not only that thing that settles today's contractual obligations but it is also that thing in which future liabilities (for example, the money cost of future production, the future cost of living, and so on) will fall due. Money, therefore, possesses the capability of acting as a vehicle for moving generalized (nonspecific) purchasing power into the indefinite future. Money is a one-way (present to future) time vehicle or *time machine* for store of value purposes. Today's money can always be held to pay for future purchases, as long as the carrying cost in the shape of storage, wastage, and so on of today's money is lower than any other thing that has some degree of liquidity. Money is, as far as the private sector is concerned, a time machine *par excellence*. Durables other than money can also possess this time machine store of value function (liquidity) in various degrees. Nevertheless, any durable besides money cannot (by definition) be used as a universal means of settlement of contractual liabilities order. For any durable other than money to be considered a liquid asset for moving generalized purchasing power to the future, it must have very low carrying costs and it must be readily resalable for money in a well-organized, orderly spot market.

The degree of liquidity associated with any durable other than money depends on the degree of organization and orderliness of its spot market. A well-organized market is one where it is not costly to bring buyers and sellers together.[8] In normal times in a well-organized market, there will be many participants on both the buyers' side and the sellers' side of the market. An orderly market is one that operates under rules that are meant to assure buyers and sellers that changes in moment-to-moment market prices can be expected to be small. The difference between the last transaction price and the next transaction price will not differ by more than what the preannounced rules of the market deem appropriate.

In a world where the future is uncertain, in order to assure an orderly market, an institution known as a 'market maker' must exist. A *market maker* is defined as an institution that publicly announces a willingness to act as a residual buyer or seller to assure orderliness and continuity if an abrupt disruptive change occurs on either the demand or supply side of the market. As long as participants believe that financial markets are orderly, financial assets possess a significant degree of liquidity. Holders of financial assets can have a 'fast exit' strategy where each holder believes that if he/she wants to liquidate his/her asset position he/she can execute an immediate sale at a price that does not differ significantly from the previous market price. In other words, financial asset holders believe that their portfolio can provide an 'undated' cash inflow approximately equal to the market value of the last recorded transaction.

To assure an orderly market when a disruptive change in market sentiment is threatened, the market maker requires a *buffer stock* of the asset being traded in the market plus a significant stock of money (and/or immediate access to obtain additional money when required). If demand or supply tends toward unruly changes that threaten large swings in market prices, then the market maker must step in to buy in a declining market, or sell in an advancing market to limit the otherwise disorderly market price movements.

A credible market-making institution in every financial market is a necessary condition for the public to believe that a market is orderly.[9] Orderliness is a necessary characteristic of liquid financial markets. The existence of a market-making institution allows holders of financial assets to sleep peacefully at night 'knowing' that the opening spot price tomorrow will not differ significantly from the closing price today.

If a spot market for a specific durable is thin or nonexistent, it is not well organized. The purchase of a durable for which there is no well-organized, orderly spot resale market is likely to be 'permanent and indissoluble, like marriage, except by reason of death or other grave cause'.[10] These durables are illiquid, even though they may be capable of delivering to the holder a stream of specific services or a dated cash flow in the future.

4.3   FINANCING AND FUNDING ASSETS: WHY MONEY MATTERS

Marshall warned that the 'element of time is the center of the chief difficulty of almost every economic problem'.[11] Modern economic systems deal with the difficulty by organizing markets that operate in different time dimensions. Spot markets are equivalent to Marshall's market period or to Hicks's flexprice markets where the existing stock supply is, by definition, perfectly inelastic with regard to alternative possible spot market prices. Any change in the public's spot demand, therefore, will be immediately and completely reflected in a change in the spot prices.

Forward markets (because of the fixity of contractually agreed-upon money prices for the duration of the contract) are equivalent to Hicks's fixprice markets in a calendar time setting or Marshall's short-run period analysis. Flexprice and fixprice markets coexist in the real world, despite the often apparent impossibility of this occurring in mainstream macroeconomic models.

Classical general equilibrium is the basic theoretical model of all mainstream economic theory. In a classical general equilibrium model, as developed by Debreu, all payments (for either factors of production or products) are made simultaneously at the initial instant of time[12] whether the transaction requires immediate (spot) delivery or specifies a delivery date in the future. According to Debreu this requirement that all payments be made at the initial instant remains even in a model where the future is said to be uncertain. Debreu wrote: 'uncertainty of the environment . . . originates in the choice that nature makes among a finite number of alternatives'.[13] Even in an 'uncertain' (that is, probabilistic risky) classical world 'a contract for the transfer of a commodity now specifies, in addition to its physical properties, its location and its date, an event on the occurrence of which the transfer is conditional'.[14] Nevertheless, the payment on this conditional contract occurs at the initial instant when both parties agree. This initial instant payment, unlike contracts in the real world, is nonconditional since the price of any commodity is 'the amount paid . . . initially by . . . the agent who commits himself to accept . . . delivery of one unit of that commodity. *Payment is irrevocably made although delivery does not take place if specific events do not obtain'.*[15]

Since Debreu's general equilibrium formulation is the theoretical foundation of all mainstream models, even if orthodox models explicitly have markets for forward delivery, *all payments are made on the spot* (at the initial instant of acceptance of the contract.). No wonder that the concept of liquidity is given short-shrift in mainstream economic models. No wonder that these models stress a budget line (income) as the sole constraint on spending, and ignore the possibility of a more important liquidity constraint on spending. With liquidity having no role to play in orthodox models, it is easy to understand why the money neutrality axiom is unquestionably accepted as a fundamental truism in mainstream economics.

It cannot be stressed too much that the fundamental microfoundations of today's logically consistent mainstream economic theories presume that no economic agent needs to worry about his/her ability to meet future contractual liabilities since, by assumption, all payments occur at the initial instant of the analysis. Mainstream theory has removed the problem of matching cash inflows and outflows from their analysis. This unrealistic assumption has led to the famous businessman's jibe about economists: 'They have never had to meet a payroll'.

Logically consistent mainstream theory emasculates the importance of money, cash inflows, cash outflows and liquidity from any historical time setting. There are never any cash-flow problems in the model. This is an inevitable outcome of assuming as an 'article of faith' that *money is neutral*. In the real world, payments and receipts are contractually generated in the form of money in a sequential time setting as buyers and sellers engage in spot and forward markets. Liquidity is a fundamental recurring problem whenever people organize most of their income receipt and payment activities on a forward money contractual basis. For real world enterprises and households, the balancing of their checkbook inflows against outflows to maintain liquidity is the most serious economic problem they face every day of their lives. The fear of not being able to meet one's cash outflow commitments sometime in the future leads to a demand for liquidity (and the holding of monetary reserves) 'for a rainy day'. It is only in this real world setting that the institutions of money and money contracts have an essential role to play in determining the real output and employment of the community. It is only in this nonergodic world that cash flows over time are essential to asset-holding positions and money is never neutral as the fear of liquidity problems worries us all.

4.4   ASSET POSITION TAKING AND LIQUIDITY

Essentially there is a spectrum of assets that range from completely illiquid assets to fully liquid assets. For simplicity all assets can be categorized as belonging to one of three classes. These are:

1. *Illiquid assets* are durables whose spot (resale) markets are poorly organized, disorderly, thin or even notional so that, for all practical purposes, these assets cannot be readily resold during their useful lives. Most real capital goods are illiquid assets. These illiquid assets are used to produce output in the future that when sold are expected to yield net cash inflows at specific future dates. In other words, these illiquid assets are expected to provide a 'dated' cash inflow over their useful lives. These 'productive' assets are never held *primarily* for being able to immediately convert the present value of the dated future cash inflows into money if the holder needs funds. If the holder of an illiquid asset is unable to meet any future contractual liabilities, a distress sale of these assets may be held. But it is clear to the holder of the illiquid asset that even if such a liquidation sale of these assets is possible, the sales

receipts will involve a money sum far less than the asset's purchase price (minus any depreciation). In other words, a distress sale of illiquid assets is almost always certain to involve large capital losses for the seller and is never contemplated as a strategic option by someone planning to take a position in illiquid assets.

2. *Liquid assets* are financial assets that are traded in well-organized, orderly spot markets where spot market prices are expected to change in an orderly fashion. As long as an asset is readily resalable in an orderly market, it has some degree of liquidity. Positions in liquid assets are held for two possible reasons: (a) for a dated stream of cash inflows (dividends and/or interest payments) the asset may be expected to yield (net of carrying costs) to the holder and (b) the expected sales receipts that can be obtained by immediately reselling (liquidating) the asset at any future point of time prior to the end of the asset's useful life. If this sale price exceeds the purchase price, then the holder has made a capital gain. If the sale price is less than the purchase price, a capital loss has been incurred.

    Securitization is a process whereby a market-making institution takes an illiquid asset and by guaranteeing to 'make' an orderly spot market in that asset, converts the asset into a liquid asset.

3. *Fully liquid assets* are any assets that can be immediately converted into (resold for) money in a spot market where a market maker 'guarantees' a fixed and unchanging net spot money price. As long as the market maker has sufficient money reserves to back up his/her guarantee, then holders of a fully liquid asset can at any time sell out their position to obtain the 'guaranteed' quantity of 'undated' cash which can be used to discharge contracts at any future date. Similarly all potential buyers know they can always take a position at the price 'guaranteed' by the market maker. Money is the basic fully liquid asset of the system because the spot price of money in terms of itself is certain and unchanging (no capital gain or loss in nominal terms is possible) as long as society honors and obeys the civil law of contracts.

For individuals and business firms savings means holding unspent income as a liquid store of value that can be used at any point of time to meet contractual liabilities. Only liquid and fully liquid assets will be used by savers for store-of-value purposes. Illiquid assets may have a store of value in the sense that when they are used in production there may be a stream of future 'dated' money receipts that are expected to be received by the holder of these illiquid assets. For profit-oriented entrepreneurs, this expected 'dated' stream of future net money income flows (or quasi-rents) is the primary reason for demanding illiquid assets such as plant and equipment.[16]

The boundaries between fully liquid, liquid and illiquid assets are not watertight or even unchanging over time. The degree of liquidity associated with any asset depends on the degree of organization and orderliness of the relevant spot market at any moment of calendar time. Depending on social practices and institutions, the degree of liquidity of any asset can change from time to time if the operating rules of the market maker change. For example, securitization of a formerly illiquid asset can create liquidity for this asset if the securitized asset market maker is credible. Differences in degree of liquidity among assets are reflected in differences in the transaction costs of buying and selling and the stickiness of the money spot price over time. The smaller the transaction costs and/or the greater the stickiness, *ceteris paribus*, the greater the degree of liquidity of any asset. These factors depend, in large part, on the ability of a market maker maintaining orderliness.

4.5   REAL CAPITAL, SAVINGS, TIME PREFERENCE AND LIQUIDITY PREFERENCE

Durability is a characteristic possessed by real illiquid capital goods and by liquid financial assets including money. This quality of durability makes capital goods a primary form of wealth and a capitalized source of dated future money income. Classical economic theorists, therefore, conceive of the individual's saving out of income as taking the form of durable, producible capital goods that will yield a 'known' dated stream of future net cash inflows (income). This conflating of savings with the demand for producible illiquid durables underlies the Say's Law fallacy that today's increased desire to save on the part of households is the same thing as an increased demand to buy real producible capital goods today.

Keynes and Post Keynesians, on the other hand, argue that people save out of current income primarily in the form of nonproducible (by the use of labor in the private sector) liquid assets. The demand to use liquid assets to store one's wealth occurs because savers desire to have readily available, at any indefinite future date, sufficient funds for the discharge of any contractual commitments that may arise. Unlike the classical economy where all payments are made at the initial instant for goods and services to be delivered today and for all possible dates in the future, in a money-using economy an act of saving does 'not necessitate' the purchase of any producible durables today or 'a week hence or a year hence or to consume any specific thing at any specified time'.[17] Today's desire to save is a desire to transfer command of unspecified resources to the indefinite and uncertain future. Savers, therefore, have to engage the two-step decision process illustrated in Figure 4.1

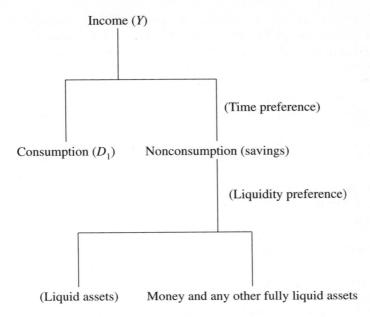

Income (*Y*)

(Time preference)

Consumption (*D*₁)   Nonconsumption (savings)

(Liquidity preference)

(Liquid assets)   Money and any other fully liquid assets

Figure 4.1   Two-step decisions about the use of current income

In the first step, *the time preference decision*, income-receiving house-holds choose how to allocate current income between spending on D_1 (con-sumption) and how much will *not* be spent on currently produced goods and services, that is, how much will be saved (nonconsumption).[18] After the consumption versus nonconsumption (saving) time preference decision is made, savers are required to make a second decision, *the liquidity preference decision*, which requires each saver to decide how to allocate unspent income (savings) among alternative *time machines* (liquid stores of value) that can transport generalized purchasing power from today to the indefi-nite future.

In a monetary economy, the possession of money always gives one the ability to exercise an immediate claim on current resources – as long as claims on resources are exercised through the use of money contracts. Money and any other asset, with negligible carrying charges, that can be readily converted into money in an orderly resale spot market can provide this time-machine store-of-value function for savers wanting to move resource claims into the uncertain future. Illiquid assets, by definition, cannot provide this time-machine function.

The saver's choice of a time-machine vehicle to transport savings to the future is limited to a choice between liquid and fully liquid assets. Unlike the products of industry, an essential and peculiar property of all liquid assets (as discussed further in Chapter 5) is that they cannot be produced by labor in the private sector (that is, they have an elasticity of production of approximately zero). Current resources are never used (employed, consumed) to satisfy this liquidity demand by savers.[19] A decision to save does not create an increase in demand for producing additional (illiquid) real capital for the latter must use current resources in its production.

This obvious conclusion that planned saving is a demand for a liquid store of value and not a demand for real capital is in stark contrast to mainstream economists' classical belief that any increase in the propensity of households to save out of current income is equivalent to an expansion in demand for newly produced real capital goods. If the classical view were applicable to the real world, then any policy that increases household savings out of each level of income automatically increases the demand for real investment. If, on the other hand, the Keynes–Post Keynesian 'liquidity preference as an allocation of savings' view is true, then a policy to increase saving will, *ceteris paribus*, reduce today's effective demand for the products of industry and therefore depress real economic activity.

In the 1950s and 1960s most well-known American (Old) 'Keynesians' ignored Keynes's taxonomic distinction between savings as a demand for liquid financial assets and entrepreneurs' investment demand as a demand for illiquid real capital goods. It became impossible to dislodge from economists' minds the classical fallacy that if the propensity to save increased, the demand for real capital increased *pari passu*. The classical sophism that the decision to save automatically means a decision to buy producible durables was quickly resurrected in the economic growth literature[20] and today often adversely affects policy choices for economies that want to stimulate real economic growth.

The Keynes–Post Keynesian anti-classical perspective of savings involving taking a position in liquid financial assets means that our entrepreneur-directed, market-oriented, monetary economy is fundamentally different from a classical world where liquidity is irrelevant. Only the Keynes–Post Keynesian view involving the use of a nonproducible money can correctly and properly explain the implications for the real economy of the development of financial markets with financial intermediaries who 'make' the market by operating as residual buyers and sellers in specific financial assets. Only under this Keynes–Post Keynesian conceptual approach can we understand why:

1. money is demanded both as a means of contractual settlement and as a liquid store of value, that is, a vehicle for transferring savings (generalized purchasing power) over time;

2. titles to capital goods, debt contracts and other financial assets, with
    negligible carrying costs, that are traded on organized orderly resale
    spot markets are demanded primarily as liquid stores of value, rather
    than to gain control of the management of any underlying real dur-
    ables. Accordingly, in any entrepreneurial economy with developed
    markets for financial assets there will be an institutional separation of
    ownership from control of real capital;[21]
3. reproducible capital goods are illiquid assets that will be demanded pri-
    marily as an input to produce goods and services that are expected to
    yield a future 'dated' stream of cash inflows. Producible durable goods
    are never demanded as a store of value of generalized purchasing
    power.

4.6   ATTRIBUTES OF ALL DURABLES

In the obscure and oft-neglected Chapters 16 and 17 of *The General
Theory*, Keynes wrestled with the problem of trying to extricate himself
from the short-period single-production period outlook of the rest of his
book. The essence of these chapters involves the problem of financing and
funding the demand for additional investment in capital goods as the real
wealth of the community accumulates.[22]

It is the durability of all assets – capital goods, money and other financial assets – that links the uncertain economic future with the present and
the past. There are four attributes that all durable assets possess in different degrees and these affect their desirability to be held. These four attributes are:

1. q, the expected quasi-rents or money value of the output, net of the
    running expenses, which can be obtained by assisting some process of
    production or supplying services to a consumer, or the expected divi-
    dend or interest payments associated from holding financial assets;
2. c, the carrying costs (including wastage) of the asset over any account-
    ing period;
3. l, the liquidity premium which arises from the quick power of disposal
    of the asset during any period.[23] In a monetary economy the power of
    disposal of an asset involves the ease of reselling the asset for money
    in a well-organized, orderly spot market. The degree of liquidity and
    hence the liquidity premium associated with an asset cannot be dis-
    cussed independently of the financial institutions that make the spot
    (resale) market for particular durables; and
4. a, the expected appreciation (or depreciation) in the money spot price

of the asset at the end of the period compared with the current market spot price.[24]

For all illiquid assets, the value of $a=0$ and $l=0$.

Keynes tended to measure the attributes of q, c, l, and a, in a unit equal to a percentage (per period) of the initial cost of the asset. This allowed Keynes to normalize for differing life expectancies of the various assets and differing initial costs. In most of what follows it will be more useful to conceive of these q, c, l, and a attributes in units of absolute monetary sums per accounting period over the lives of the various assets. This latter unit of measure can be directly converted into the demand price of the asset (in the mind of the holder) by a present value calculation.

Entrepreneur–investors are not primarily interested in titles to real capital goods or other financial assets as a liquid store of value. Their object is to acquire the services of real capital as inputs for the production process. To obtain the services of capital goods, investors must acquire control over the physical capital stock. What is relevant to the profit-maximizing firm's calculations is the marginal unit supply price of the service of the capital factor. Investors do not necessarily want title to the stock of capital. (Similarly, firms do not care whether they own their labor force (slaves) or allow others to hold title to the factor called labor. What is relevant is the marginal supply price of labor services.)

Savers, on the other hand, are interested in protecting and possibly increasing the value of their liquid asset holdings. Savers want an *undated* source of liquidity, that is, readily resalable assets that assure that cash will be available to them at anytime in the future. Even if a well-organized spot resale market for plant and equipment existed, the market value of these capital goods would be less than the spot price of the associated debt and equity securities. If a saver possessed a physical capital instrument and intended to convert his/her store of value (for example, a sausage machine) into future consumption goods in a different time pattern from the 'dated' stream of anticipated quasi-rents over the life of the sausage machine he/she would, at some point of time, have to find a sausage machine buyer. In selling, he/she would almost certainly disrupt the machine's physical (and value) productivity yield and incur delivery costs to dismantle and transport the equipment to the buyer.

Moreover, since real capital assets are normally large indivisible physical units, the saver may be required to search out a buyer of the whole unit in a future period, even if he/she desires only to increase consumption in that period by some amount smaller than the expected value of the whole physical asset. The smaller the unit of an asset, *ceteris paribus*, the greater its salability is likely to be. Thus, as Makower and Marschak have shown in a model where the probability distribution of future quasi-rents is given, sales of large units 'not only increase the dispersion of future yields, but also reduce their actuarial values'.[25]

Accordingly, the problem of finding a buyer for a secondhand piece of equipment is likely to be complex and costly. It is here that financial assets are clearly superior to real physical goods as liquid stores of value for financial assets can be quickly resold in orderly markets with little or no transaction costs for delivering the asset to the buyer. Financial assets can be bought and sold without any physical disruption to the usage of any underlying real capital. To the surprise of mainstream economists, the market values of fractionalized titles to physical goods are often worth more than the book value of new indivisible physical goods themselves.

Since savers are interested in titles to real capital as a liquid store of value and typically do not have the expertise to operate the underlying real assets, while entrepreneurs have the knowledge to manage the flow of productive services from capital goods to obtain quasi-rents, savers' liquidity preference decisions and entrepreneurs' investment decisions will look toward different price levels. Capital investment decisions depend on the market demand price (that is, the present value of the expected 'dated' flow of future money quasi-rents) relative to the flow-supply price (money cost of production) of real capital goods. Savers's liquidity decisions, on the other hand, depend on the price of securities relative to their expected future price and the fear of being illiquid. The only common determinant between the investment decision and the liquidity decision is the interest rate that is (a) the basis for the discounting factor in calculating present values of expected future quasi-rents, and (b) basis of the liquidity premium savers require to give up their holding of money to hold a less liquid financial asset.

NOTES

1. J.M. Keynes, *The General Theory of Employment, Interest and Money*, Harcourt, Brace, New York, 1936, p. 29.
2. Elsewhere I have explained how the terms 'consumption' and 'income' resulted in a semantic dispute regarding alternative consumption hypothesis. See P. Davidson, *Post Keynesian Macroeconomic Theory*, Edward Elgar, Cheltenham, 1994, pp. 44–6.
3. The development of the contractual category concepts in this section benefitted greatly from private correspondence with Sir John Hicks in the 1970s and 1980s.
4. But even in the retail market, the seller may exercise a 'reservation price' below which he/she refuses to sell. Marshall associated this reservation demand price with the seller's fear of 'spoiling the market' for future sales. Retail spot market clearing prices are usually associated with 'clearance sales'.
5. Whether to hold in inventory or to sell (liquidate) the product today at the spot price will depend on the concept of 'user costs'. See Keynes, *The General Theory*, pp. 66–73.

6. *The Collected Writings of John Maynard Keynes*, vol. 29, edited by D. Moggridge, Macmillan, London, 1979, p. 80. Keynes defined consumption goods as finished 'when they are ready for sale to the consumer, or to a Capitalist for the purpose of holding them in stock for speculation [for later sale on a spot market]' while capital goods are 'finished' when they are ready for use by consumers as consumption-capital (for example, houses) or by producers as instrumental capital.

7. Fixed money forward contracts are an essential aspect of all production processes organized by entrepreneurs. Since Arrow and Hahn have demonstrated that classical theory is not applicable to systems using money contracts, it should be obvious that classical theory, despite its popularity among mainstream New Classical and New Keynesian economists alike, is not a useful tool for resolving the real economic problems that our entrepreneurial, contract-oriented, system faces.

8. A well-organized market deals in a standardized 'product' so that each buyer 'knows' the characteristics of the unit he/she buys without having to make a detailed examination of each unit.

9. In organized financial asset markets, whenever the market maker finds he/she is unable to carry out his/her function of maintaining orderliness, trading is suspended to permit the market maker to reorganize his/her resources sufficiently so that order can be restored when the market is reopened. 'Circuit breakers' in financial markets such as the New York Stock Exchange are preannounced rules that stop trading if the market maker is unable to prevent the market from getting too disorderly. Until the market is opened again, the liquidity of assets traded on the market has to virtually disappear. Circuit breakers and suspended trading rules therefore are a form of capital flow regulations and controls.

10. Keynes, *The General Theory*, p. 160.

11. A. Marshall, *Principle of Economics*, 1st edn, London, Macmillan, 1890, p. viii.

12. G. Debreu, *Theory of Value*, University of Yale Press, New Haven, CT, 1959, p. 32.

13. Ibid., p. 98. As already indicated, in the classical model uncertainty is conflated with probabilistic risk.

14. Ibid., p. 98.

15. Ibid., p.100. Emphasis added.

16. Technically this is true for all fixed capital illiquid assets. Working capital illiquid assets may yield up their entire quasi-rents at a single future date.

17. Keynes, *The General Theory*, p. 210.

18. Classical theory presumes that the time preference decision is the only one that utility-maximizing savers make regarding the use of their current earned income claims. In classical analysis time preference involves allocating income between currently produced consumption goods and currently produced investment goods.

19. See the essential elasticity properties of money and liquid assets in Chapter 5 *infra*.

20. For example, see J. Tobin, 'Money and economic growth', *Econometrica*, **33**, 1965, pp. 671–84.

21. Since A.A. Berle and G.C. Means's landmark study (*The Modern Corporation and Private Property*, Commerce Clearing House, New York, 1932), applied economists have recognized this separation of ownership from control as an important problem for developed capitalist economies. Since classical theory does not make the distinction between time preference and liquidity preference, it is not surprising that mainstream economic theorists have provided little guidance on this problem.

22. For similar views on these chapters, see J. Robinson, 'Own rates of interest', *Economic Journal*, **71**, (1961) pp. 596–600, and R. Turvey, 'Does the rate of interest rule the roost', in *The Theory of Interest Rates*, edited by F.H. Hahn and F.P.R. Brechling, Macmillan, London, 1965.

23. According to Keynes, a nonmonetary economy is one where there is no asset whose *l* is always greater than *c*. See Keynes, *The General Theory*, p. 239.

24. Keynes, *The General Theory*, pp. 225–6.

25. H. Makower and J. Marschak, 'Assets, prices, and monetary theory', *Economics* **5**, 1938, p. 279.

5.   Why liquidity preference?

The fundamental question for any monetary analysis applicable to a money-using, market-oriented economy is: 'Why do people prefer to hold money which is barren or even interest bearing or dividend yielding securities as a store of value rather than real "productive" physical goods?' Our response involves explaining that the use of money contracts to organize production and exchange processes is the way an entrepreneur system deals with an uncertain (nonergodic) economic future. This use of money contracts requires economic decision makers to maintain a liquid cash position in order to avoid the malady of illiquidity or the gallows of bankruptcy. Money is the liquid asset *par excellence* in that tendering it will always legally discharge a contractual obligation. The demand for liquidity involves either the demand for money directly or the demand for any other financial asset with low carrying costs that can be readily converted into money rapidly and without significant transaction costs.

5.1   THE FOUR MOTIVES FOR HOLDING MONEY

> Without money [as a liquid store of wealth], we cannot put off deciding what to buy with the thing we are in the act of selling. If we do not know precisely what use a thing will be to us, we are compelled nevertheless, by an absence of money, to override and ignore this ignorance. It is *money* which enables decisions to be deferred.[1]

In *The General Theory*, Keynes distinguishes three motives for holding money:

> (i) the transactions-motive, i.e., the need for cash for the current transaction of personal and business exchanges; (ii) the precautionary-motive, i.e., the desire for security as to the future cash equivalent of a certain proportion of total resources; and (iii) the speculative-motive, i.e., the object of securing profit from knowing better than the market what the future will bring forth.[2]

Keynes recognized that

> money held for each of these three purposes forms, nevertheless, a single pool, which the holder is under no necessity to segregate into three watertight

compartments for they need not be sharply divided even in his own mind, and the same sum can be held primarily for one purpose and secondarily for another. Thus we can – equally well, and perhaps, better – consider the individual's aggregate demand for money in given circumstances as a single decision though the composite result of a number of different motives.[3]

There is only a *single* demand for money for liquidity purposes. For expositional reasons it is useful to study each motive for holding money as if it was separate and independent of the others, even though in reality it need not be. In 1936 Keynes suggested that the three motives formed an exhaustive set and that all other reasons for holding money (for example, the income motive or the business motive) are merely subcategories of these three major divisions. By 1937, however, Keynes was forced to admit that one of the three motives, the transactions demand for money, was misspecified in *The General Theory*. He rectified this error by adding a fourth motive for demanding liquidity, the *finance motive*.

Unfortunately, this respecification of the demand for money went unnoticed as most economists were still trying to understand Keynes's liquidity preference theory as it had been set out in *The General Theory*. Keynes's 1936 triumvirate analysis of the demand for money was hailed by his followers as 'a study in depth of a magisterial quality not matched in the present century'.[4] Yet, by ignoring Keynes's 1937 finance motive correction to the theory of liquidity preference, many admirers of Keynes fostered a retrograde analysis that was incompatible with his earlier *Treatise on Money* where his 'views about all the details of the complex subject of money are . . . to be found'.[5] By the 1960s, what had evolved as mainstream Neoclassical Synthesis (Old) Keynesianism was so different from Keynes's corrected monetary analysis that Milton Friedman's claim, that these 'Keynesians' were championing a theory in which money does not matter, was quite accurate.

As Keynes's first biographer, Roy Harrod, pointed out: 'it is a paradox that the man whose worldwide fame during most of his lifetime arose from his specific contributions to monetary theory, which were rich and varied, should be studied mainly in one of his books which contains little about money as such'.[6] Although in 1937, Keynes admitted that his abbreviated *General Theory* monetary analysis was misspecified, most Old 'Keynesians' ignored Keynes's 1937 correction as they regressed into a classical analysis which implicitly assumed the neutrality of money. The Keynesian Revolution was aborted by those who claimed to be Keynesians but who disregarded Keynes's *Treatise on Money* and his finance motive revision that requires a nonneutral monetary view.

Keynes's most recent biographer, Lord Skidelsky, has noted that only the modern Post Keynesian school has followed Keynes's monetary approach by developing a research agenda that has been directed to judiciously blending Keynes's monetary analysis of his *Treatise on Money* with his 1937 corrected version of liquidity preference. In Skidelsky's words:

> The Post Keynesian school has continued to emphasize the stress on the importance of time and uncertainty, the use of money as a store of value, and the 'animal spirit' theory of investment. Conventional behavior by capitalists or workers which produces perverse results for the economy as a whole is seen as a sensible response to uncertainty.[7]

5.2 THE DEMAND FOR THE MEDIUM OF CONTRACTUAL SETTLEMENT[8]

Keynes's 1936 conception of the transactions demand for money involved the need 'to bridge the interval between the receipt of income and its disbursement'.[9] This calendar time interval is determined by institutional contractual payments arrangements. For example, hourly wage workers are often paid at the end of each week, while salaried employees are paid at the end of each month, credit card balances are due on a certain date each month, the rent is due at the beginning of each month, and so on.

Households hold transaction balances to avoid the possibility of being unable to meet their contractual purchase liabilities that come due between income receipt dates. The quantity of transaction balances held by households depend on (a) the length of time between well-established contractual pay receipt intervals, and (b) the *planned* household spending during the pay interval.

Similarly, business firms require transaction cash balances to meet their contractual obligations for the purchase of productive inputs into the operation of the enterprise. The quantity of business transaction balances held by entrepreneurs depends on (a) the *planned* spending of firms during the period between cash inflows from sales receipts, (b) the length of time between sales receipts, and (c) the degree of vertical integration of the firms.

While defining the transactions motive as the 'need for cash for the current transaction of personal and business exchanges',[10] Keynes's 1936 analysis encouraged viewing this demand for money for transaction balances primarily from the householders' position to the neglect of any separate business motive. In *The General Theory*, household consumption expenditures are identified with D_1 expenditures which were to be primarily financed out of current income. Consequently, many 'Keynesians' (and, in 1936, Keynes himself[11]) were misled by this cursory treatment to incorrectly specify the demand for transaction balances as uniquely and directly related to the level of income per accounting period. In other words, in the 1936 *General Theory*, the only cause for a change in the volume of cash balances demanded for transactions per period purposes is a change in the actual level of income in that period.

Before discussing Keynes's finance motive correction for his 1936 misspecified transactions demand for money, it will be helpful to discuss the other motives for demanding money in *The General Theory*, the precautionary and the speculative demands for money.

5.3   THE DEMAND FOR A LIQUID TIME MACHINE

Keynes's precautionary motive for holding cash balances concept is usually given perfunctory treatment in most economic models. Typically, the precautionary motive demand is, like the incorrectly specified transactions demand, assumed to be directly related to one's income. The only significant difference between the transactions and precautionary demands for money is that the former involved contractual liabilities that are expected (or planned for) during the current income receipts period while the latter involved unplanned liabilities that might be expected or feared in general even if unplanned in specifics.[12] This precautionary motive is a demand to have liquidity immediately to meet all unplanned liabilities.

Chapter 4 indicated that all income recipients have to make two sequential decisions regarding their currently earned claims on resources. These decisions are:

1.   the time preference decision of how to allocate current income between current (consumption) expenditures and planned nonconsumption (saving); and
2.   the liquidity preference decision of how to allocate savings out of current income among various time machines (liquid assets) to transport purchasing power to the indefinite and uncertain future.

This time-machine decision where savers choose to store their savings among alternative liquid assets (including money) involves the speculative demand for money. In the absence of well-organized and orderly spot markets for financial assets there can be no speculative motive for there are no alternatives to money as a liquid store of value. In the absence of the speculative motive, the precautionary motive would come to the fore as the rationale for holding the only possible liquid store of value money into the indefinite future.

In all but the most primitive of money-using economies, however, there are at least some well-organized and orderly spot markets where durables can be resold. Liquid financial assets, by definition, are durables traded on well-organized, orderly spot financial markets. Since the spot market price of any liquid financial asset can differ, in an orderly manner, each day, any liquid asset is a potential object of speculation to serve as a possible alternative to money as a time machine for transferring liquidity to the future. In making a choice as to which financial assets to use as stores of value, savers face two potential uncertainties: an income uncertainty and a capital value uncertainty. In an uncertain world, savers must choose how much of each uncertainty they wish to bear.

1. *Income uncertainty*   Issuers of many liquid assets either contractually or conditionally quasi-contractually agreed to provide a cash inflow at specific calendar dates to the holders of the assets (for example, interest payments on bonds, dividends on equity securities). The longer the saver holds a liquid asset, the larger total cash inflow that the holder may receive. From this cash income flow the holder will have to subtract the carrying costs of holding the asset to arrive at an estimate of the net cash inflow accruing to taking a position in the specific asset. In a world of uncertainty, savers also must consider whether the issuer of each specific liquid asset will be able to meet this future cash contractual or quasi-contractual obligation. For the saver the income uncertainty involves how the saver compares the expected net income from taking a position in any liquid asset *vis-à-vis* holding cash where the latter typically yields a zero net cash inflow to the holder.[13] There is no income uncertainty for the holder of cash.

2. *Capital uncertainty*   Since the spot market price of liquid assets can change over time, savers must contemplate the possibility of an increase or decrease in the asset's market price at a future date when the holder wishes to liquidate his/her holdings. This potential capital gain or loss is obtained by subtracting today's spot price (p_s^{t0}) from the expected spot price at a future date (p_s^{t1}) when the asset will be resold. If ($p_s^{t1} - p_s^{t0}$) > 0, a capital gain is expected from holding the asset until $t1$ and the holder is said to be bullish on the asset. If ($p_s^{t1} - p_s^{t0}$) < 0, a capital loss will be expected. If the saver holds money instead, there will be no capital uncertainty. The price of money in terms of itself can never change.

Both income uncertainty and capital uncertainty are vexatious to savers who can avoid these uncertainties only if they hold all their stores of value in the form of money. The cost of this option is to give up all possible income earnings on one's savings as well as the possibility of capital gains.[14]

Buying liquid assets with one's savings, however, exposes the saver to the uncertainty of possible capital loss.

Moreover, there are usually transaction costs (T_s) incurred in both buying and reselling (that is, liquidating) any liquid asset. These transaction costs are usually independent of the time interval that the liquid asset is held. If an unforeseen liability should come due in the immediate future, then the transaction cost of taking a position in a liquid asset and then liquidating it can easily swamp any income flow that can be expected to be received from holding the asset for such a short time. It is, therefore, normal to prefer to hold some saving in the form of money to cover planned (and possibly unforeseen) obligations that can come due in the very near future.[15]

The more uncertain the future appears, the more unplanned contractual liabilities may come due and the greater the fear of possible capital loss on financial assets. The more savers fear the uncertain future, the more they will desire to store their savings in the form of money rather than other liquid assets. Holding money always soothes the savers' fear of becoming illiquid if anything unpredictable occurs.[16]

5.4   BULLS VERSUS BEARS

All savers find a capital loss repugnant. To induce a saver to exchange his/her money holdings for a liquid asset whose spot market resale price can change over time, the saver must expect that in so doing he/she will receive a liquidity premium in terms of promised future income payments less carrying costs that exceed the possible capital loss plus transaction costs of getting into and out of the liquid asset.

Let q be the future expected income (or quasi-rents) to be received over a period of time, c is the carrying costs, p_s^{t0} the current spot market price of the asset, p_s^{t1} the expected spot market price at some future date, and T_s the transaction cost of taking and then liquidating a position. If one holds money there is no income ($(q - c) = 0$), no capital gain or loss[17] ($(p_s^{t1} - p_s^{t0}) = 0$), and no transaction costs ($T_s = 0$). Savers will estimate the expected future income plus capital gain or loss plus transaction costs associated with holding a liquid asset and compare this result with that of a zero return on money.

If, for a specific liquid asset the saver expects

$$(q - c) + (p_s^{t1} - p_s^{t0}) + T_s > 0, \tag{5.1}$$

then the saver is a 'bull' and should buy all the assets that he/she currently can afford. If it is expected that

$$(q - c) + (p_s^{t1} - p_s^{t0}) + T_s < 0, \tag{5.2}$$

then the saver is a 'bear' and would prefer to hold money rather than the liquid asset for speculative purposes. Of course, in a world of uncertainty, most people are unlikely to have absolute confidence in any expectation of future capital gains or losses they might hold. Few savers are, therefore, likely to be a complete bull or a complete bear. Most sensible people will hold a mixed portfolio of money and other liquid assets – rather than putting all their liquidity eggs in one basket. The larger the positive evaluation a saver puts on $(p_s^{t1} - p_s^{t0})$, the more bullish he/she is and the more he/she will alter his/her portfolio from money toward other liquid assets.

This bull–bear evaluation applies to any easily resalable durable. In *The General Theory*, Keynes ignored the availability of equities, options, derivatives and other financial assets and used bonds and money as the only alternative liquid assets that savers would consider using as a time-machine store of value. This simplification permitted Keynes to provide an easy explanation of how the price of bonds and hence the nominal rate of interest was determined in the marketplace.

For long-term negotiable bonds where the annual monetary interest payment is fixed, the effective rate of interest is inversely related to the spot price of the bond, that is, $i = f(1/P_B)$ where i is the market rate of interest and P_B is the spot price of the bond. If most participants in the bond market think today's interest rate on outstanding bonds is 'high' (bond prices are 'low'), then they will tend to be bullish on bonds. Since the term 'high' connotes the expectation that the interest rate is normally lower and therefore bond prices are normally higher, the market must think bond prices should rise and the interest rate decline. Consequently savers will be bullish on bonds and will hold very little of their total savings in the form of money (for store of value purposes).

Figure 5.1 is a hypothetical diagram that displays the aggregate demand curve for money held for speculative purposes at alternative rates of interest. At the 'high' interest rate of i_a of Figure 5.1, point A indicates the relatively small (that is, close to the ordinate axis) quantity of money demanded for speculative purposes as most bond market participants are bullish on bonds. If most people believe interest rates are 'low' at the interest rate i_b in Figure 5.1 (bond prices are high), then most savers will expect interest rates to increase and bond prices to decline. People will be bearish on bonds. The further from the y-axis is any point on the demand curve for money for speculative purposes (Figure 5.1), the more bearish on bonds are market participants as a group. The quantity of money demanded for speculative purposes will be greater at the i_b interest rate than at interest rate i_a. Connecting points such as A and B produces a downward-sloping demand

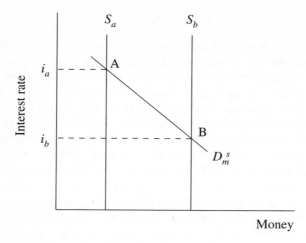

Figure 5.1   The speculative demand for money

for money for speculative purposes curve $D_m{}^s$ in Figure 5.1. In other words the demand for money for speculative purposes is, in this simple two-asset model, inversely related to the rate of interest, that is,

$$D_m{}^s = f(-i). \tag{5.3}$$

If the money supply is determined exogenously by the actions of the central bank, then the supply of money can be represented as the vertical curve, S_a, in Figure 5.1. Any exogenous increase in the supply of money will shift the money supply curve outward, say from S_a to S_b. The rate of interest will decline from i_a to i_b.

Every fall in the interest rate reduces the current earnings from holding a bond. The reduced earnings of bondholders will offset a smaller possible capital loss if the price of bonds falls (the interest rate to rise) in the future. If, for example, there are no transaction costs of buying or reselling bonds, then if the interest rate is 4 per cent, it is worthwhile to invest in bonds as long as the saver does not think the rate of interest 'will rise faster than by 4 per cent of itself per annum, i.e., by an amount greater than 0.16 per cent per annum. If, however, the interest rate is already as low as 2 per cent, the running yield will only offset a rise of as little as 0.04 per cent per annum'.[18] This implies that the speculative demand for money curve is a downward-sloping rectangular hyperbola that approaches the abscissa asymptotically.[19] The lower the rate of interest the more to fear that the rate of interest will return to a more normal level while the smaller the running yield is available to offset this fear.

In contrast to this rectangular hyperbola formulation of Keynes's speculative demand for money curve, Old Keynesians claimed that, at some low,
but positive, interest rate, the demand curve for speculative money balances
becomes infinitely elastic (horizontal).[20] This horizontal segment of the
speculative demand curve was designated the liquidity trap by Old
Keynesians such as Paul Samuelson and James Tobin. These mainstream
Old Keynesians made the liquidity trap the hallmark of what Samuelson
labeled Neoclassical Synthesis Keynesianism. If the economy is enmeshed
in the liquidity trap, then Old Keynesians argued that the Monetary
Authority is powerless to lower the rate of interest to stimulate the economy
no matter how much the central bank exogenously increased the supply of
money. This view of the impotence of monetary policy was succinctly summarized in the motto 'you can't push on a string'.

The liquidity trap implied that monetary policy would be powerless to
stimulate the economy if it fell into recession. These Old Keynesians, therefore, proclaimed that deficit spending fiscal policy was the only policy
action available to pull an economy out of a recession. This faith in deficit
spending as the only solution for recessions became the policy theme for
'Keynesians', even though Keynes's speculative motive analysis denies the
existence of a 'liquidity trap'. Nor was Keynes enamored with government
deficits *per se*. Indeed Keynes was a firm believer in pursuing a 'cheap
money' policy to its practical limits before any fiscal stimulus was undertaken. Moreover Keynes believed that government should always try to
maintain a balanced operating budget. If fiscal deficits were required to
stimulate the economy, they should always be associated with capital
budget spending on productive investment projects that hopefully permitted government to 'co-operate with private initiative'.[21]

In the decade after the Second World War, econometricians searched in
vain to demonstrate the existence of a liquidity trap (that is, a horizontal
segment of the speculative demand for money) where monetary policy
could not affect the interest rate. In a stunning *volte face* of the history of
economic thought, Milton Friedman and his followers who accept the neutrality of money as an article of faith used this failure of econometricians
as an attack on Keynes's theory. Friedman's motto 'Money Matters'
became an anti-Keynesian weapon. This may have been an effective argument against Old Keynesians who followed Samuelson's lead in accepting
the neutral money axiom. Keynes, however, explicitly declared that in his
analysis money was never neutral, that is, that money matters in both the
short run and the long run in the real world.

5.5   THE FINANCE MOTIVE AND ENDOGENOUS MONEY

In the early 1930s, Keynes searched for a simplification of his *Treatise on Money* after he concluded that his critics 'simply failed to grasp' the *Treatise*'s elaborate monetary analysis.[22] The result was a less rigorous monetary specification in *The General Theory* where 'money enters into the economic scheme in an essential and peculiar manner, [but] technical monetary detail falls into the background'.[23] This deliberate ensconcement of monetary analysis led Keynes into incorrectly specifying the transaction demand for money in his 1936 *General Theory*. This error encouraged mainstream Old 'Keynesians' to develop a 'Bastard Keynesian' model (to use Joan Robinson's felicitous phrase) that fit better with the classical axiomatic microfoundations that Samuelson asserted in the *Foundations of Economic Analysis* (1947). Bastard Keynesianism is a perversion of Keynes's monetary analysis.

In 1937, Bertil Ohlin quickly spotted the error in Keynes's 1936 simplification of the transactions demand for money. In reply to Ohlin's criticism, Keynes introduced a new and what appeared to be a somewhat novel purpose for demanding money, namely the *finance motive*.[24] Keynes argued that if *planned* investment expenditures per period are unchanged, that is, contractual commitments to buy new real capital goods each period are constant, then the demand for money to be used to 'finance' the production of the investment goods each period would be unchanged and could be lumped under a subcategory of the transactions motive where capital goods production transactions are involved.

Producers of capital goods had to assure themselves that when they entered into forward contracts for the hiring of inputs for production of capital goods they would be able to meet all these contractual liabilities until the product was finished, delivered and paid for. The quantity of cash balances needed each period by capital goods producers to meet these forward contracts for producing investment goods would be unchanged as long as planned investment production was unchanged.

'But if decisions to invest are (e.g.,) increasing, the extra finance involved will constitute an additional demand for money'.[25] Any increase in profit expectations will induce entrepreneur–investors to enter into ordering more investment goods if they believe they can obtain funding for the purchase of these investment goods when they are delivered. When the producers of investment goods receive more contractual orders, they will require more working capital loan finance (the finance motive) to meet their expanded contractual payrolls, raw material and semifinished material costs.

Capital goods producers will contact their bankers to request these larger working-capital loans. The producers can show their greater volume of contractual orders as 'collateral' for these working-capital loans. The bankers, having experience that in the past these customers repaid their previous working-capital loans, will be agreeable to make these additional loans since the borrowers have met the 'three C's' criteria – creditworthiness, collateral and character. In an uncertain world, this three C's standard is the rule of thumb that bankers use to determine whether they should make a loan.

If this greater quantity of requests for working-capital loans are approved by the bankers, the money supply will increase endogenously. The resulting working-capital loans will be outstanding until the investment project goods are finished and delivered to the buyers. The resulting sales receipts will repay the outstanding working-capital loan finance advanced by bankers (or other financial intermediary institutions). These repayments will make the equivalent volume of finance available for new working-capital loans. Keynes's finance motive analysis recognizes that there will be an increased demand for money in terms of working-capital loans to finance the production of the higher volume of investments at any given interest rate – even before any additional employment and income are generated[26] in the capital-producing industries.

The next question that this analysis has to answer is where will the entrepreneur-investor buyers of these newly produced capital goods obtain the funds to pay for these costly, durable investment goods at the time of delivery. The buyers of long-lived investment goods rarely have enough liquid savings to pay the entire purchase price at the delivery date. Typically the buyers will have to externally 'fund' most (if not all) of the purchase price by selling long-term debt (for example, a mortgage bond) and/or by floating new equity securities to savers.

5.6   THE FINANCE MOTIVE, FINANCE AND FUNDING

To understand the different roles that money-finance *vis-à-vis* saving-funding play in the capital accumulation process, it is vital to draw a sharp distinction between working-capital loan finance and funding. Working-capital loan finance provides the capital producer with money to pay for inputs in the production of long-lived durables during the production period, while 'funding' provides the investor with money to pay the purchase price of a completed investment project. In this funding process the investor–buyer sells a liquid financial asset (a bond or an equity security) to obtain directly, or more typically through financial intermediaries, the small pools of savings in the economy. Financial asset markets therefore play a major role in permitting external funding of large-scale investments. This role will be discussed in detail in Chapter 6.

To clarify the essence of the finance motive, and to indicate why it is not properly taken into account in his *General Theory* discussion of the transactions motive, in 1937 Keynes wrote:

> It follows that, if the liquidity-preferences of the public (as distinct from the entrepreneurial investors) and of the banks are unchanged, an excess in the finance required by current ex-ante output (it is not necessary to write 'investment', since the same is true of *any* output which has to be planned ahead) over the finance released by current ex-post output will lead to a rise in the rate of interest; and a decrease will lead to a fall. I should not have previously overlooked this point, since it is the coping-stone of the liquidity theory of the rate of interest. I allowed, it is true, for the effect of an increase in *actual* activity on the demand for money. But I did not allow for the effect of an increase in *planned* activity, which is superimposed on the former. . . . Just as an increase in actual activity must (as I have always explained) raise the rate of interest unless either the banks or the rest of the public become more willing to release cash, so (as I now add) an increase in planned activity must have a similar, superimposed influence.[27]

Since Keynes felt that the finance motive was the coping-stone of his liquidity preference theory, it is surprising that the concept was never adopted in the mainstream Keynesian economic literature.

The introduction of the finance motive involves relating the demand for transaction balances to finance planned increased production to meet increased spending propensities. If the supply of money does not change in response to an increase in planned spending to increase production, then producers' demand for additional working-capital loans will increase the rate of interest before there is any additional production undertaken[28] as the additional borrowers tend to crowd out others in the loan market. If, on the other hand, the Monetary Authority and the banking system attempt to maintain the interest rate in response to an increased demand for finance, then the money supply will endogenously expand before there is any increase in the production flow from the nation's enterprises. This increase in the money supply (to finance additional working capital loans) before production actually expands has been wrongly interpreted by Monetarist economists as demonstrating that an increase in the money supply 'causes' an increase in output.

The finance motive is the macro analogue of the microeconomic maxim 'Demand means want plus the ability to pay'. The demand for money, therefore, is *not* independent of demand in the real sector. This interdependence of the real and monetary sector demand functions violates the so-called 'classical dichotomy' where the neutral money axiom assures the independence of the real and monetary sectors.

When Keynes linked the finance motive with changes in the decision to invest, he was, as he readily admitted, discussing 'only a special case' of the finance motive. Keynes's justification for linking the finance motive to changes in planned investment contractual orders was his belief that planned investment is 'subject to special fluctuation of its own'. In his discussion of war finance, Keynes generalized the application of the finance motive to other exogenous components of aggregate demand. In a letter printed in the 18 April 1939 edition of *The Times*, Keynes elucidated his reasoning still further. The immediate question was how the government was going to fund the additional expenditures for rearmament. Keynes argued that

> If an attempt is made to borrow them [the savings which will result from the increased production of nonconsumption (war) goods] before they exist, as the Treasury has done once or twice lately, a stringency in the money market must result, since pending the expenditure, the liquid resources acquired by the Treasury must be at the expense of the normal liquid resources of the banks and of the public.'

In other words, an increase in the letting of government contracts will increase the aggregate demand for working-capital (transactions) balances by the suppliers of government (for example, war) goods, even before the increased expenditures on production are undertaken.[29] Once the additional production is finished, additional income will have been paid out from which there will be an additional pool of saving in the community. The government can tap this pool of savings to fund the government's purchases by selling government bonds to the savers.

The finance motive makes clear the need for an endogenous increase in the money supply if increases in planned spending are to be translated into increases in production flows without any constraints raised by increasing interest rates. Keynes noted an overdraft system 'is an ideal system'[30] for mitigating the effects on the banking system of an increased demand for *ex ante* finance; for bank 'credit is the pavement along which production travels, and the bankers if they knew their duty, would provide the transport facilities to just the extent that is required in order that the productive powers of the community can be employed at their full capacity'.[31]

The inevitable conclusion of the correctly specified liquidity preference analysis (to include the finance motive) is that the money-contract-based, entrepreneurial system in which we live cannot be dichotomized into independent real and monetary subsets. The classical dichotomy based on the neutrality of money axiom does not apply.

Keynes's finance motive analysis emphasizes the importance of banking and financial institutions in facilitating expansion in the real world. In the absence of an endogenous money supply system:

> a heavy demand for investment can exhaust the market and be held up by the lack of financial facilities on reasonable terms. It is, to an important extent, the 'financial' facilities which regulate the *pace* of new investment. Some people find it a paradox that, up to the point of full employment, no amount of actual investment, however great, can exhaust and exceed the supply of savings. . . . If this is found paradoxical, it is because it is confused with the fact that too great a press of uncompleted investment decisions is quite capable of exhausting the available finance if the banking system is unwilling to increase the supply of money and the supply from existing holders is inelastic. It is the supply of available finance which, in practice, holds up from time to time the onrush of 'new issues'. But if the banking system chooses to make the finance available and the investment projected by the new issues actually takes place, the appropriate level of incomes will be generated out of which there will necessarily remain over an amount of saving exactly sufficient to take care of the new investment. The control of finance is, indeed, a potent, though sometimes dangerous, method for regulating the rate of investment (though much more potent when used as a curb than as a stimulus).[32]

5.7   ENDOGENOUS VERSUS EXOGENOUS MONEY

Money does not enter the system exogenously like manna from heaven, nor is it dropped from a helicopter as Milton Friedman often presumes. Nor does the money supply increase come from the hiring of additional labor in the private sector to produce the money commodity. In our world the supply of money can increase only through two distinct institutional processes – both of which are related to the institution of money contracts.

1. *The income-generating-finance process* Whenever entrepreneurs expect demand for their output to increase, they will have a profit incentive to increase borrowing to obtain more working-capital loans to meet the higher costs of the increased flow of output. If the banking system is designed to accommodate this increased demand for working-capital loans, then the bankers will be responding positively to the 'needs of trade'.[33] Bank money supply will expand endogenously.[34] Depending on the short-run production flow-supply elasticities of the industries thus stimulated, changes in real income and/or prices will follow (with varying time lags) this endogenous increase in the money supply. Once a new higher level of equilibrium output is reached there is no further need to increase the money supply (due to the finance motive) as the needs of trade are no longer expanding.

Of course, if entrepreneurs expect demand for producible goods to decline, then the finance process will work in reverse. Firms will use some of their current sales proceeds to pay off last period's working-capital loans and reduce their demand for this period's loans. In the absence of other borrowers willing to expand loan obligations, the total supply of money will endogenously decline.

2. *The portfolio change process* The Monetary Authority can exogenously initiate action (open-market operations) to induce the public to hold more or less money balances. By bidding up the price of outstanding government debt (lowering the rate of interest), the Monetary Authority makes it profitable for bondholders to sell some government securities to the central bank and substitute additional bank deposits as their alternative liquid store of value. Alternatively, by selling bonds and depressing their price, the Monetary Authority can raise the interest rate sufficiently to induce the public to reduce its holdings of money by purchasing bonds from the central bank.

In sum, under the income-generating-finance process, an increase in the demand for money induces an endogenous increase in supply if bankers are willing and able to expand under the rules of the game that regulate banking operations. This endogenous money supply increase occurs *pari passu* with additional contractual purchase orders for resources and goods. Changes in the money supply and changes in resource utilization can be directly correlated through the income-generating-finance process. Because production takes time, however, changes in measured output flows will tend to lag changes in the volume of outstanding bank loans. This calendar sequence of events has led some empiricists to incorrectly infer that an increase in the money supply 'causes' an increase in output. Rather it is the endogenous increase in the supply of money that permits an increase in production that is induced by increasing order books of capital goods producers.

In the portfolio change process, increases in the supply of money are immediately used by the bond-selling public as a substitute for securities as a time-machine liquid store of value. If both money and securities have zero elasticities of production, and if they are good substitutes for each other but poor substitutes with respect to producibles, then this exogenous increase in the quantity of money will not necessarily be associated with any increased demand for output and resource utilization. An exogenous increase in the money supply initiated by the Monetary Authority can increase the demand for producible capital goods only if it (a) lowers the discount rate used by firms to evaluate an assumed unchanged expected stream of future quasi-rents associated with investment projects, or (b) reduces the amount of credit rationing to a previously unsatisfied fringe of borrowers, or (c) induces an improvement in the expected flow of quasi-rents.[35] There is no requirement that exogenous policy induced increases in the money supply must induce a *pari passu* increase in aggregate demand.

NOTES

1. G.L.S. Shackle, *The Years of High Theory*, Cambridge University Press, Cambridge, 1967, p. 290. In a nonmonetary economy, no asset exists whose ability to carry purchasing power over time exceeds the carrying cost associated with the asset's physical and value deterioration and/or inventory storage costs. (See J.M. Keynes, *The General Theory of Employment, Interest and Money*, Harcourt, Brace, New York, 1936, p. 239.)
2. Keynes, *The General Theory*, p. 170.
3. Ibid., p. 195.
4. R.F. Harrod, *Money*, London, Macmillan, p. 151.
5. R.F. Harrod, *The Life of John Maynard Keynes*, London, Macmillan, 1951.
6. R.F. Harrod, 'Themes in dynamic theory', *Economic Journal*, **73**, 1963, p. 442.
7. R. Skidelsky, *Keynes*, Oxford University Press, Oxford, 1995.
8. This section is based on P. Davidson, 'Keynes's finance motive', *Oxford Economic Papers*, **17**, 1965, reprinted in Louise Davidson (ed.), *Money and Employment, The Collected Writings of Paul Davidson*, vol. 1, London, Macmillan, 1990.
9. Keynes, *The General Theory*, p. 195. Also see J.M. Keynes, *A Treatise on Money*, vol. I, London, Macmillan, 1930, Ch. 24.
10. Ibid., p. 170.
11. Ibid., p. 199.
12. For example, you may not know whether, during the period, your child will get hurt and need medical attention, or you will smash your car fender and need to get it repaired, and so on, but you 'know' that some unforeseen contingency could arise which requires cash to make a payment during the period.
13. Though the holders of currency receive no income, the holders of bank money may receive some interest income against which the potential cash inflow from the financial asset must be compared.
14. For those individuals who are afraid of any capital losses – the complete bear – saving will be held entirely in money or other fully liquid assets. For those savers, sometimes characterized as widows and orphans – who would never 'live off their capital', except for transactions and precautionary balances, saving will be invested entirely in income-bearing securities where the fear of default is at a minimum.
15. Cf. J.R. Hicks, 'A suggestion for simplifying the theory of money', *Economica*, **2**, 1935, pp. 1–19, reprinted in *Critical Essays in Monetary Theory*, Oxford, Oxford University Press, 1967.
16. If all assets were instantaneously resalable without any costs, there would never be a need to hold 'barren money' rather than a productive asset, except for the necessary nanosecond before it was necessary to meet a contractual commitment that came due. In the real world, the magnitude of actual costs of moving between liquid assets and the medium of contractual settlement is related to the degree of spot market organization and the existence of financial institutions that 'make' spot markets and that thereby assure reasonable moment-to-moment stickiness in spot prices.
17. If money is held in the form of bank deposits, then $(q-c)$ will equal the net interest earnings (net of any bank charges) on bank accounts. In what follows, for simplicity we assume that for money $(q-c)=0$.
18. Keynes, *The General Theory*, p. 202.
19. Ibid., p. 202. Of course if there are transaction costs in buying and selling bonds, then

this rectangular hyperbola will shift up and asymptotically approach a positive value related to the total market transaction costs.

20. In terms of Figure 5.1, the liquidity trap would be represented by the downward-sloping curve becoming horizontal at some low but positive interest rate.

21. *Ibid.*, p. 378.

22. Harrod, *The Life of John Maynard Keynes*, p. 435, also see p. 437.

23. Keynes, *The General Theory*, p. vii.

24. J.M. Keynes, 'Alternative theories of the rate of interest', *Economic Journal*, **47**, 1937, reprinted in *The Collected Writings of John Maynard Keynes*, vol. 14, edited by D. Moggridge, London, Macmillan, 1973, pp. 201–14.

25. *Ibid.*, p. 209.

26. J. Robinson, *The Rate of Interest and Other Essays*, London, Macmillan, 1952, pp. 20–22.

27. J.M. Keynes. 'The ex-ante theory of the rate of interest', *Economic Journal*, **47**, 1937, reprinted in *The Collected Writings*, vol. 14, pp. 220–21.

28. And concomitant additional cash inflows for the owners of the additional hired inputs.

29. Thus Keynes anticipated and explicitly responded to the so-called 'crowding-out' argument almost three decades before it was developed as an anti-Keynesian argument by Monetarists in the 1970s.

30. Keynes, 'The ex-ante theory of the rate of interest', reprinted in *The Collected Writings*, p. 223.

31. Keynes, *A Treatise on Money,* vol. II, p. 220.

32. Keynes, 'Alternative theories of the rate of interest', reprinted in *The Collected Writings*, vol. 14, pp. 210–11. Of course, if there was some queuing initially (before the increase in the demand for finance), then the length of the queue will increase as planned transactions rise as a result of entrepreneurs attempting to finance more investment projects than before.

33. The nineteenth-century real bills doctrine argued that the banking system should be designed to respond positively to the 'needs of trade'.

34. Sometimes it is claimed that this endogenous money supply must be done at an unchanging rate of interest. See B.J. Moore, *Horizontalists and Verticalists*, Cambridge, MA, MIT Press, 1988.

35. A vivid illustration of the possibility that an exogenous increase in the money supply will not stimulate additional spending for producibles was provided in the 1990–92 period. During that period, the Federal Reserve lowered interest rates more than 20 times, while aggregate demand in the private sector increased less than 2 per cent in real terms, while real investment declined. Apparently, lower interest rates were accompanied by lower entrepreneurial expectations of future quasi-rents, and therefore the demand for investment goods fell, while real consumption increased slightly as real income increased by 2 per cent.

6. Financial markets, liquidity and fast exits

In modern entrepreneurial economies, the development of well-organized, orderly markets for financial assets sever the direct link between ownership and control of real capital assets. In the modern corporation, ownership is typically widely dispersed among a population that holds its savings in the form of financial assets. Owners of these enterprises hold legal titles primarily for the expected capital gain they expect from changes in financial market prices and secondarily for the dividend yield that accrues to them while they hold legal title. Most owners would know little about managing the real capital goods that enterprises use.

6.1 THE DOUBLE-EDGED SWORD OF FINANCIAL MARKETS

For the real economy, the existence of liquidity-creating financial markets is a double-edged sword that in good times facilitates investment in real capital goods but in bad times 'adds greatly to the instability of the system'.[1]

The good edge of the financial market sword is that the existence of financial markets makes real investments that are fixed for the community appear to be liquid for the individual. This prospect of liquidity encourages today's savers to transfer their command of existing real resources to entrepreneur-investors who require funding in order to command real resources in excess of what their own earned claims will permit. In good times, the expectation of high returns[2] associated with the possession of financial assets encourages many savers to surrender the full liquidity of their money holdings. The result is that very large investment projects – projects often too large to be funded by any single individual or small group of partners – can be funded by pooling the small sums of many savers.

As long as financial markets are orderly, financial asset holders believe they have a readily available *fast exit strategy* for liquidating their 'investment' the moment they become dissatisfied with the way matters are developing. Without the liquidity provided by orderly markets, fast exits, even if they were possible, would involve very large costs and therefore the 'risk of making an investment as a minority owner would be intolerable'.[3] In the absence of liquid financial markets, the small sums of many savers could not be readily pooled and mobilized to fund the accumulation of large capital-using projects.

The bad edge of the double-edged financial market sword is that the existence of financial markets makes investments that are fixed for the community only appear to be liquid for the individual. The fast exit strategy that calms all financial asset holders' fears of the uncertain future is available to all only as long as the vast majority of these people do not simultaneously try to execute this strategy. When fear of the uncertain future is rampant, many holders of financial assets may simultaneously rush for the exit. The result is a market liquidity crisis. The resulting market crash adds to the instability of the real economy

6.2   MARKET LIQUIDITY, FAST EXITS AND FUNDING INVESTMENTS

Because of the absence of any precise knowledge of the prospective yield of any long-lived asset, the daily reevaluations of equities on the organized exchanges are based on a tacitly agreed upon convention, that is,

> The existing market valuation, however arrived at, is uniquely correct in relation to our existing knowledge of the facts which will influence the yield of the investment and that it will only change in proportion to changes in this knowledge; though, philosophically speaking it cannot be uniquely correct, since our existing knowledge does not provide a sufficient basis for a calculated mathematical expectation.[4]

Because each holder of financial assets believes he/she has a fast exit strategy, the only question is at what price can one sell one's holdings. If there were no transaction costs in converting securities into money and vice versa, then the expected spot price of an asset at the next moment of time *vis-à-vis* this moment's price would be the only relevant price comparison for deciding on whether to hold one's position or to execute a fast exit at this moment. The decision to buy or hold securities today would simply depend on what the individual expected to happen between today and tomorrow, and expectations about the spot price the day after tomorrow would not be relevant until tomorrow became today. Decisions can be made afresh in the light of tomorrow's spot price and expectations about the spot price that will occur in the market the day after tomorrow.

It is because the spot markets for securities are so well organized in modern economies, that is, the transaction costs of moving between money and financial assets are so very low, that each potential buyer believes that his/her store of wealth is extremely liquid. This appearance of being able to immediately sell a liquid asset with very low transaction costs attracts many persons who, as minority shareholders in an enterprise, do not, and could not, manage the production process of the firm. Moreover these minority shareholders have little knowledge (or even interest) in the long-run prospective yield of the capital assets that they legally own. The result is that financial asset market valuations are a result of a convention established on 'the mass psychology of a large number of ignorant individuals'.[5]

The prices of equities need bear little relationship to entrepreneurial views of future profit opportunities. The appearance of a high degree of liquidity of securities means that those current owners of the underlying capital goods are under no moral or legal obligation to see that the real capital assets are used efficiently whenever there is an unexpected perceived change in the external reality.

This ubiquitous belief in the possibility of a fast exit for closing out one's position in liquid securities means that portfolio balance decisions of savers are typically oriented toward expected short-term capital gains (or losses) via spot market purchases and sales, rather than the expected, but uncertain, long-term income flows that the underlying capital goods might yield. Moreover, the daily market value of any financial asset is determined, not by the terms one could expect to pay for all the outstanding units held by the general public, but only by the small volume that is actually traded on any day. It should not be surprising, therefore, to find the total market value of securities is unrelated to either entrepreneurs' estimates of the present value of the underlying real capital goods or the market's long-run expected dividend yield. In times of either euphoria or fear of the future, *there are no market 'fundamentals' that determine the market price of the equities of any specific enterprise.*

The valuation ratio is the total market value of the outstanding titles to the enterprise relative to the cost of production of the real assets of the enterprise. If the price of equities is depressed (because households have increased their bearish preference for money *vis-à-vis* titles to capital goods for any reason), then it may be possible to buy titles to capital goods at a price far below the replacement (cost of production) price of the underlying real capital. The valuation ratio is, in this case, less than unity.

When the valuation ratio is less than one, an individual entrepreneur, who can obtain the funding for a merger or acquisition, can obtain control of the flow of services from the enterprise's existing capital stock less expensively by a take-over than either by purchasing the equivalent real secondhand capital assets directly on a spot market (if it exists) or by ordering the equivalent in new capital goods.[6] This merger and acquisition process retards the rate of real capital formation for society by reducing the demand for ordering new capital goods to be produced.

Depressed security prices also retard the rate of investment because financial intermediaries may be unwilling to float new issues in security markets where prices have fallen significantly. Financial intermediaries such as investment bankers and underwriters, whose function it is to bring new issues to the market, are often concerned with the goodwill of their customers who have previously purchased new issues that the intermediaries have sponsored. These financial institutions, therefore, may be reluctant to provide arrangements for an entrepreneur who wishes to embark on a new large investment project if recent previous new issues are showing a loss when the current spot price is compared to their initial public offering (IPO) price. These financial middlemen may well 'try to protect the market for their previous issues by restricting the output of new ones'.[7] The result will be to create an 'unsatisfied fringe' of would-be entrepreneurs needing funding as sponsors are loathed to add pressure to an already depressed market.

If the spot price of titles to capital goods is high relative to the flow-supply (or production) price for real capital so that the market value of equities exceeds the replacement value of the underlying capital goods (that is, the valuation ratio exceeds unity), then entrepreneurs will find it cheaper to order new equipment rather than attempt to gain control over the flow of services from existing capital goods via the merger and acquisition purchases of secondhand equities. If equity prices are high, then 'there is an inducement to spend on a new project what may seem an extravagant sum if it can be floated off on the stock exchange at an immediate profit'.[8] The profit opportunities from floating IPOs during the NASDAQ dot-com bubble of the 1990s induced investment bankers and venture capitalists to actively search out and encourage entrepreneurial plans for capital expansion. As a result, the number of entrepreneurial investors who were assured funding increased, raising the demand for capital goods and the accumulation of real capital goods that created the boom years of 1993–2000.

Keynes used 'the term speculation for the activity of forecasting the psychology of the [financial] market, and the term enterprise for the activity of forecasting the prospective yield of assets over their whole life'.[9] For the most part financial market activity is speculative and independent of both real investment activity and the rate at which new securities are being floated since the latter is very small relative to the total number of transactions and the outstanding stock of existing securities. The lower the transaction costs of organized security market activity, the more the focus of market participants will be on the capital gains or losses due to expected changes in the very near future spot market prices of financial assets. In essence, stock market activity and financial markets prices depend almost entirely on people's view about how rich (or poor) they are likely to be in the near future, that is, changes in the public's expectations of future spot security prices are much more important than such 'fundamentals' as price-earnings ratios.

Because the cost of moving into and out of financial markets has been reduced so much in the last two decades, the foundation for the public's daily reevaluations of securities has become ever more evanescent. The growth of day traders who continuously churned over their portfolios in hopes of short-term capital appreciation became more prevalent in the 1990s. Active financial market participants, including many mutual fund managers, held securities at any moment only for capital gains rather than for income.[10] This idea that people buy securities primarily for capital gains and not for the income-producing potential is sometimes known under the derogatory terminology as 'selling to the bigger-fool' theory.

In modern entrepreneurial economies, security markets are organized so that the majority of traders can gamble on unknown and unknowable future changes in the conventional basis of valuation of securities with a minimum of transactions costs.[11] As a consequence the market value of equities will often appear to be quite absurd to 'a rational observer from the outside . . . [as] the vast majority of those who are concerned with the buying and selling of securities know almost nothing whatever about what they are doing'.[12] Perhaps, this is what Federal Reserve Chairman Alan Greenspan meant when he noted, in 1996, that the stock market valuations were being driven by 'irrational exuberance'. Moreover, the fund manager who does try to focus the long-term prospects of the enterprise

> will in practice come in for the most criticism . . . For it is the essence of his beha-viour that he should be eccentric, unconventional and rash in the eyes of average opinion. If he is successful that will only confirm the general belief in his rash-ness; and if in the short run he is unsuccessful, which is very likely, he will not receive much mercy. Worldly wisdom teaches it is better for reputation to fail conventionally than succeed unconventionally.[13]

The vast majority of owners of corporate enterprises are, for the most part amateurs or professional speculators interested only in taking advan-tage of the expected misguided views of the crowd.[14] Nor need holders of financial assets possess real capital managerial skills as long as transaction and carrying costs are so small that the potentially profitable date for liqui-dating one's specific asset holdings, for given expectations, is near enough in the future so that the money dividend or interest yield on the securities and/or the underlying capital goods is relatively negligible.[15]

The only unequivocal links between the liquidity preference behavioral decision and the investment demand decision for the hire-purchase of capital goods are those changes in the interest rate affecting (a) the rate of discount used by entrepreneurs to evaluate future expected net cash inflows or their optimism regarding future cash inflows, or (b) the public's bearishness propensity which in turn may affect the number of unsatisfied entrepreneurs who cannot obtain funding commitments from nonbank financial intermediaries.

The existence of a money-creating banking system and well-organized liquidity-creating financial markets permit today's entrepreneurs to make investment expenditure decisions that may be incompatible with the public's portfolio allocation preferences at the current rate of interest. If entrepreneurial investors can obtain funding commitments from financial intermediaries such as investment bankers, then they can sign purchase order contracts for capital goods that will stimulate capital goods producers to employ necessary resources to meet these forward contractual orders. Ultimately it will be the spot market price of securities that will be the adjusting mechanism that brings the public's portfolio balance decision into harmony with the outstanding volume of securities representing past and present needs for external funding for the investment projects undertaken. In a monetary economy, it is finance and funding that provide the energy fuel that permits the investment tail to wag the portfolio balance dog.

No matter what the current portfolio holdings desire of the public is, or what changes may occur in the public's bullish–bearish balance in the immediate future, the Monetary Authority and the banking system can act as a balancing factor to stabilize the prices of financial assets. By operating either directly or indirectly through financial intermediaries on the spot market for securities, and by laying down (either by law or custom) rules and regulations of the financial markets game, the Monetary Authority can affect the spot price of securities and the volume of securities and money available for the public to hold.[16] The banking system can permit (encourage?) entrepreneurs to undertake any level of expenditure on newly produced capital goods that their animal spirits desire – as long as the public has confidence in the existing money-contractual system for organizing production and exchange activities. In a closed economy, this confidence in the ongoing contractual system depends, in large part, on the expectation that the contractual money–wage rate (relative to productivity), that is, unit labor costs of production, will remain relatively more sticky in terms of money than in terms of anything else. This expectation of money price of

the products of industry being sticky in terms of money encourages individuals to enter into money contracts and store purchasing power in terms
of domestic liquid financial assets. In an open economy where different
nations use different chartalist monies, if the exchange rate between monies
can vary then it is possible for the expected domestic unit labor costs to be
more sticky in terms of some foreign nation's money rather than the domestic money. This can lead to a 'flight of capital' or 'hot-money' flows as
people speculate on the exchange rate and store purchasing power in terms
of foreign financial assets. This open economy case will be discussed in later
chapters.

6.3   THE MARKET FOR SECURITIES

Money and liquid securities are the primary vehicles used to transfer generalized purchasing power over time.[17] Each individual saver's disposition
to allocate his/her savings between money and other liquid assets depends
on many factors including the saver's desire to maximize generalized purchasing power for unspecified claims on resources in the future; the saver's
fears of income and capital losses; the saver's vision as to future spot prices
of financial assets, and the saver's confidence in his/her ability to foresee an
unforeseeable future better than other financial market participants.

If the public (a) increases its fear of capital loss or (b) lowers its expectations about the rate of increase in future spot securities prices, or (c) has less
confidence in its expectations of changes in security prices or (d) shortens
the time period until the expected date of liquidation of a position in financial assets, then the public has become more bearish (because of either speculative or precautionary factors).[18] This will cause a fall in security prices,
thereby reducing the aggregate value of the public's liquid store of wealth.

A change in the market value of the liquid store of wealth *per se* can have
an effect on the public's bull–bear balance. A fall in the market value of
securities can make the public even more bearish and a rise, more bullish.[19]
Changes in the price of financial assets can also generate a wealth effect that
can have an impact on households' demand for real goods and services.[20]
As Keynes noted, 'A country is no richer when it swaps titles to capital at a
higher price than a lower one, but the citizens, beyond question, *feel*
richer'.[21] When spot prices of financial assets rise, households may believe
it is less necessary to save out of current income and therefore aggregate
consumption at all levels of income may increase. This increment in the
propensity to consume is likely to come at the expense of 'normal' savings
out of income, rather than, in the aggregate, the liquidation of paper profits
in the spot markets for securities. In the United States, for example, there

was an example of such a wealth effect during the 1990s when NASDAQ stock prices rose dramatically while there was a recorded fall in the personal savings rate to zero and even to negative levels.[22]

In the absence of central bank actions to create or destroy liquidity by directly (or indirectly through the banking system) buying or selling securities to the public, it is the flexibility of the spot price of marketable financial assets that permits each decision-making unit to hold as much of its liquid store of wealth in securities as it desires and to alter its portfolio as often as it desires, while in the aggregate the public holds exactly the quantity of financial assets and money that is made available to it.

Any decline in the spot price of securities can be offset by the banking system if the central bank regulators encourage depository institutions or other financial intermediaries to purchase financial assets on the spot market and simultaneously create bank deposits for the public. During the stock market crash of October 1987, for example, the Federal Reserve flooded banks, government bond market makers, and other financial intermediaries with liquidity in order to encourage them to buy from the general public financial assets overhanging the markets.

A similar but stronger action flooding the financial system with liquidity was taken by the Federal Reserve immediately after the September 11, 2001 terrorist attacks on the World Trade Center and the Pentagon. In the two days following the attack, the Federal Reserve pumped $45 billion into the banking system. Simultaneously,

> to ease cash concerns among primary dealers in bonds – which include investment banks that aren't able to borrow money directly from the Fed – the Fed on Thursday [September 13, 20001] snapped up all the government securities offered by dealers, $70.2 billion worth. On Friday it poured even more into the system, buying a record $81.25 billion of government securities.[23]

In effect, these actions of the Federal Reserve removed securities from the general public by making liquidity available to financial intermediaries who would purchase securities from those members of the general public who wanted to make a fast exit.

The *Wall Street Journal* reported that just before the stock market opened in New York after the terrorist attack, investment banker Goldman Sachs, loaded with liquidity due to Fed activities, phoned the chief investment officer of a large mutual fund group to tell him that Goldman was willing to buy any stocks the mutual fund managers wanted to sell. Similarly, the *Journal* notes that corporations 'also jumped in, taking advantage of regulators' newly relaxed stock buyback rules'.[24] These corporations bought back securities that the general public had held, thereby propping up the price of their securities.

The post-September 11, 2001 activities of the Federal Reserve flooding the banking and financial system with liquidity vividly demonstrate that the Monetary Authority can either directly or indirectly reduce the outstanding supply of securities available to the general public. The public could then satisfy its increased bearish tendencies by increasing its money holdings without depressing the spot market price for financial assets in a disorderly manner. Until, and unless, the public's increase in bearishness recedes, the Monetary Authority and the banking and financial intermediaries can hold that portion of the total titles to the underlying real capital of enterprises that the public does not want to own.

Although the public shifted its portfolio holdings from titles to real capital goods toward money and other safe haven financial assets after the terrorist attack, the community cannot alter its holdings of aggregate real capital at all in the short run. Accordingly, the total market value of titles to capital goods held by the public at any point of time does not necessarily bear any particular unique relationship to the total stock of capital goods in the economy, despite the claims of some financial market 'experts' that there is a long-run fundamental price–earnings ratio.[25] The actual market value of securities will largely depend on (a) the historical accidents of the past needs of firms to externally fund investment expenditures; (b) the net buy back of securities by enterprise; (c) the current sentiment of the wealth-holding public and (d) the behavior of the Monetary Authority, the banking system and financial intermediaries in response to changes in the bull–bear sentiment of the public.

In an economy where the major form of money is bank deposits, portfolio decisions in combination with the operations of the financial system will determine what proportion of the community's total of real wealth is owned by households and what proportion is owned or looked after by the banking and financial system.

6.4   THE DIFFERENT ROLE OF BANKS AND NONBANK FINANCIAL INTERMEDIARIES

It is often difficult to explain the nuances of an economic theory – especially a revolutionary theory such as Keynes's *General Theory* – to politicians, to central bankers and to other decision makers who are engaged in important real world economic decisions. Keynes noted that the famous nineteenth-century economist and founder of *The Economist* magazine, Walter Bagehot, once complained that the directors of the Bank of England were not acquainted with the correct theoretical principles under which a central bank should operate. Bagehot wrote:

They could not be expected themselves to discover such principles. The abstract thinking of the world is never to be expected from persons in high places; the administration of first-rate current transactions is a most engrossing business, and those charged with them are usually but little inclined to think on points of theory, even when such thinking most nearly concerns those transactions.[26]

In trying to explain to policy makers the implications of his revolutionary analysis, Keynes wrote that his proposals involved 'an extension . . . of the essential principles of *banking* by which, when one chap wants to leave his resources idle, those resources are not withdrawn from circulation but are made available to another chap who is prepared to use them – and to make this possible without the former losing his liquidity'.[27]

Those savers who, at the moment, do not want to exercise their earned income claims on the real resources of the system but do not want to give up the option of being able to exercise these claims immediately at any future moment, should hold their unexercised claims in the form of fully liquid bank deposit money. A well-designed monetary system should be able to create additional monetary claims (bank deposit liabilities) on resources for those borrowers who are prepared to exercise them immediately without having to extinguish the bank deposit claims of savers who want the complete freedom of full liquidity.

Nonbank financial intermediaries cannot create additional claims to be used to command resources. Instead nonbank intermediaries can only act as transfer agents moving liquidity from savers to entrepreneurial investment spenders. This transfer is accomplished by inducing savers to give up the liquidity of their bank deposits in return for the promise that the savers will receive a positive return (a liquidity premium) in excess of what the savers could 'earn' if they kept their savings in the form of bank demand deposits. This liquidity premium is offered if savers hold either the nonbank intermediaries' liabilities, or other securitized assets issued by the investor-spenders. To minimize the liquidity premium that savers will demand to surrender their bank deposits to the nonbank financial intermediaries, the latter often securitize their own liabilities that they sell to savers while attempting to convince the public that the financial assets they offer are almost as good as money.

In the case of securitized money market funds, for example, the market maker typically suggests that the market price for the securities of the fund is fixed and unchanging and that conversion can be made within the day. The small type in the money-market equity contract, however, usually indicates that (a) the redemption of money-market shares can be postponed at the option of the issuers for several business days if the fund manager does not have sufficient money to repurchase the securities and (b) the redemption price of money-market funds is not guaranteed.[28]

Liquidity is the essential focus of Keynes's revolutionary analysis. Too great a demand for liquidity by the public can saddle the system with persistent involuntarily unemployed resources. It is the public's demand for liquidity combined with the actions (and reactions to this demand) of the bank and nonbank financial community that rules the roost (that is, the path of the real economy) for good (that is, rapid economic growth and the rapid accumulation of capital) or for evil (stagnation, persistent unemployment and persistent poverty).

For rapid economic growth, two conditions are necessary:

1. entrepreneurs must have strong 'animal spirits' that encourage them to see additional significant profit opportunities in the future that can be obtained by innovation and investment today, and
2. as long as there are idle resources available, liquidity desires on the part of savers must not be allowed to prevent 'animal spirited' entrepreneurs from having sufficient access to liquidity to be able to sign purchase order contracts for all the new capital goods they desire.

Animal spirits depend in large part on the creative imagination of the entrepreneurial class. Obtaining the claims on resources necessary to put creative ideas into capital facilities requires the positive cooperation of the central bank, the banking system and the nonbank financial community. Financial markets can help promote economic progress if they are organized as closely as possible to Keynes's banking principles in that they permit savers to believe they have not lost any significant liquidity when they transfer their claims to entrepreneurs who want to command resources that otherwise would remain idle. The presence of a properly designed accommodating (endogenous money) banking system and associated financial intermediary institutions provide the potential to contribute significantly to a golden age of economic development and growth. On the other hand, unregulated 'liberalized' financial markets that encourage topsy-turvy growth of financial institutions can, at times of stress, experience liquidity crises that produce poor economic performance.

In order to understand the mechanics of how the financial system can produce prosperity or provoke havoc, it is essential to understand how banks and nonbank institutions link the entrepreneurial demand for finance and funding of large, costly investment projects with the household demand for savings and liquidity. Once the relationship between financial markets and the public's liquidity preference are taken into account, it can be demonstrated that even if society plans to save a proportion of its full employment income that is compatible with the entrepreneurial planned proportion of total output devoted to the production of investment goods, a stable economic growth rate may not be attainable unless certain actions are taken by these financial intermediaries and accommodated by the Monetary Authority.[29]

6.5 BANK LOANS AND MONEY-MARKET FINANCIAL INTERMEDIARIES

Throughout most of the twentieth century, there has been a clear division between the role of commercial banks and the role of nonbank financial intermediaries. Commercial banks were the primary providers of working-capital loans to producers of capital goods. The resulting producers' debt contracts were nonmarketable assets that were held by banks. The interest received on these loans was the primary source of profits for the banks.

Nonbank financial intermediary promoters (such as investment bankers) made contractual commitments to entrepreneur-investors to float new issues that would provide funding for large investment projects by the date when payment was due to the producers of the investment projects.[30] Trust companies, insurance companies and other financial intermediaries that collected small pools of savings from many saving households were willing buyers of the new issues promoted by investment bankers. In return for their custom, the investment bankers typically offered options on forth-coming flotations of new issues to these good customers. Any unsubscribed portion of the new issue flotation was then offered on the over-the-counter market to the general public.

Until the 1990s, nonbank financial intermediaries such as insurance companies, mutual funds and so on rarely bought and held positions in the short-term (working capital) debt obligations of producing enterprises. In the 1990s a trend developed where banks, who are the originators of short-term working-capital loans to enterprises as well as household loans on credit card purchases, sold their short-term loan portfolio. According to a report in the July 23, 2001 *Wall Street Journal*, US banks sold off $1.2 trillion dollars of their loan portfolio in 2000 'up from $234 billion a decade earlier'.

Nearly half of the outstanding loans initiated by banks in 2001 are now held by nonbank financial intermediaries, especially mutual funds. This resale of loans to nonbank intermediaries permits banks to shed much of their default uncertainty arising from the large volume of working capital and consumer loans that the banks originate. The effect has been to shift banks' profit orientation from earning interest on outstanding loans to earning fees for making, servicing and reselling short-term loans to mutual fund managers and ultimately to individual investors in these funds.

The downside aspect of this shift in the source of bank profits from interest earnings to originating and servicing fees is that bank loan officers do not worry as much about the creditworthiness of borrowers as long as there is a strong market for these loans. There is therefore an incentive for bank loan officers to become 'loan pushers' and loan traders rather than investigators of the soundness of the borrower's use of loan money.[31]

This selling of bank-originated loans to nonbank financial intermediaries has permitted banks to make more loans per period without increasing their total loan portfolio holdings. By advertising, but not guaranteeing, larger yields and by suggesting the safety of principal (but not providing insured deposits), the mutual fund intermediaries have been able to attract the medium of contractual settlement from the bear hoards of abstaining households and even, on occasion, leveraging these bear hoards with additional loans to purchase additional loans from banks.

Saver households are willing to accept an equity position in money-market mutual funds (rather than holding fully liquid interest-bearing insured bank deposits) because they believe that holding a position in a money-market fund promises (a) a greater reward (yield) without any fear of capital loss than can be expected from holding savings in the form of a bank deposit, while (b) if mutual fund holders decide on a fast exit, they have greater confidence in the ability of the managers of the mutual fund to readily redeem its shares than the confidence that the household saver would have if the householder had to liquidate the underlying loan contracts directly; and (c) the very low transaction costs of buying and reselling the mutual fund's securities encourages the belief in the cheapness of a fast exit strategy.

The greater the confidence the saver has in the money-market fund manager's ability to repurchase its outstanding mutual shares at a fixed price with very low transactions costs the higher the value of the marginal propensity to purchase securities (m) out of current household savings. At the limit, $m = 1$, that is, all increments in income that are not spent will be stored in securities that are presumed to be fully liquid rather than bank deposits.

Although both nonbank financial intermediaries' liabilities and bank deposit liabilities are evidence of private debt, a major difference between them is that only the bank liabilities can be generally used to discharge a contract. Only banks can directly use the central bank's clearing facilities and are specially favored by the central bank in the sense that the latter guarantees converting bank liabilities into legal tender at the option of the holder. Banks' demand deposit liabilities are a 'tap issue' in the sense that each holder of the banks' deposit liabilities is assured of being able to convert his/her deposits into legal tender (central bank liabilities) at his/her initiative and without costs or the possibility of capital loss. Bank deposits therefore represent the preeminent fast exit strategy asset.[32] Nonbank financial intermediaries' liabilities are denied this tap issue status and the direct use of a central bank clearing system. Hence the securities of nonbank financial intermediaries such as mutual funds, while being a good substitute for money as a store of value, cannot be directly used in settlement of a contractual obligation. As a consequence there will always be some transactions cost involved in converting nonbank financial intermediaries' liabilities that are used as a store of value into the medium of settlement – a cost which does not exist for legal tender money or bank money.

6.6 CONCLUSION

Recent trends in the growth of mutual funds and other nonbank financial intermediaries have encouraged saver households to reallocate their saving portfolio from holding less (government insured) bank deposits toward holding more liabilities of nonbank financial intermediaries. This has permitted a significant expansion of debt obligations on the part of debtor households and enterprises. This suggests that a sudden switch by many households to a fast exit strategy at a future date could cause a horrific liquidity problem, unless the central bank is alert to the need for pouring as much liquidity into the system as necessary, quickly and promptly. The experiences of October 1987 and September 2001, suggest that the Federal Reserve bank has, on an unsystematic *ad hoc* basis, responded adequately to individual financial market liquidity crisis. It is not clear that the central banks of other nations or currency unions will respond similarly, or that the Federal Reserve might fail to respond adequately in some future crisis. It does suggest that a more systematic response to such liquidity experiences should be built into the organization of central banks.

NOTES

1. J.M. Keynes, *The General Theory of Employment, Interest and Money,* Harcourt, Brace, New York, 1936, p. 151.
2. Including expected capital gains.
3. Peter L. Bernstein, 'Stock Market Risk in a Post Keynesian Setting', *Journal of Post Keynesian Economics,* **21**, 1998, p. 18.
4. Keynes, *The General Theory*, p. 152.
5. Ibid., p. 154.
6. This may occur if poor management of a firm has caused equity holders to have a pessimistic view of the future. Thus a stock take-over by a more efficient management may improve the 'productivity' of the real capital of the firm that has been swallowed up.

7. J.M. Keynes, *A Treatise on Money*, vol. II, London, Macmillan, 1930, p. 368.
8. Keynes, *The General Theory*, p. 151.
9. Ibid., p. 158.
10. This has resulted in a drastic reduction in the dividend yield of liquid securities traded on organized exchanges.
11. Keynes, *The General Theory*, p. 159, also *A Treatise on Money*, vol. II, p. 361.
12. Keynes, *A Treatise on Money*, vol. II, p. 361.
13. Keynes, *The General Theory*, pp. 157–8.
14. Ibid., pp. 154–8
15. Thus, the lower the transactions cost, the more households are likely to ignore future income expectations for expected capital gains. No wonder, with the growth of discount brokerage firms via the Internet, the volume of day traders grew substantially – as did the daily volatility in the market in the 1990s.
16. Not surprisingly, in a world of uncertainty, the spot price in the securities market need not be an equilibrium one in the sense that all the public's potential borrowers and lenders are being satisfied at the current price. Financial intermediaries and the banking system operate as buffers by building up and/or discharging inventories of securities.
17. Basic to the classical school's view is the belief that producible consumer durables are good stores of value (for example, M. Friedman and A. Schwartz, 'Money and business cycles', *Review of Economics and Statistics supplement*, 1963, pp. 59–63; D. Patinkin, *On the Nature of the Money Mechanism*, Stockholm, Almquist & Wicksell, 1967, p. 260) even though carrying costs mount steeply for produced durables after some minimum stock level per household has been obtained. Consequently, except where there is expectation of very rapid inflation in future offer prices (that is, expectations of rapid rises in money-wages and flow-supply prices) so that expectations of rising spot prices for consumer durables are sufficient to more than offset the increasing carrying cost, the classical model will be irrelevant. Such expectations, however, are incompatible with the essential properties of money and, as already suggested, are incompatible with a viable monetary economy. Hence the classical fable is only applicable to either a world of perfect certainty, or to real world episodes of flight from money. The latter case is extremely rare and it is unlikely that the classical general equilibrium theories had such a perverse case in mind.
18. This increase in bearishness may result from the fact that rapidly fluctuating stock prices may decrease the public's confidence in their expectations about the future. On the other hand, steadily increasing stock prices may increase the public's confidence and therefore increase their bullishness. Thus, changes in portfolio balance decisions may be the result of either the rapidity of fluctuations in security prices or the expected rate of change, or a combination of these factors. (Cf. Keynes, *A Treatise on Money*, vol. II, p. 252.)
19. F.P.R. Brechling, 'A note on bond holding and the liquidity preference theory of interest', *Review of Economic Studies*, **24**, 1957, p. 191.
20. This wealth effect on the demand for consumer goods may be more powerful than the wealth effect that Pigou and Patinkin associated with the change in real money balances for a given stock supply of money when there is a change in the price of consumer goods.
21. Keynes, *A Treatise on Money*, vol. II, p. 197.
22. Since the securities one owns may be pledged as collateral against a loan, households might actually spend more than they earn without liquidating their position in equities during a roaring bull market.
23. *Wall Street Journal*, October 18, 2001, p. 1.
24. Ibid., p. 1.
25. Thus Kaldor's (and others') use of the valuation ratio as a determinant of long-run equilibrium growth is highly misleading since there is no necessary relationship between the market value of the outstanding stock of titles in the hands of the public relative to the value of the net finance committed to the purchase of capital goods until both the marginal propensity to buy placements out of household savings and the actions of the Monetary Authority and the financial intermediaries who 'make' spot security markets are specified. Cf. N. Kaldor, 'Marginal productivity and macroeconomic theories of

distribution', *Review of Economic Studies*, 1966, **33**, pp. 309–19, also J. Robinson, *The Accumulation of Capital*, London, Macmillan, 1956, p. 230.

26. Keynes, *A Treatise on Money*, vol. II, p. 364.
27. R. Skidelsky, *John Maynard Keynes, Fighting For Britain 1937–1946*, London, Macmillan, 2000, p. 222.
28. Assets issued by nonbank financial intermediaries always have a lower degree of liquidity than bank demand deposits. Ultimately the central bank acts as a market maker who guarantees an unchanging exchange rate between banks' demand deposit liabilities and legal tender (the liabilities of the central bank). Liabilities of nonbank financial intermediaries do not have the same backing of the central bank. Accordingly, nonbank financial intermediaries must act as the market maker in their own outstanding liabilities. This requires nonbank financial intermediaries who act as market makers to have either a significant inventory of cash reserves or to be able to exercise a fast exit strategy in the particular assets in their own portfolios.
29. See Chapter 7 *infra*.
30. Other financial intermediaries such as mutual savings institutions, credit unions, savings and loan associations provided the contractual commitments for funding homeowners mortgaged purchases of new (and old) homes.
31. Securitization may account for the explosion of consumer credit card debt in the last decade.
32. Thus in an earlier era, when fear of the future became overwhelming, there were 'runs' on banks. With the development of federally insured bank deposits, the perceived need for a fast exit from insured deposits has disappeared.

7. Planned investment, planned savings, liquidity and economic growth

7.1 HARROD'S ACTUAL, WARRANTED AND NATURAL RATES OF GROWTH

Drawing on Keynes's *General Theory*, Sir Roy Harrod developed formulations that appeared to demonstrate that to maintain a stable (equilibrium) rate of economic growth there was a necessary equality between the proportion of planned savings out of income and the proportion of current output devoted to the production of investment goods. Although Harrod recognized that economic 'growth is the aggregated effect of a great number of individual decisions . . . based on trial and error',[1] he failed to see that the liquidity preference of the public can alter the rate of economic growth even if the public's planned savings ratio is equal to the ratio of planned investment production to total output. In this chapter we shall demonstrate why the existence of liquid financial markets creates many a slip between the planned savings cup and the planned investment lip. But first we should review Harrod's taxonomic approach to the theory of economic growth.

Harrod developed three concepts of economic growth of output:

1. *the warranted rate of growth* occurs when growth would be in an 'equilibrium of steady advance'[2] as entrepreneurs' expectations of sales growth are just being met by contractual purchases (realized demand) of buyers;
2. *the actual rate of growth* at any point of time may not be an equilibrium rate. Instead the growth rate may be changing as entrepreneurs revise their investment plans if they discover that realized demands of buyers differ from the entrepreneurial expectations of sales; and
3. *the natural rate of growth*, is the growth rate that would maintain full employment of labor and capital.

Harrod showed that the warranted or equilibrium rate of growth (G_w) of total production in the economic system could be formulated as

$$G_w = s_d / C_r \tag{7.1}$$

where s_d is the 'desired' or expected ratio of aggregate planned savings to aggregate income implicit in entrepreneurial expectations of short-period sales proceeds, and C_r is the required stock of capital facilities that are necessary to produce a volume of output that just meets entrepreneurs' expected short-period sales proceeds. In other words, the warranted rate of growth in effective demand is defined as that rate which will justify or validate the sales expectations that are the basis for the capacity that producers are installing in each period. As long as net investment is positive, new capacity is being added to the system and there will be some increment in demand that will make entrepreneurs satisfied with the investment commitments they are currently undertaking.

The actual (or realized) rate of growth of an economy depends on the realized change in effective demand between periods. If the realized change in aggregate effective demand between production periods is equal to that which entrepreneurs expect, then the actual and warranted growth rates coincide as the 'desired' saving ratio (s_d) exactly equals what income recipients are planning to save out of income. If on the other hand, the planned saving ratio is greater (less) than the expected or desired savings ratio, then, in the aggregate, buyers will be spending less (more) out of income than entrepreneurs expected.

Harrod's natural rate of growth (G_n) concept is the growth in total production and sales necessary to maintain full employment. The natural rate of growth 'is not determined by the wishes of persons and companies as regards savings'.[3] The natural rate of growth depends solely on the aggregate supply factors of (a) the growth in the working population and (b) the improvement of productivity of workers due to changes in the capital–labor ratio and technological progress. Chapter 2 indicated that the determinants of aggregate demand are not identical with the factors determining aggregate supply. Consequently, in a free market economy, it would be fortuitous if either the warranted or the actual rate of growth equaled the natural (or full employment) rate of growth.

If individuals, in the aggregate, plan to save more out of full employment income than the savings ratio associated with the natural rate of growth, then aggregate demand will be less than can be produced at full employment. The warranted growth rate will be less than the natural growth rate. If the aggregate planned savings ratio is less than the savings ratio compatible with the natural rate of growth, then aggregate demand will exceed aggregate supply at full employment. In Harrod's growth analysis there is no automatic mechanism that assures that aggregation of individual savings decisions and entrepreneurial investment spending decisions will result in a golden age of full employment economic growth.

Harrod's growth analysis did not inquire into the role played by financial markets and financial intermediaries in achieving and maintaining any specific warranted growth rate when planned savings equals planned investment. The rest of this chapter addresses that problem.

7.2   PLANNED SAVINGS AND THE SUPPLY OF FINANCIAL ASSETS

All economic models are simplifications of reality. To explain the relationship between planned savings, the role of financial markets and planned investment, some simplifications will be made at this stage of the analysis. Initially assume that all financial assets are in the form of equities (titles to ownership of real capital). At any point of time, there is a given stock of equity securities available to the general public equal to all the previously issued securities net of those repurchased by the issuer or purchased and held by the banking system.

Any increase in the stock of equities available in the marketplace will come through initial public offerings (IPOs) or 'new issues' that are floated to fund a new investment project that has just come 'on stream'.[4] Since a portion of the cost of these investment projects may be internally funded by the firm,[5] it is only to the extent that the firm uses external sources of funding that there will be an increase in the supply of securities available in the market.

Each period, the quantity of additional equity securities offered in the marketplace will depend upon (a) entrepreneurial demands for newly produced capital goods, (b) the necessity to externally fund some portion of that demand and (c) the behavior of financial intermediaries who raise the funds by floating the new issues to the public.

If only a fraction (g) of all investment spending is externally funded and if h is the fraction of long-term external funding provided directly by the banking system,[6] then the value of new issues offered to the general public will be equal to a fraction of the market value of net investment expenditures per period. If g and h are taken as exogenous, while I_n is net investment spending, then the quantity of new issues necessary to fully fund the external funding requirement is

$$Q_s = [(1-h)(g)(I_n)]/(p_s) \qquad (7.2)$$

where Q_s is the quantity of newly issued securities and p_s is the spot market price of equities.[7] Equation (7.2) indicates that given the fraction of net investment that must be externally funded via 'new issues' each period, the quantity of securities that must be sold to the public will be greater the lower the market price. At the end of each period, the total market supply of securities being held by the public depends on (a) the pre-existing stock supply of previously issued securities plus (b) new issues floated in the market during the current accounting period.[8]

The fact that the volume of new issues floated on the market is related to the need to externally fund net investment expenditures indicates that the supply of equities available to the public is not completely independent of the demand for net real investment. The existence of g and h as exogenous variables which depend partly on financial institutions' behavior, and partly on the financial rules of the game, suggests that real investment expenditures and the flow of new issues are independent 'at least in the sense that any degree, positive or negative, of the one is compatible in appropriate circumstances with any degree, positive or negative of the other'.[9] Accordingly, when the relationship between planned savings and planned investment spending is analysed to obtain generalizations about economic growth, it is necessary to provide an explicit hypothesis regarding the actions of the banking system, the magnitudes of g and h, the behavior of financial intermediaries, the liquidity preference of the public for allocating current savings between equities and money, and the price of IPOs.

When households have positive savings out of income, they must decide in what liquid 'time machines' to store their savings. If households plan to hold some of their savings in the form of financial securities, then we can posit that there is a marginal propensity to buy securities (m) out of household savings (S_h). This propensity to use savings to purchase additional securities was called the 'non-speculative demand for securities' by Kaldor.[10] In modern times, this non-speculative demand for securities can be closely associated with institutional arrangements and tax policies that encourage income recipients to put a fixed proportion of their income into 401(k) and other tax sheltered pension plans. The administrators of these pension plans 'invest' these funds in financial securities.

The magnitude of this marginal propensity, to buy (the non-speculative demand for) securities, Keynes assumed, would be between zero and unity.[11] Old and new classical economists and old and new Keynesians, on the other hand, implicitly assume that the marginal propensity to buy securities out of household savings equals one. If this marginal propensity for 'non-speculative demand for securities' is less than unity, then there is a potential slip so that even if planned savings equals planned investment, a warranted rate of growth may not be possible to maintain.[12]

7.3   OWNERSHIP AND LIQUIDITY

The business of the daily exchanging of existing financial titles to wealth that occurs in modern security markets absorbs a significant volume of human energy and attracts worldwide attention, yet the role of organized security markets and related institutions as the link between the desire to accumulate capital goods by firms and the desire to store wealth by households is only vaguely perceived in mainstream economic texts. The existence of a banking system and continuous well-organized spot markets in titles to real capital makes the investment decision independent of the decision to save and to own equity securities. When, centuries ago, there were no organized, orderly securities markets, then

> Decisions to invest in private business were . . . largely irrevocable, not only for the community as a whole, but also for the individual. With the separation between ownership and management which prevails today . . . a new factor of great importance has entered in, which sometimes facilitates investment but sometimes adds greatly to the instability of the system . . . the daily revaluations of the Stock Exchange, though they are primarily made to facilitate transfers of old investments between one individual and another, inevitably exert a decisive influence on the rate of current investment.[13]

In a world of perfect foreknowledge, of course, there would be no need for continuous reevaluation of the market value of existing titles and outstanding debt contracts that occurs in real world financial markets. In a world of actuarial certainty (in the sense that the sum of the 'known' objective probabilities of all possible events equals unity) insurance markets could produce an actuarial certain market valuation for equities.[14] Organized security markets, however, are not insurance markets – nor do the financial intermediaries connecting savers and investors in these markets operate on actuarial principles.

Some nonbank financial intermediaries have developed semi-privileged arrangements with the banking system and the central bank. The existence of semi-privileged liquidity-creating arrangements between some financial market intermediaries and the Monetary Authority either directly or indirectly[15] (via commercial banks) has meant that, *under certain conditions*, if central bankers understand their job, the money supply will respond endogenously to both changes in the needs of trade and changes in financial (liquidity) conditions.[16] Let us examine the possible relations between planned savings decisions, planned investments, financial intermediaries, and financial markets and liquidity demands.

7.4 EXTERNAL FUNDING AND SAVERS' 'NONSPECULATIVE' DEMAND FOR SECURITIES

To simplify the following analysis of external funding requirements and economic growth, assume that (a) neither the central bank nor commercial banks engage in any open-market operations to affect the supply of (equity) securities available to the general public and (b) no changes occur in the public's liquidity preference (changes in the precautionary and speculative demand for securities) during the period of analysis. For the purpose of analytically separating 'independent' economic factors, the following analysis emphasizes first, household decisions about what time machines households plan to use to store their current savings (Kaldor's non speculative demand for securities) and second, entrepreneurial decisions on how much net investment spending must be externally funded and how much will be internally funded. These decisions will determine the increments in the market demand and supply of financial assets.[17] The price of financial assets will increase (be constant, decline), if the nonspeculative demand for securities out of current savings exceeds (equals, falls short of) the volume of new issues required to externally fund the planned investment projects during the current accounting period.

If entrepreneurs expect sales to grow, they will plan to increase production and capacity. Typically a firm plans to fund externally a significant portion of its large investment projects. By selling long-term securities to obtain the external funding, capital-accumulating enterprises attempt to mobilize the pools of savings that are being generated as the capital goods are produced and the owners of the productive inputs are paid. Before placing an order for the investment project, any prudent firm will make sure that sufficient external funding will be available when the investment project is delivered and payment is required. To that end an investment banker (or a venture capitalist, or promoter) is engaged to float a new issue at the date when external funding will be required.

Once assured of long-term funding, the investing firm does not have to worry whether it will have sufficient liquidity to pay for the delivery of the goods. It can enter into contractual agreements for the delivery of plant and equipment from the capital goods producers 'knowing' it will have the funds when the bills come due. Armed with these orders, the producers of capital goods obtain short-term working-capital loans from their bankers to pay for their required labor and raw material inputs in the production process. Upon delivery, receipts from floating the new issue are combined with any internal funding the entrepreneur has undertaken. The payment received by the capital goods suppliers is used to repay the bankers for the working-capital bank loans and to make final payroll and material supply payments.[18] The repayments to the banks of the working-capital loans become a revolving pool of finance which can be used to maintain a similar level of investment expenditures in the next period.

If, at the initial financial asset price level, the aggregate planned net external funding (or quasi-debtor) position of firms is growing *pari passu* with the aggregate planned net creditor position of households, then the volume of new issues just equals the (nonspeculative) demand for securities out of current household savings,

$$iI = m \, s_h \, Y_h \qquad\qquad (7.3)$$

where i is the fraction of investment expenditures (I) which entrepreneurs, in the aggregate must finance externally, m is the marginal propensity to purchase securities out of aggregate household savings, and s_h, is the public's planned savings ratio out of household income (Y_h).

If the funds used to internally finance investment spending are equal to corporate savings out of profits ($s_c P$), then,

$$s_c P = (1 - i) \, I. \qquad\qquad (7.4)$$

If entrepreneurial expectations of sales proceeds from current production are being realized, then aggregate savings out of household income must be equal to the fraction of investment spending that is being externally financed, that is, $m s_h \, Y_h = iI$ and $m = 1$. Given these conditions, the equilibrium growth path (Harrod's warranted growth rate) will be maintained while new issues are being floated at an equal pace with the (nonspeculative) demand for securities out of household savings.

Mainstream growth models assume that the equilibrium growth path will be maintained as long as the planned savings ratio equals the planned investment ratio. Consequently our analysis shows that mainstream economic models must implicitly be assuming that the marginal propensity to buy securities from household saving equals unity. If, however, households desire to hold some of their saving each period in the form of bank deposits[19] (that is, $m < 1$), then the supply of new issues coming to market will exceed the nonspeculative demand for securities. The price of securities will have to decline (the interest rate will increase) as firms struggle to raise sufficient external funding to pay for the capital goods they ordered. This increase in the cost of financial capital will induce entrepreneurs to reduce their planned investment spending.

7.5 ACTUAL GROWTH WHEN NEW ISSUES EXCEED THE NONSPECULATIVE DEMAND FOR SECURITIES

In a monetary economy, there is no reason to expect the marginal propensity to buy securities out of saving to equal unity. In fact it is more reasonable to assume that as household wealth increases a portion of saving will go to the accumulation of additional bank balances.[20] Accordingly even if sales expectations are being justified as planned savings equals planned investment, that is,

$$s_c P + s_h \, Y_h = (1 - i)I + iI \qquad (7.5)$$

if the marginal propensity to buy securities (m) out of household saving is less than unity, then

$$s_c P + m \, s_h \, Y_h < (1 - i)I + iI \qquad (7.6)$$

and, at the current market price of securities, the value of the new issues that is necessary to externally fund the planned investment spending will exceed the demand for securities out of household saving. As a result the market price of equities will fall, the cost of capital funding will rise and some planned investment project will be choked off.[21]

The financial intermediaries who float new issues will interpret the decline in the market price of equities as a resistance to buy their new offerings by their usual customers. In an attempt to protect this goodwill with their best customers for new issues, the bankers, underwriters and venture capitalists will reduce the future flow of new issues coming to market. They will reduce their commitments to float new issues and perhaps even actively encourage investor firms to postpone their investment plans (thereby forcing firms to reduce their planned investment spending). Also, investment bankers and other promoters of IPOs may, in the very short run, hold some of the already committed new issues off the market. They will finance this unplanned increase in their inventories of new issues by increasing their indebtedness to the banking system. These actions will tend to support the financial market against this unforeseen slump[22] and to maintain a more orderly market for new issues. The banking and financial system is looking after that portion of the real wealth of the community that the public does not wish to own.[23]

Even if the real forces in the economy are such that the planned savings ratio at a given level of income is equal to the proportion of aggregate production that entrepreneurs want in the form of capital goods production, as long as $iI > m\,s_h\,Y_h$, then the liquidity needs of the public are not being entirely met by the banking system and this excessive demand for fully liquid assets will constrain the rate of real economic growth. To remove this liquidity constraint will require either (a) the central bank directly, or indirectly through the banking system, accommodating the 'bears' by increasing the money supply via market purchases of outstanding securities from the public, or (b) investment underwriters financing their excessive new issue security inventories. In other words, the banking system must endogenously respond to these needs of the financial circulation (in excess of the needs of trade) by increasing the money supply.

If the Monetary Authority does not permit the banks to expand the money supply at the initial security price level and the bearish tendencies of the public are unchanged, then as promoters borrow to finance their swollen inventories, the banks will have to ration the remaining credit among the borrowers from the industrial circulation.[24] This rationing of credit to the industrial sector will obviously reduce growth and may even induce a slump, even if financial intermediaries took no voluntary actions of their own to staunch the forthcoming flow of new issues.

Even if the banking system increased loans to encourage financial middlemen to hold unplanned inventories of new issues, these financial intermediaries would not be willing to hold their excessive inventories for any length of time. This is especially true if there is a persistent flow of new issues coming to market that exceeds the demand for securities out of household saving. Instead, encumbered by increasing indebtedness to the banks, the financial intermediaries would basically turn off the spigot of new issues so that they can disgorge their swollen inventories with a minimum of adverse effect on security prices. As long as the quantity of new issues reaching the market exceeds the 'nonspeculative demand' for financial assets, funded orders for new capital goods will be reduced by such Procrustean devices as rationing access to long-term funding.[25]

In sum, an excessive demand for liquidity by the public can restrict expenditures on new capital goods even if the public proposes to be sufficiently thrifty out of a given level of income to maintain the warranted rate of growth. If the planned savings ratio is compatible with a full employment growth of real effective demand, a golden age of economic growth may be interrupted or prevented solely by an excessive demand for liquidity by savers. In such circumstances the Monetary Authority should redress immediately the financial constraints on growth by accommodating this excessive liquidity demand. The central bank must be ready to supply sufficient cash to meet all the bearish desires of savers and to provide adequate funding for all planned investment projects. As Keynes declared:

The banks hold the key in the transition from a lower to a higher scale of activity. . . . The investment market can become congested through a shortage of cash. It can never become congested through a shortage of savings. This is the most fundamental of my conclusions in this field.[26]

Since expectations of future spot prices of securities can greatly affect the current financial market conditions,[27] it may be necessary and desirable for monetary policy to make a pre-emptive strike on excessive liquidity preference tendencies before adverse expectations are generated in the financial market. By removing securities from either the public or the dealers just before the excessive market bearishness appears, the Monetary Authority can create positive financial conditions so that all the new issues offered on the market will be voluntarily taken up by the public without depressing the market price.

A growth-oriented monetary policy necessitates providing increases in the money supply in anticipation of all the needs of trade *and* finance as long as the point of effective demand does not exceed full employment. Of course, to diagnose these monetary needs in advance and to achieve an exact balance is not possible via either any simple quantitative rule for expanding the money supply, or using an econometric analysis of past events. Instead, if the Monetary Authority is to promote a financial atmosphere which is compatible with a golden age, it should err on the side of 'cheap money' and the 'best' judgment forecasts of the trend of liquidity forces in the financial markets. The Monetary Authority will need flexibility and discretion if it is to anticipate, or at least not frustrate, the 'needs' for the financial 'paving stones' that permit the real factors to achieve an equilibrium rate of growth that approaches full employment of resources. On balance, it will be desirable for the Monetary Authority to provide in advance all the credit paving stones that enterprise might need at full employment.[28]

7.6 THE CONTRACTIONARY CASE WITH A BULL MARKET

If the 'nonspeculative' demand for securities out of household savings exceeds the flow of new issues coming to market, that is, $iI < m \, s_h \, Y_h$, then although there is a tendency for the spot price of securities to increase (interest rates to fall), this liquidity imbalance will slow the economy below the equilibrium (warranted) rate of growth.

This seemingly paradoxical result of a recessionary economy in the presence of a bullish security market is, however, easily explainable. Since internally financed investment expenditures are equal to total corporate savings (retentions) out of profit income, then, if the nonspeculative demand for

securities from household savings exceeds the demand for external funding
for investment by firms, then household savings plus corporate savings
must exceed aggregate investment at the given level of income.[29] It therefore follows that since m is equal to, or less than, unity when $iI < m\, s_h\, Y_h$,
entrepreneurial short-period sales expectations associated with the given
level of employment must be disappointed. In this case, some firms will
decide to produce a flow of output that would equal Harrod's warranted
growth rate where planned savings equals planned investment, some firms
will be saddled with losses, or at least, they will have lower sales receipts
than expected and will be earning less than expected profits. This will
induce firms to retrench even if the costs of capital are declining.

Faced with disappointing sales and possessing existing capacity that is
excessive for current levels of realized sales, entrepreneurs are unlikely to
have visions of additional investment opportunities which can become
profitable solely because of a decline in the market cost of capital. Of
course, with rising security prices, investment underwriters will find it easy
and profitable to float new issues and they therefore may 'beat the bushes'
to flush out additional investment projects from entrepreneurs, particularly
from those who might, under other circumstances, be part of the unsatisfied fringe of entrepreneurs who desire funding. If these financial intermediaries are successful, they may be able to increase real investment and the
demand for external finances sufficiently so that a slowdown is avoided.

7.7   ECONOMIC GROWTH, LIQUIDITY AND FUNDING 'OTHER' SPENDING SECTORS

As long as the public's planned saving ratio out of current income exceeds
the entrepreneurial demand for the quantity of newly produced capital
goods necessary to maintain effective demand at the current level of
employment, it does not matter whether households desire money or securities as a time machine for transferring purchasing power to the future,
entrepreneurial sales expectations must be disappointed. Realized profits
and cash flows will be lower than expected and under the pressure of slack
markets entrepreneurs will retrench.[30]

If the private sector's planned saving is in excess of planned investment,
then economic growth can be maintained only if there are other sectors that
want to spend in excess of their income and can find liquid funding for the
resulting excess of expenditure. In a closed economy, the 'other' sector is
government, since the federal government as a buyer can always spend and
fund more than it takes in as tax receipts. In an open economy, an 'other'
sector is foreign buyers. If foreigners want to spend in excess of their foreign

earnings, the domestic economy can experience export-led growth, where an excess of exports over imports not only creates jobs domestically but is funded by domestic savers either directly, or indirectly through nonbank financial intermediaries (a) making loans to foreigners or (b) purchasing foreign financial assets. This open economy aspect of seeking economic prosperity through export-led growth, rather than government deficit spending, will be discussed in detail in later chapters.

Harrod succinctly summarized this central theme of the operation of a monetary economy:

'It was Keynes's contention, which was both a novelty and source of endless confusion among commentators that a tendency for savings to exceed investment had nothing whatever to do with people putting money into a stocking or even with their leaving it idle in a banking account. Savings might exceed investment even if all savers immediately invested their money in securities, and investment might exceed saving even if a great many savers were putting their money into stockings.[31]

To this we might add that a warranted rate of growth may not persist even if planned savings equals planned investment, if the liquidity desires of savers are not compatible with the needs for external funding by enterprise and the banking system does not create sufficient liquidity to satisfy the desires of savers while providing for all the external funding needed by entrepreneurs. An accommodating money-supply policy to meet the needs of industry and finance is a necessary, but not a sufficient condition for a golden age of full employment growth. If the central bank provides sufficient liquidity to drive interest rates close to zero, and still effective demand for the products of industry is not sufficient to bring about a golden age, then easier financial conditions cannot *per se* induce the economy to expand to its full employment rate of growth.

There is an asymmetry about money matters. If demand for securities out of current savings is less than the need for external funding requirements of enterprise, then a more rapid expansion of the money supply is necessary to maintain growth while the banking system looks after the portion of the real wealth of society that the public does not wish to currently own. If the demand for securities out of household savings exceeds the needs for external funding, monetary policy may be powerless to encourage an expansion. This is the analysis which ultimately lies beyond the old monetary theory adage 'You can't push on a string.'

The financial arrangements between firms, investment underwriters, stock specialists and other market makers and commercial banks and the central bank provide a mechanism both for communicating the monetary needs of industry and finance, and a way for the Monetary Authority to respond to the current and anticipated monetary needs of the financial community. Unfortunately, the various financial institutions operating on this two-way street are often misguided by the principles of classical conventional wisdom. It is, therefore, not surprising that these human financial institutions have often acted in a way that constrained the rate of accumulation while real resources remained involuntarily idle. The financial system as it has developed with a rationalization provided by the *laissez-faire* philosophy of mainstream economic theory has led to procedures where the services of the productive resources of society are often dissipated in ways that are adverse to the social interests. It is the separation of ownership from control that is due to the growth of organized orderly security markets and not the lack of perfect competition in the traditional microeconomic sense which leads to unemployment and the major misallocation of resources in real world economies.

In the absence of financial institutions which operate as residual buyers and sellers in financial markets to maintain orderliness, there would be no liquid financial assets. Then money alone would possess liquidity and display those essential elasticity attributes which assure that Say's Law is not applicable. The existence of market makers who offer savers a choice of many liquid time machines, assures greater liquidity for financial assets than to the real capital goods underlying these securities. The access these financial institutions have via the banking system to ultimately the lender of last resort that is supporting the organized financial asset market structure, is the institutional *coup de grâce* to the classical view that, in the long run, (a) underemployment equilibrium is impossible, and (b) income distribution and the rate of interest will always adjust real consumption spending to assure full employment growth.

7.8   SOME CONCLUSIONS

For wealth-holding households the portfolio balance decision as to what proportion of their liquid store of value to hold in the form of uncertain deferred claims (securities) and what proportion to hold as immediate claims (money), relate to their whole block of wealth at each moment[32] and not to their current increment of wealth we call saving. The guidelines for monetary policy involving iI and $ms_h Y_h$, as developed in this chapter, are much too simple. These rules were developed merely as a convenient analytical way of separating out the diverse financial forces creating complications for the smooth operation of monetary economy.

In the real world, new issues and household savings are trifling elements in the securities market. Changes in total demand for securities (the speculative and precautionary demand) that are induced by changes in public confidence and opinion about future spot securities prices can dominate the needs of the financial circulation and the spot price of newly issued financial assets. Any discrepancy between iI and $m\, s_h\, Y_h$, can be swamped by the eddies of speculative movements by the whole body of wealth-holders who are constantly sifting and shifting their portfolio composition.

In an uncertain world, where financial market expectations are especially volatile and unpredictable, the relationship between increases in the quantity of money and the needs of the financial circulation are too complex and capricious to be handled by any simple rule, even if growth in the real factors underlying the needs of the industrial circulation could be accurately forecast. The solution lies:

> in letting Finance and Industry have all the money they want, but at a rate of interest which in its effect on the rate of new [externally financed] investment . . . exactly balances the effect of bullish sentiment. To diagnose the position precisely at every stage and to achieve this exact balance may sometimes be, however, beyond the wits of man.[33]

Any rule for expanding the money supply at the same rate as the growth in output will only fortuitously promote a steady rate of accumulation. If the Monetary Authority, as the ultimate creator of the medium of contractual settlement gears its policy to maintaining the purchasing power of its creation in periods of rising money production costs of reproducible goods (inflation) before full employment growth is achieved, then the resulting constraint on the growth of the money supply will severely restrict output growth. It will be impossible to expand the revolving fund of finance even to meet the needs of a growing industrial circulation, and accumulation will be retarded even though households and entrepreneurs propose to behave in a manner consistent with maintaining a steady rate of real growth.

If there are strong social and political forces causing spontaneous rises in the money production costs of reproducible goods, 'then the control of the price-level may pass beyond the power of the banking system'[34] even if the Monetary Authority holds the rate of growth of the money supply far below the growth in potential output. Accordingly, a monetary policy compatible with a socially desirable stable rate of growth and a relatively stable price level, must be coordinated with a fiscal policy which assures the proper balance of the real forces underlying aggregate demand, and a government policy on incomes oriented toward stabilizing the production costs of reproducible goods over time.

> If we have complete control of the Earnings (or Wages) System and of the Currency System, so that we can alter the rate of earnings by *fiat*, can accommodate the supply of money to the rate of earnings we have decreed, and can

control the rate of investment, then we can follow our fancy as to what we stabilise – the purchasing power of money . . . its labour power, or anything else – without running the risk of setting up social and economic frictions or causing waste . . . But if . . . we have at least a partial control of the Currency System but not of the Earnings System, . . . [then] we have some power to decide what the equilibrium price level and rate of earnings is to be, but no power of bringing about this equilibrium except by setting into operation the mechanism of induced changes [to depress the economy].[35]

NOTES

1. R.F. Harrod, *Towards A Dynamic Economics*, Macmillan, London, 1948, pp. 76–7.
2. Ibid., p. 81.
3. R.F. Harrod, *Money*, Macmillan, London, 1969, p. 196.
4. We assume that business firms can finance replacement investment spending entirely from depreciation allowances and hence do not have to dilute equity values by selling additional securities to fund replacement investment.
5. In a world of uncertainty, institutional rules may require that some portion of net investment be internally financed.
6. In the United States banks rarely hold long-term equity securities so that h is approximately zero. In other countries, however, banks often do hold substantial amounts of equity securities so that $0 < h < 1$.
7. The supply curve of new issues with respect to the market price is a rectangular hyperbola for any given level of investment spending.
8. If there is a large degree of homogeneity between the new issue securities and the previously outstanding stock of securities, then there will be a single market price for both the new issues and the already existing securities.
9. J.M. Keynes, *A Treatise on Money*, vol. I, Macmillan, London, 1930, p. 145.
10. N. Kaldor, 'Speculation and economic stability', *Review of Economic Studies*, 7, 1939, pp. 1–27, reprinted in N. Kaldor, *Essays on Economic Stability and Growth*, Duckworth, London, 1960, p. 48.
11. See J.M. Keynes, 'The ex-ante theory', *Economic Journal*, 47, 1937, p. 668. Both the classical and the Old and New Keynesian economists implicitly assume that $m = 1$, that is, that all household savings are used to buy securities. Such an assumption requires that increases in the quantity of money are never held as a store of value.
12. Of course, the decision as to what time machine to use to transfer command purchasing power into the future is relevant not only in determining what vehicle is used to hold the current saving, but also to the whole block of households' existing wealth. Indeed since today's savings 'is but a trifling proportion of the block of existing wealth, it is but a minor element in the matter'. At each point of time, 'saver' asset holders have to decide how much of their total postponed command of resources to hold in the form of financial assets (equities in our simple model) and how much in the form of money (bank deposits and/or currency). This is the relevance of the portfolio balance decision.
13. J.M. Keynes, *The General Theory of Employment, Interest and Money*, Harcourt, Brace, New York, 1936, pp. 150–51.
14. The popular view among mainstream academics that observed market prices for securities is a random walk implicitly presumes an actuarial market valuation process.
15. Certain government bond houses in New York have obvious connections with the central bank through the market for repos and so on. With the 'informal' intervention of the Federal Reserve Bank of New York between the Long Term Capital Management hedge fund and its banker creditors, it should be obvious that other types of large financial intermediary funds can have, in times of stress, a special relationship with the central

bank. Thus the 'too big to fail' doctrine that was applied to member banks in the 1980s has now spread to other nonbank financial intermediaries.

16. A prime example was the days immediately following the September 11, 2001 terrorist attack on the World Trade Center and the Pentagon. See Chapter 6 *supra*.

17. In reality, these are only a trifling proportion of the existing stock of savers' liquid wealth and firm's total outstanding external funding obligations.

18. Any remaining sales revenue becomes the gross profits of the capital goods producer.

19. Or, in an open economy, in financial assets traded on a foreign securities market.

20. The greater one's income, *ceteris paribus*, the larger one's average bank balance over the accounting period.

21. As we have already noted, this assumes that the normal factors affecting liquidity preference, for example, expectations about future spot prices of securities and so on are unaltered, so only the minor increments in liquid wealth holding demand affect the market price of securities.

22. Cf. J.R. Hicks, *Critical Essays in Monetary Theory*, Oxford University Press, Oxford, 1967, p. 48.

23. Of course, if the underwriters were to draw down their precautionary cash balances to finance the undesired increment in financial asset inventories (perhaps because they think the downward price pressure is only temporary) the immediate impact would be to offset the excessive bear mentality of the public. If the downward pressure does not disappear quickly, the underwriters will be forced to slow the flow of new issues to the market and/or borrow additional funds from the banking system. Cf. R.F. Kahn, 'Some notes on liquidity preference', *Manchester School*, 1954, pp. 237–8.

24. This may take the form of raising the cost of bank loans in general and/or discriminating against small or new firms without a track record of prompt repayment of previous loans.

25. Cf. R.F. Hawtry, *The Art of Central Banking*, Longmans, Green, London, 1932, p. 382.

26. Keynes, 'The ex-ane theory', pp. 668–9.

27. A complication that we have, by assumption, previously avoided.

28. This will require removing much of the burden of fighting inflation from the shoulders of the central bank. Instead domestic inflationary pressures should be constrained via an incomes policy while inflationary pressures coming from international transactions should be constrained by adopting the reforms outlined in Chapter 14 *infra*. (For a further discussion of alternative views for preventing inflation, see P. Davidson, *Post Keynesian Macroeconomic Theory*, Edward Elgar, Cheltenham, 1994, Chapter 9.

29. Since $Sc = (1 - i)I$, if $iI < m \, s_h \, Y_h$ then total savings $(S) = Sc + s_h \, Y_h$, and therefore total planned savings exceeds planned investment, that is, $S > I$.

30. To the extent that firms are making out-of-pocket losses, they may partly finance these by additional borrowings from the banks (who, however, are unlikely to be willing to make such loans even if they have excess reserves). Cf. Keynes, *A Treatise on Money*, vol. I, p. 145. Even if firms finance losses by borrowing, they will be under financial pressure to cut costs and therefore production and hiring in the future.

31. R.F. Harrod, *The Life of John Maynard Keynes*, Macmillan, London, 1951, pp. 404–5. Also see p. 372, n.1.

32. As long as there are continuous well-organized spot markets for deferred claims (securities).

33. Keynes, *A Treatise on Money*, vol. I, pp. 254–5.

34. Ibid., vol. II, p. 351.

35. Ibid., vol. I, p. 169.

8. Complicating the picture: money and international liquidity

In the previous chapters, a closed economy was discussed where all transactors resided in the same nation and all contractual commitments were expressed in terms of a single monetary unit. In the following chapters, the analysis is expanded to deal with international contractual transactions. The use of different monies by parties to international contracts has important implications for the demand for liquidity in a global economy.

8.1 OPEN VERSUS CLOSED AND UNIONIZED VERSUS NON-UNIONIZED MONETARY SYSTEMS

A precise taxonomy is a necessary precondition for all scientific inquiry. Distinctions are made between open and closed economies and between unionized monetary systems (UMS) and non-unionized monetary systems (NUMS). Table 8.1 presents the four possible combinations of these features.

Table 8.1   A classification of economic systems by trading patterns and monetary systems

Economy monetary system	Closed economy ($\varphi = 0$)	Open economy ($\varphi > 0$)
Unionized monetary system (UMS) ($\Theta = 0$)	1. no external trading partners 2. single money for all contracts	1. external trading partners 2. single money for all contracts
Non-unionized monetary system (NUMS) ($\Theta > 0$)	1. no external trading partners 2. various monies for contracts 3. no fixed exchange rate	1. external trading partners 2. various monies for contracts 3. no fixed exchange rate

The first cell of Table 8.1 involves a closed economy utilizing a single money to settle all contractual obligations between residents. This cell is the equivalent of the traditional closed economy model used by Keynes in *The General Theory* to demonstrate the possibility of underemployment equilibrium in a simple market-oriented, entrepreneurial economy. More complicated economies, therefore, are even more likely to exhibit persistent unemployment problems without some governmental and private institutional planning and control.

The open economy UMS cell in Table 8.1 involves a home (local) regional economy trading with other regions where the same monetary unit is used to denominate and settle all private contracts between transactors. Examples of economies that will fall within this cell are regions within the same nation that trade with each other (for example, transactions between residents of the New York Federal Reserve District and the Atlanta Federal Reserve District) or trade among member nations in a common currency union, for example, the euro nations, or trade among nations with a permanently fixed exchange rate.

The closed economy NUMS cell in Table 8.1 is applicable to the global economy where one monetary unit is used for contracts between residents in a single region or nation and different monetary units for contracts between residents in different regions. The exchange rate between any two monies may vary over the life of the contract.

Finally, the last cell of Table 8.1 (open NUMS) is applicable to the analysis of an individual real world national economy that has foreign trading partners with different currencies and a floating exchange rate system among the various currencies.

The four-way classification scheme of Table 8.1 depends on: (a) the theory of aggregate accounting to distinguish between open and closed economies; and (b) the laws and customs of society that determine the medium of contractual settlement to distinguish between a UMS and a NUMS.

8.2 AGGREGATE ACCOUNTING AS A BASIS FOR THE CLOSED–OPEN DICHOTOMY

For the most part, aggregate economic income measures can have no meaning other than that assigned to them by aggregate accounting theory. The aggregate (or social) accounts do not measure conventionally existing items. Rather, they are a way of accounting for particular abstract theoretical concepts.[1]

A closed economy is one where there are no transactions between individuals in the domestic economy and individuals outside the economy's accounting system. There are no external trading partners who (a) sell raw materials, labor, or finished goods to domestic firms and residents, or (b) purchase the products of domestic industries, or (c) buy and/or sell assets from/to domestic economic agents. In a closed system, the aggregation of the accounting records of all transactors is included in the single set of books on aggregate or national accounts. All payments (except currency transactions) are entirely recorded via the accounting records of this closed economy's banking and clearing-house system.

For a closed economy, a double-entry record-keeping system[2] of aggregate accounts ensures that the total money expenditure of domestic residents on new goods and services equals the total gross money income receipts of residents as well as the value of gross production of all domestic enterprises (see equation (8.4) *infra*).

An open economy, by its very nature, involves a significant volume of transactions between domestic residents in nation A and inhabitants in other nations. In the accounting system of an open economy all the simple equalities between aggregate expenditures and income receipts of domestic residents (as expressed in equation (8.4)) need not necessarily hold. The market value of production of final goods by domestically located enterprises need not equal either the gross income earned by domestic residents or the total expenditures of domestic residents on final goods and services. The following accounting relationships are useful in sorting out the differences between closed and open economies where:

V_c=the market value of domestically produced final consumer goods purchased for domestic use net of the value of foreign components,[3]

V_i=the market value of domestically produced investment goods for domestic use, net of foreign components,

V_g=the market value of domestically produced government-purchased goods for domestic use, net of foreign components,[4]

V_x=the market value of domestically produced goods for export net of foreign components,

V_m=the market value of all foreign-produced goods imported into the domestic economy net of domestically produced components.

All values are expressed in terms of the domestic monetary unit. The value of aggregate expenditures on all final goods by domestic residents (E_D), or gross domestic purchases is

$$E_D = V_c + V_i + V_g + V_m. \qquad (8.1)$$

The value of aggregate domestic production emerging from domestically located enterprises (V_{GDP}) or income generated domestically is called gross domestic product (GDP). It is

$$V_{GDP} = V_c + V_i + V_g + V_x. \tag{8.2}$$

GDP measures all income produced within the borders of a nation whether the income generated from this domestic production is to be received by domestic residents or by foreigners.

Gross national product (GNP) is the gross aggregate income earned by domestic residents, whether from domestic production or foreign production. To obtain the value of GNP one must add to GDP the foreign-generated income earned by domestic firms and households ($Y^g_{f \to d}$) and subtract the domestically generated income earned by foreign firms and households ($Y^g_{d \to f}$) to obtain *aggregate income earned by domestic residents* (V_{GNP}), that is,

$$V_{GNP} = V_{GDP} - Y^g_{d \to f} + Y^g_{f \to d}. \tag{8.3}$$

In a closed economy, $V_X = 0$, $V_M = 0$, $Y^g_{d \to f} = 0$, $Y^g_{f \to d} = 0$, so that

$$V_{GDP} = V_{GNP} = E_D. \tag{8.4}$$

In an open economy, there can be a net inflow or outflow of payments between economy A and its trading partners. If, for example, nation A earns more than it produces domestically (GNP>GDP) this difference is accounted for by presuming a net positive export of a real productive service (capital) to foreigners who pay for this capital either by repatriating profits (for equity capital) or by interest payments (for debt capital loans). Income earned by residents of nation A might therefore be more (or less) than income generated domestically because of foreign ownership of business enterprises located in nation A (or foreign loans to domestic enterprises) and domestic residents' ownership (or loans) to foreign-based enterprises.[5]

The difference between the aggregate domestic output (or GDP) and aggregate expenditures by domestic residents is obtained by subtracting equation (8.1) from (8.2). In a closed economy where there are no exports or imports, the difference is zero. In an open economy, this difference is equal to the exports minus imports, or the economy's savings on its foreign earnings account

$$V_{GDP} - E_D = V_x - V_m = B \tag{8.5}$$

where B is the balance of goods and services.

In an open economy there will always be contractual payments between residents (and/or governments) of different nations. There can therefore be a net inflow or outflow of payments between economy A and its trading partners. In any accounting period, the balance between total in payments and total out payments is called the current account (*CA*) balance, where

$$CA = B + (- Y^g_{d \to f} + Y^g_{f \to d}) + UTP \tag{8.6}$$

where $(- Y^g_{d \to f} + Y^g_{f \to d})$ is net foreign income and UTP is unilateral transfer payments. Unilateral transfer payments are international payments from residents of one nation to residents of another nation (or from one national government to another) with no reciprocal obligation on the part of the latter to ship goods or services in return, for example, gifts.

The current account balance is a measure of overall international payments imbalances. The current account balance measures the value of home-owned output of goods and services (whether produced domestically or abroad) placed at the disposal of foreigners minus the value of foreign-owned output (produced at home or abroad) placed at the disposal of domestic residents.[6]

If residents of nation A are making more payments to foreigners than foreigners make payments to domestic residents, then the current account balance will be in deficit. Nation A will face a liquidity question of how to finance its payments deficit.

8.3　THE ACCOUNTING VALUE OF EXPORTS AND IMPORTS AND TRANSFER PRICING

In the national income accounts of an economy, the value of exports and imports is based on market prices. In the nineteenth and early twentieth centuries, most exports and imports were sold or purchased in open markets. With the advent of multinational corporations, however, a considerable portion of a nation's imports and/or exports may be represented by a transfer of goods from a subsidiary of a multinational corporation in one country to another subsidiary of the same multinational in another country. When a multinational transfers goods from one of its subsidiaries in nation A to another in nation B, then there is a question of at what price should this shipment be evaluated. The transfer price will affect the value of exports from A and imports into B in the balance of payments accounts of nations A and B. The transfer price recorded in the multinational corporation's accounting books need not be a market price. Rather, it can reflect a valuation picked by the multinational's comptroller.

Transfer prices can be arbitrarily set to avoid national tax liabilities in a nation or avoid currency and capital export restrictions or other government regulations.[7] If shipments by multinationals are significant in a nation's balance of payments, then transfer prices can bias the national accounts measurements of trade and current account balances. Caution must be exercised before interpreting any balance of trade statistics as symptomatic of a fundamental national disequilibrium, rather than as an accounting imbalance due in some part to decisions of a multinational comptroller to take advantage of different regulations or tax laws in various national jurisdictions.

8.4 THE BALANCE OF PAYMENTS ACCOUNTING STATEMENT

The items that make up a balance of payments accounting statement are illustrated in Table 8.2. This balance of payments statement involves a double-entry bookkeeping system. For the United States, every item in the statement that puts the United States into debt to foreigners is recorded in the debit column, and every item that provides the United States with a claim on foreigners is recorded as a credit entry.[8]

Table 8.2   A balance of payments statement

Credits (claims on foreigners)	Debits (debts to foreigners)
1. Merchandise exports	Merchandise imports
2. Exports of services	Import of services
3. Investment income on US assets abroad	Income payments on foreign assets in the US
4. Unilateral transfers to the US from foreigners	Unilateral transfer from the US to foreigners
5. Short-term credit from foreigners	Short-term credit to foreigners
6. Long-term investment of foreigners in the US	Long-term investment of US residents abroad
7. Foreign reserve changes	

Line 1 on Table 8.2 indicates that all US exports of merchandise during the accounting period provide the United States with claims on foreigners while all merchandise imports put the United States into debt to foreigners. Except for smuggling, the import and export of merchandise goods can be readily recorded at ports of entry and exit. The value of merchandise credits minus debits on line 1 is often referred to as the *balance of trade*.

Line 2 records the exports and imports of services. Exports of services (for example, foreigners flying on US airlines) produce claims on foreigners, while the import of services (for example, US residents purchasing insurance from Lloyd's of London) puts the United States in debt to foreigners.

Line 3 records income received by US residents from production abroad (claims), and income payments to foreigners (debts) from production occurring in the United States.

The net value of the sum of lines 1, 2 and 3 is called the *balance on goods, services and income account*. It is a measure of the savings of the nation on its total foreign earnings. A positive balance indicates that the nation is spending less than it is earning from transactions with its foreign trading partners. If the balance is negative, the domestic nation is spending more than it is earning (during this accounting period).

Line 4 records unilateral transfer payments between residents of different nations during the accounting period. A *unilateral transfer payment* is payment made from one person to another residing in a different country without any offsetting sales of goods, services or assets. For example, if a foreign student is studying at the University of Tennessee and he/she receives money from his/her parents overseas to pay for living expenses in the United States, that transaction is a unilateral transfer credit in the US balance of payments. Similarly, if a Mexican working in the United States sends part of his/her wages back to his/her family in Mexico that gives rise to a debit unilateral transfer payment for the United States.

Unilateral transfer payments can be between either individuals or governments. For example, when Germany and Japan paid their contribution to the US war against Iraq ('*Desert Storm*') in 1991, these payments were recorded as unilateral government transfer credits on line 4 of the US balance of payments statement.

Lines 1, 2, 3 and 4 together are called the *current account*. If the current account balance is negative, then the domestic nation is spending more than its international earnings plus unilateral transfers. A negative current account balance is often characterized as evidence that a nation is living beyond its means. A nation's 'means' is defined as the net export earnings on goods and services plus net investment income plus net unilateral transfer payments. If the deficit in the current account balance persists, conventional wisdom suggests that the nation must 'tighten its belt' and lower its 'riotous' living by reducing dependence on imports.

Lines 5, 6 and 7 in Table 8.2 represent the *Capital Account*. If the current account is in deficit then the capital account must be in surplus. Changes in the capital account indicate how any current account deficit or surplus is being financed by (i) short-term credits, or (ii) direct investments (by buying or selling assets), or (iii) sales or purchases of foreign reserves.

8.5   MEASURING THE DEGREE OF OPENNESS

One possible measure of the degree of openness (φ) of an economy is the ratio of the market value of imports denominated in local currency terms to the total amount of domestic expenditures on final goods and services, that is,

$$\varphi = (V_M/E_D). \tag{8.7}$$

If $\varphi = 0$, the economy is closed and there are no purchases by domestic residents from any foreigners. The greater the value of φ, the more open is the economy. At the limit, when $\varphi = 1$, the economy is completely open and residents do not purchase any home-produced goods. They buy only imported products.

The degree of openness is not only a measure of the relative importance of the balance of payments in determining employment and economic growth but it is also a measure of the economy's susceptibility to importing inflation. Concerns about inflation involve the price level of the things residents buy. The more open the economy, the less the overlap of the price level of the things residents buy with the things residents produce and the more important is the price of imports (in terms of the domestic currency) in determining the real wage and standard of living of the nation's residents.

The aggregate expenditure on final goods and services (E_d) of a nation is the sum of expenditures of domestically produced goods and imports, that is,

$$E_d = (P_D Q_D) + (P_M Q_M) = PQ, \tag{8.8}$$

where P is a weighted average of P_D, the price level of domestic goods and services, and P_M, the price level of imports, where the weights represent the importance of domestic goods and imports in the total purchases (or the degree of openness).

$$P = (P_D)(1 - \varphi) + (P_M) (\varphi). \tag{8.9}$$

The degree of inflation faced by residents in a nation therefore depends not only on the costs of domestically produced goods but also on the price of imports and the degree of openness in the economy.

The greater the degree of openness of the economy, the greater the potential for importing inflation. For example, if $\varphi = 0.2$, then a 10 per cent rise in the price level of imports (P_M) in terms of domestic currency will lead to a 2 per cent increase in the average price level (P) of things residents buy.[9] If P_D is to remain unchanged, then the price level of domestically produced goods (P_D) has to decline by 2.5 per cent to offset the imported inflation. If P is directly related to unit labor costs and if domestic productivity was rising by, say 3 per cent per annum, then price stability would require that money-wages increase by no more than 0.5 per cent per annum. In other words, if import prices rise over time, domestic money-wages must rise by less than the growth in productivity to offset this imported inflationary force.

During the 12 months of 1979, for example, the price of imported Saudi marker crude oil in terms of dollars increased approximately 65 per cent. The value of imported oil into the United States at that time was approximately equal to 2.3 per cent of US aggregate domestic expenditure so that φ in terms of oil was equal to 0.023. Assuming the increase in Saudi prices is representative of the price of all imported crude, then the contribution of this oil price shock to US inflation in 1979 was 1.5 per cent (that is, $0.65 \times 0.023 = 0.015$). The price of domestic goods would have had to decline by 1.5 per cent during 1979 if the price level of all things purchased by US residents (P) was to remain unchanged in 1979. This means that if labor productivity had been rising at its traditional postwar 3 per cent per annum during 1979, domestic money-wages would have been able to rise by no more than 1.5 per cent on average if inflation in the United States was to be avoided.

Labor productivity declined by approximately 3 per cent in 1979. Consequently, if the inflationary impact of the OPEC (Organization of Petroleum-Exporting Countries) oil price increase in 1979 was to be offset in the United States, money-wages would have had to decline by approximately 4.5 per cent. Even if it were possible to convince American workers that an 'across-the-board' reduction of 4.5 per cent in money-wages would have eliminated inflation and hence would not affect real wages (other than through the real adverse effects of lower productivity and the adverse change in oil terms of trade *vis-à-vis* OPEC, both of these factors being taken as parameters in this case), American workers would not have accepted a decline in their money-wages.

This refusal to accept lower money (not real) wages would not be due to a money illusion, that is, to workers confusing a money-wage decline for a further decline in real wages. Instead, workers' resistance to money-wage cuts is due to their engaging in long-term contractual cash outflow commitments in terms of mortgages on their houses, rental leases on their apartments, and even loan obligations to finance children's college education. Any reduction of workers' cash (wage) inflows, even if it does not imply a further reduction in today's real wage, would immediately create a serious liquidity shortage threatening families with insolvency. Lower cash inflows, even when they do not mean further reduction of purchasing power, are not willingly accepted by households and firms operating in an entrepreneur economy that organizes production and consumption activities on a forward nominal contracting basis.[10]

8.6   THE UMS–NUMS CLASSIFICATION

As has already been stressed, money is that thing that discharges legal contractual obligations. In modern societies money is anything 'the State or the Central Bank undertakes to accept in payments to itself or to exchange for compulsory legal-tender money'.[11] If things other than legal tender instruments are customarily accepted in discharge of tax obligations to the state or by the central bank in exchange for the central bank's liabilities (legal tender),[12] then those other things will be accepted to discharge private contractual obligations. These other things are as good as legal tender and therefore they are money.

If all spot and forward contracts between transactors (in either a closed or open economy) are denominated in the same nominal unit, such a contracting system is a pure unionized monetary system (UMS). The system is still essentially a UMS even if various nominal units are used in different contracts between different transactors, as long as the exchange rates among the various nominal units are (a) fixed *and* (b) expected to remain unchanged over the life of private contracts. Any system that permits different contracts denominated in various nominal units while maintaining a fixed exchange rate among these units can be considered an UMS where the various currencies are fully liquid assets.

If there is more than one fully liquid asset and if law or custom permits contractual settlement of any contract with any of the available fully liquid assets at the option of the payer, then the system can be considered a pure UMS. If law or custom requires fully liquid assets to be converted into a specific money for contractual settlement, then the system is one step removed from a pure UMS where the size of the step depends on the cost of conversion.[13]

Where different contracts are denominated in different nominal units, expectations of fixed exchange rates are therefore a necessary requirement for any system to approach UMS status. Moreover, since forward contracts for production, hiring, investment and other economic activities do not have any uniform duration, and since an ongoing economy is always operating under a myriad of existing catenated spot and forward contracts, the exchange rate must be expected to remain unchanged for the foreseeable (contracted for) future.

For example, one can conceive of the State of Tennessee as an open economy ($\varphi > 0$) dealing with the rest of the United States in a pure UMS since all contracts between Tennessee residents and trading partners throughout the United States are in dollar terms. Each Federal Reserve district bank issues its own bank notes. Until the mid-1970s, Federal Reserve notes found circulating in the United States but outside the district of issue were sent back to the issuing Federal Reserve district bank for redemption. Nevertheless, notes from any Federal Reserve district bank are legal tender for paying any contractual obligations within the United States. Furthermore, the exchange rate between one Federal Reserve district bank's dollars and any other Federal Reserve district's dollars are fixed and unchanging no matter what the payment flow imbalance between these districts. Thus, the 12 Federal Reserve districts are part of one single UMS, even though each district can be considered an open economy trading with the other 11 districts in a UMS (and with the rest of the world in a NUMS).

Similarly, Scotland and England can be looked upon as open economies trading with each other (and others), even though the Scots use different-looking banknotes compared to English currency. These two 'nations' are part of the UMS of Great Britain and even if devolution ultimately comes to Scotland and the political openness of the two nations increases, this should not *per se* affect either the magnitude of the degree of openness or the basic UMS of Great Britain.

In a non-unionized monetary system (NUMS), regional or national contracts are denominated and settled in local monetary units, while interregional or international contracts are denominated in various other nominal units. The exchange rate between different monies is expected to exhibit significant variability over the contract period. In essence then, any UMS can be thought of as a limiting case of a NUMS when any domestic currency can be used as the means of contractual settlement, for the exchange rates are expected to remain absolutely unchanged during the period.

The degree of unionization of any real world trading system depends on expectations about the fixity of future exchange rates. In the absence of an institution that either guarantees fixity, the degree of 'non-unionization' (Θ) of the monetary system cannot be measured *ex ante*; it can only be measured *ex post*. The variability of exchange rates between trading partners over past periods (looking back) need not reflect what past populations expected the future to be (looking forward). If for a significant period of calendar time the historical record showed $\Theta = 0$, as in the case of the exchange rate between the English and Scottish pounds, then it seems reasonable to suppose that past populations considered the two nations to be in a UMS. If the historical record shows $\Theta > 0$, it may also be reasonable to believe that in the past people thought they operated in a less than perfect

UMS. The past expected degree of non-unionization cannot be known. Only given the unrealistic assumption of rational expectations can the historical record be interpreted as accurately tracking the average expectations of the population in the past.[14]

8.7   EXCHANGE UNCERTAINTY

The most obvious advantage for decision makers residing in a UMS over those in a NUMS is that there is one less uncertainty (unpredictability) that entrepreneurs in the former need worry about when they enter into long-term contractual commitments across regions. In a NUMS, possible changes in exchange rates (and/or conversion cost changes) can wipe out any expected profit for an entrepreneur *vis-à-vis* the same contractual arrangement if the firm operated in a UMS. The uncertainty regarding possible exchange rate changes in a NUMS represents a real cost of operating in a NUMS that does not exist in a UMS.

The real cost of a NUMS that must be borne by someone is due solely to the way economies organize the medium for discharging a contract in a NUMS.[15] Organized forward exchange markets permit hedging that shifts the costs of uncertainty from the entrepreneur to the speculator. Still there are additional transaction costs to the entrepreneurs who enter into hedging contracts in the forward exchange market. Moreover, since most forward exchange markets are limited to a 90- or 180-day forward duration, exchange uncertainties associated with longer-term contracts cannot be shifted but must be willingly borne by at least one of the original transactors if they are to consummate a 'deal'.

8.8   WAS THE GOLD STANDARD A UMS?

Under a gold standard the exchange rate between domestic currencies is fixed except for the movements between gold export and gold import points. As long as each nation's central bank defines the domestic monetary unit in terms of a weight of gold and is obligated to 'make' a market in gold, that is, to maintain two-way convertibility between domestic money and gold, the gold price of each currency can fluctuate only between the gold import and export points. These gold points depended on (a) the difference between the buy and sell prices of gold at the central bank, and (b) the cost of shipping gold.[16] As long as two-way convertibility was maintained, the exchange rate could never fall below the gold export point in A (above the gold import point in B). If the public was confident that existing parities would be maintained under the gold system, then as soon as the market exchange rate moved close to the gold export point in economy A, commercial banks and business firms that deal in international trade can move in to buy the relatively 'weak' domestic currency of A by selling some of the 'strong' currency of B. Hence, the private sector's liquidity desires provide helpful exchange movements provided 'there is a fixed rate of exchange and complete confidence that it will not be altered'.[17] The gold standard, except for fluctuations between the gold points, is a UMS. The closer the gold points are to each other, the more the trading partners are linked into a UMS.

NOTES

1. For a complete discussion of the importance of theory before measurement, see P. Davidson and E. Smolensky, *Aggregate Supply and Demand Analysis*, Harper & Row, New York, 1964, Ch. 15.
2. It is not an exaggeration to suggest that the most important invention ever made by man was double-entry bookkeeping. This system provides a method of control over complex economic production and exchange activities. Without such controls, modern economies could not exist. Many societies have developed other important inventions such as the wheel, gunpowder and so on, but it was only after the development of double-entry bookkeeping in the Italian merchant states that Western European nations (and later their territorial positions) led the world into the commercial and industrial revolutions. After centuries of economic stagnation, those economies that adopted a double-entry bookkeeping system to organize and control production and exchange processes enjoyed tremendous rates of growth in living standards. Those economies that do not use a double-entry bookkeeping system (for example, tribes in Africa and the Amazon) continue to stagnate.
3. For example, suppose a household purchased an IBM personal computer in New York for $1000. The value of the computer component produced in Asia (say $300) plus the value of the assembly overseas of parts (say $400) should be subtracted from the purchase price to obtain the V_c of this computer. In this case $V_c = \$1000 - \$600 = \$400$.
4. Calculations involved in estimating such items can be very complicated. For example, the costs of US personnel that staff the embassy in Mexico is part of V_g, but the cost of the Mexican cleaning help for this embassy is a foreign component which would not be computed here, but rather as an import.
5. For example, in 2000, the United States earned $14 billion less from overseas investments than it paid to foreigners who owned US investments.
6. *The Collected Writings of John Maynard Keynes*, vol. 5, edited by D. Moggridge, Macmillan, London, 1973, p. 118.
7. Multinational corporations have sometimes set up what has been labeled a 'daisy-chain' of transfer prices. In a daisy-chain, if nation A has high corporate profit taxes, then the multinational can transfer price the export at a loss and ship it to a subsidiary in nation B, a 'tax-haven' nation (that is, a nation that has very low or negligible corporate profit taxes). The subsidiary in B can then ship the product at a high price to a subsidiary in nation C where the subsidiary in C sells the product to the public for a loss. All the profits have been transferred to the subsidiary in the tax-haven nation. As losses have been inflicted in the subsidiaries in nations A and C. These losses can be used to offset profits on strictly domestic operations in nations A and C and thereby avoid most of the corporate profit tax liabilities. In reality the product can be shipped from A to C and never

physically land in nation B. As long as the subsidiary in B takes legal title to the product while it is in international waters and resells to the subsidiary in C, then the daisy-chain has been used.

During the period of price controls under President Richard Nixon in 1972–73, multinational oil companies set up daisy-chains in order to bring oil imports into the United States at high prices in an attempt to circumvent domestic oil-price controls.

8. A simply formula for remembering where to place any item is: credit is for claims, and debit is for debts.

9. As all prices indices do, we are measuring price-level changes for a given market basket of goods. The composition of this initial market basket was determined in part by the initial ratio (P_D/P_M). We are not accounting for any substitution effects that may occur after the initial instant due to a change in relative prices. (Nor would we account for an exogenous change in relative demands and, hence, the composition of the original market basket.)

10. If cash-flow problems become pervasive in the economy, then a cumulative debt deflation process can occur which will threaten the very structure of capitalist financial institutions. See H.P. Minsky, *John Maynard Keynes*, Columbia University Press, New York, 1975.

11. *The Collected Writings*, vol. 5, p. 6.

12. Since banks have deposits at the central bank that can be immediately converted into legal tender (where the latter is the liabilities of the central bank), holders of demand deposits at banks can convert these deposits into legal tender at their option at zero costs. Consequently demand deposits are money.

13. In a modern, bank money economy, the ability to write sight drafts for the immediate transfer of ownership of particular fully liquid assets through the clearing mechanism of the national banking system in effect 'monetizes' the fully liquid assets known as bank demand deposit liabilities.

14. Of course, the same degree of unionization need not exist between the domestic economy and all its trading partners, since the exchange rate could be unchanged between some trading partners (for example, the US and Mexico in the 1960s) while in the same period it varied with others (for example, the US and Canada).

15. Thus there is the potential for a 'free lunch' in international trade if nations organize their laws of contract on a UMS basis.

16. Keynes argued that it was the spread between the gold points which permitted interest differential between financial centers in different nations. The greater the spread between the points, the greater the possible differential interest rates; hence the greater the leeway for some independence of interest rate policies in the two nations. Keynes recommended a spread of at least 2 per cent between bid and ask prices for gold.

17. R.F. Harrod, *Money*, Macmillan, London, 1969, p. 75.

9. Trade imbalances and international payments

A Keynes-Post Keynesian monetary view of transactions between nations, whether the nations are in an unionized monetary system (UMS) or a non-unionized monetary system (NUMS), suggests that any persistent payments imbalance creates a liquidity problem for both nations. The liquidity problem for the (deficit) nation that cannot pay for all its imports with its current export earnings (plus net investment income and net unilateral transfer payments) is how the nation is to finance the excess of payment obligations over its international receipts. Initially exporters in the export surplus nation provide net short-term trade credit (finance) to the importers. This temporary short-term trade credit gives the deficit nation time to obtain longer-term funding of any persistent international payment liabilities. For the export surplus nation the less pressing liquidity issue involves choosing which international liquid time machines it should use to store its surplus international earnings (international resource claims).

Classical economic theory argues that any observed international payments imbalance is only temporary and cannot persist. Some classical real adjustment mechanism will automatically eliminate the payments imbalance. Both surplus and deficit nations have equal roles to play in this hypothetical classical adjustment mechanism. Classical theorists believe that any liquidity problem, if it exists at all, is transitory and will not affect the global real income in the long run.

In discussing classical adjustment mechanisms, Harry Johnson claimed that any liquidity problem, as suggested by Keynes's monetary theory, is irrelevant. 'In fact the difficulty of monetary theory can be seen as [merely] an extra complication of a problem in "real" or "barter" theory that has always given economists trouble'.[1] On the other hand, whether the analysis dealt with a closed or an open economy, Keynes denied that money was simply an 'extra complication' on the operation of a barter economic system. Keynes stated that:

> [M]oney plays a part of its own and affects motives and decisions and is, in short, one of the operative factors in the situation, so that the course of events cannot be predicted either in the long period or the short, without a knowledge of the behaviour of money between the first state and the last.[2]

In the real world, recommended classical free market solutions to international payments imbalances, including those advocated by international institutions such as the International Monetary Fund, places the major onus for making adjustments on the nation faced with a shortage of international liquidity. Unfortunately, this one-sided pressure on the deficit nation to solve the problem by 'tightening its belt' produces a global deflationary bias that can reduce the well-being of the surplus trading partner(s) as well.

In this chapter, the hypothesized classical adjustment mechanisms to international payments imbalances are discussed. Also it will be shown that the hypothesized classical adjustment mechanisms are inapplicable to a world – our world – where money is never neutral. Monetary changes are not Johnson's mere 'complications', but are instead real constraints on the system. In an open economy setting, nations must maintain a position in liquid foreign reserves to meet international payment obligations whenever an international payments deficit occurs.

9.1   CLASSICAL REAL ADJUSTMENT PROCESSES

Classical trade theory has always relied on some variant of David Hume's specie (gold)-flow mechanism to resolve trade payment imbalance problems. Classical theorists argue that under a gold standard an excess of imports over exports is financed by an outflow of specie (gold)[3] from the deficit to the surplus nation. In the classical system, this redistribution of gold holdings among the nations alters the money supply in each nation. The loss of gold by a deficit nation forces it to reduce the domestic money supply. The inflow of gold to a surplus trade nation automatically increases the supply of money. According to the classical 'quantity theory of [neutral] money,' relative changes in the money supply cause relative change in national price levels and/or cost levels (in terms of a single currency) between the surplus and deficit nations. The rising relative price level of goods produced in surplus (gold-importing) nation B *vis-à-vis* goods produced in nation A reduces A's demand for imports from B and increases B's demand for imports from A. This change in relative prices continues until the payments deficit is eliminated without altering the long-run global level of real income.

In one form or another Hume's argument is incorporated in the 'monetary approach to the balance of payments' adjustment mechanism that was developed by classical economists at the University of Chicago in the middle of the twentieth century. This Chicago 'monetary approach' does not rely on the nations actually operating on a gold standard. It does, however, hypothesize the same adjustment mechanism to any payments imbalance where the price level of the deficit nation will decline and that of the surplus nation will increase. This monetary approach, it is claimed, demonstrates that a free market global economy does not need to worry about persistent international payments imbalances. Johnson succinctly summed up this monetary approach by claiming that:

> [*All*] balance of payments deficits or surpluses are by their nature *transient and self-correcting*, requiring no deliberate policy to correct them. . . . The reason is simply that deficits reduce money stocks whose excessive size underlies the deficit, and surpluses build up the money stocks whose deficiency underlies the surplus.[4]

In other words, it is the 'excessive size' of the domestic money supply in nation A that is always the initiating cause of an international payments imbalance. Given an initial price level, this excess issuing of money causes households to believe that their real wealth has increased. This real wealth effect induces an increase in demand in A for *all* goods including imports. The hypothesized rise in imports was the initiating cause of nation A's trade deficit.

By postulating that trade deficits are always and only the result of an excessive supply of money in a nation, and by assuming that there must exist a general equilibrium set of prices (including the exchange rate) that assures the simultaneous clearing of all markets when goods trade for goods, Johnson and other classical theorists have loaded the deck. An observed trade imbalance must be a *temporary* phenomenon readily resolved through an unfettered market system with perfectly flexible money-wages and prices in each country. Given these conditions, trade imbalances are always eliminated by (presumably small) relative price level movements between the trading partners. The entire problem is resolved by assuming gross substitution adjustments and the absence of any income effects.

If imports are near-perfect substitutes for domestically produced goods and residents in each nation maintain their same level of real income, then the payment imbalance is assumed to be eliminated when the relative price of imports changes slightly compared to the price of domestically produced goods. In the deficit economy, the relative price of imports rises compared to home production, while in the surplus nation, the relative price of imports declines. The classical gross substitution axiom requires that residents in the surplus nation increase their import purchases and residents in the deficit nation reduce their import demand sufficiently until a long-run export–import balance in each nation is established. In the long-run, exports will pay for imports, without changing the long-run global real income or wealth total.

This 'monetary approach to the balance of payments' is firmly based on the classical axioms of gross substitution and the neutrality of money.

These presumptions assure that flexible prices (and exchange rates) will always resolve the problem without any significant effect on the combined aggregate real income and wealth of the trading nations. All of this is accomplished in the name of a monetary approach that analyses the operation of a real or barter economy in which (a) money has no real role to play and (b) liquidity considerations are irrelevant.

9.2 TRADE ADJUSTMENTS, PAYMENTS ADJUSTMENTS AND THE MARSHALL–LERNER CONDITION

In a NUMS system, an exchange rate devaluation is another classical mechanism for invoking relative price movements between imports and domestically produced goods. The classical argument is that due to adjustment lags in money-wages and prices, the deficit nation may run out of its international reserve asset (gold or hard currencies) before the relative prices have changed sufficiently to expand exports and reduce imports to bring them into balance. The fear of running out of international liquid assets can force the government of trade-deficit nation A to devalue its exchange rate immediately. This raises the costs (in terms of A's currency) of A's imports relative to substitutes produced within nation A. For households in B, the exchange rate change simultaneously reduces the costs of purchasing A's exports compared to buying substitute goods from B's factories. The result will be an increase in export quantities and a reduction in import quantities for A, and vice versa for B.

It is true that any exchange rate devaluation typically reduces the physical volume of imports and increases the physical volume of exports. A devaluation, however, lowers the price of each good exported and increases the price of each import. Consequently, a devaluation will reduce the nation's international payments deficit only if there is a resulting increase in the total monetary value of exports minus the aggregate monetary value of imports. This aggregate change in the monetary value of exports minus imports is determined by the magnitude of the absolute sum of the price elasticity of demand for imports plus the price elasticity of demand for exports. Assuming no change in aggregate income, when the exchange rate for nation A's money declines if, *and only if*, the sum of these price elasticities exceeds unity (the Marshall–Lerner condition), then the total monetary value of nation A's imports will decline relative to the total market value of A's exports; nation A's balance of payments position will improve. If the sum of these price elasticities is less than unity, then a fall in the exchange rate worsens the nation's payment imbalance.

To illustrate why this is so let us assume that deficit nation A devalues its currency by 25 per cent. In the extreme case where A's price elasticity of demand for imports is zero there is no change in the physical (real) volume of imports coming into A. The total market value of imports *in monetary terms* therefore increases by the full 25 per cent devaluation. If there is to be any improvement in A's balance of payments in this case, then the price elasticity of demand for A's exports must be greater than unity, so that the monetary value of total exports increases by more than the 25 per cent devaluation in the exchange rate.

In a less extreme case, if each price elasticity is less than unity but the sum exceeds unity, then the expansion of exports in local currency value terms will exceed the increase in the market value of imports in local currency terms. There will therefore be some improvement in the balance of payments. Nevertheless, if the sum of the elasticities is only slightly greater than unity, it may take a horrendous change in the relative prices of exports and imports (assuming no income effects) to substantially close the international payments imbalance. If the economy is a very open one and if the value of domestically produced goods and money-wages declines significantly relative to the domestic price of imports, then the real income of the residents of the domestic economy will decline significantly.

Classical theorists usually merely presume that the price elasticities for both imports and exports in each country are close to infinite so that a very small change in the exchange rate brings about a balance between the value of imports and the value of exports. These presumed close to infinite elasticities based on the classical axiom of gross substitution are the foundation of the claim that the depreciation of the exchange rate will always cure the international payments imbalance without affecting the long-run global real income.

In moments of candor, mainstream economists will admit that in the short run, the Marshall–Lerner conditions may not be applicable. In the short run, consumers and business firms may not have a chance to adjust their spending patterns in response to an exchange rate change. As one popular textbook puts it,

> [A] fall in the exchange rate tends to reduce [the value] of net exports in the very short run. . . . After consumers and firms have had more time to change the quantities of imports bought and exports sold, the Marshall–Lerner condition is more likely to hold, and a fall in the exchange rate is likely to lead to an increased [value of] net exports.[5]

Mainstream economists will admit that the typical response of the magnitude of a payments imbalance to an exchange rate depreciation is in the form of a 'J-curve', where for an unspecified length of time, the deficit in the balance of payments worsens (the downward slope of the J-curve), before an improvement (upward movement on the J-curve) can be expected. Of course, this short-run worsening in the payments balance, can force another devaluation. A new J-curve will be encountered with a further immediate decline in the value of net exports. In a series of short runs it is possible that devaluation provokes continued devaluation, and an improved trade balance is never achieved. For who knows how long a period of calendar time is required until the consumers and firms make the sufficient (presumed gross substitution) adjustments so that the Marshall–Lerner conditions prevail?

To avoid this perverse and unsettling possibility, orthodox macro economists merely 'assume that the time period is long enough so that the Marshall-Lerner condition holds'.[6] In other words, the problem of an adverse trade deficit is solved by the classical assumption that gross substitution effects are sufficiently strong to solve the problem. In a moment of candor, Abel and Bernanke remind the reader, 'Keep in mind, though, that this assumption [that the Marshall–Lerner condition prevails] may not be valid for shorter periods – and in some cases, even for several years'.[7]

Table 9.1 shows the United States International Payments record since 1981. Although the merchandise trade balance of the United States had been in persistent deficit since the first oil price shock in 1973, the current account remained in slight surplus or close to balance until 1981. In 1982 through 1984 the United States experienced three years of large and increasing trade deficits. By 1985 these international payments problems had aroused attention in Washington. Classical economist advisors to the executive and legislative branches of the government as well as many academics claimed that only a devaluation of the US dollar would resolve this persistent payments problem. In late September of 1985, under public pressure fermented by the persistent demands for a devaluation, Treasury Secretary James Baker launched an initiative to 'talk down' the value of the dollar in the foreign exchange market. Secretary Baker's economic advisors spoke about a 'soft landing' where a 35 per cent devaluation of the dollar would cure the US trade deficit without unleashing any inflationary or depressionary forces.

One week before this Baker initiative, testimony[8] presented to the Joint Economic Committee of the US Congress indicated why a deliberate lowering of the dollar exchange rate by 35 per cent would not, by itself, significantly reduce the US trade deficit. The facts since 1985 (see Table 9.1), when the United States deliberately undertook to talk down the dollar, tend to support this testimony rather than the orthodox argument that a devaluation would provide a soft-landing solution to the persistent US trade

Table 9.1.   US international payments balances (in billions of dollars)

Year	Merchandise balance	Goods, services, income balance	Current account balance
1981	−28.0	16.7	5.0
1982	−36.5	5.6	−11.4
1983	−67.1	−25.9	−43.6
1984	−112.5	−78.2	−98.8
1985	−122.2	−98.8	−121.7
1986	−145.1	−123.4	−147.5
1987	−159.6	−140.4	−163.5
1988	−127.0	−101.8	−126.7
1989	−115.7	−75.5	−101.1
1990	−108.8	−57.5	−90.4
1991	−74.0	−28.3	+3.8
1992	−96.1	−35.6	−48.5
1993	−132.6	−68.9	−82.7
1994	−166.1	−97.0	−118.6
1995	−173.7	−95.9	−109.5
1996	−191.3	−102.1	−123.3
1997	−196.7	−105.9	−140.5
1998	−246.9	−166.9	−217.1
1999	−345.6	−265.0	−331.5
2000	−449.5	−368.5	−435.4

Sources: Economic Indicators, Council of Economic Advisors, Washington, DC, May 1993 and *Economic Indicators*, Council of Economic Advisors, Washington, DC, May 2001.

deficit. In 1986, despite a drop of more than 30 per cent in the value of the dollar, the total market value of imports grew by 11 per cent while the value of exports rose less than 2 per cent. In 1987 with another 10 per cent drop in the dollar, the value of both exports and imports expanded by 11 per cent. In 1988 the dollar dropped again, bottoming out at almost 50 per cent below its 1985 peak value while the US payments deficit was approximately at the same level it was three years earlier.

Only by the winter of 1988–89, when the dollar price of imported oil collapsed on world markets (imported oil equaled almost half of the total dollar value of all US imports) did the value of US exports rise significantly more than the value of US imports. Thus it took more than 2½ years after the dollar was 'talked down' by almost 50 per cent, and a fall in the dollar price of international oil, before there was any significant reduction in the US export–import payments deficit.

In 1991, the United States experienced a substantial improvement as its current account balance turned positive and showed a $3.8 billion surplus. Unfortunately most of this improvement in the US payments balance is traceable to two factors. First, the United States slipped into recession in 1991 causing imports to decline, while exports continued to rise. Second, the current account balance improved dramatically, as Japan, Germany and some other nations made large unilateral transfer payments to the United States as their contribution to financing the short war against Iraq – *Desert Storm* – in 1991.

In 1992, these one-time unilateral transfers disappeared while by mid-1992 the United States began a long period of expansion while Europe and Japan slipped toward recession. The result was that the current account balance significantly worsened to a $48.5 billion deficit in 1992. With economic growth of approximately 3 per cent per annum between 1993 and 2000 (while the rest of the world grew at a slower rate), the US payments imbalance has continued to slide further into deficit. By 2000 the deficit exceeded $435 billion and the United States was the world's largest international debtor.

This historical record suggests that the substitution effects (implied in the Marshall–Lerner condition) necessary to assure that a devalued exchange rate will cure an international payments deficit was not applicable for the United States between 1981 and 1991. Moreover, since 1993, income effects involving changes in differential growth rates between the United States and its major trading partners appear to have a more significant impact on the US payments deficit than substitution effects.[9]

In the real world, trade between nations does not normally involve the large price elasticity (gross substitution) effects presumed by the Marshall–Lerner condition of classical theory. Moreover, to assume a decline in the exchange rate will cure an international payments deficit without reducing the income of the residents of the nation is naive. The effect of changes in income can have a significant, immediate, direct and unambiguous effect on the balance of payments.

9.3 INCOME EFFECTS AND PAYMENTS IMBALANCES

In 1933, Harrod[10] demonstrated that if the only component of autonomous demand was exports, then there could be a foreign trade multiplier such that

$$y_a = (1/mpm)(x_a) \qquad (9.1)$$

where y_a is the change in aggregate income in nation A, and x_a is the change in A's exports, and *mpm* is the marginal propensity to import of A's residents, that is, the increase in imports for an increase in income of A's residents. Harrod's trade multiplier indicated that if there was an increase in exports, the income of the nation would rise by even more than the income and employment generated by the expanding export industries.

Harrod's insight preceded Keynes's *General Theory*. Consequently, Harrod had not made consumption a function of income, and therefore the marginal propensity to consume was implicitly assumed to be zero. After the *General Theory* this Harrod formulation was recast into a Keynesian more complex foreign trade multiplier mechanism[11] that involved both the marginal propensity to import and the marginal propensity to consume in both the exporting and importing nations.

In the resulting Keynesian trade multiplier discussion, the Harrod emphasis on exogenous exports was lost. Instead the focus was placed on an exogenous increase in some internal component of A's aggregate demand function inducing, through the propensity to import, an increase in import demand. The expansion of domestic effective demand, it was noted, always spills over into an increased demand for imports in excess of any increase in demand for exports. This growth in imports stimulated economic expansion in the nation's trading partners, thereby inducing some, but not enough, expansion of nation A's exports. This feedback effect merely reduced the magnitude of the balance of payments problem. It did not solve it, even in the long run.

9.4   THIRLWALL'S LAW: EXTENDING HARROD'S TRADE MULTIPLIER ANALYSIS

Thirlwall[12] developed a demand-driven model of international payments from Harrod's trade multiplier insight. Thirlwall's analysis provides guidelines on the rate of economic growth a nation can achieve without suffering a deterioration in its international payments balance. A demand-driven model is a model where employment is determined by the point of effective demand. It does not employ the classical presumption of continuous global full employment. Nor do demand-driven models assume that long-run economic growth is exogenously determined by technological progress and labor force growth.

In Thirlwall's model, export and import functions are represented by:

$$X_a = (P_d/P_f)^z Y^{erw} \tag{9.2}$$

$$M_a = (P_d/P_f)^u Y^{ea} \tag{9.3}$$

where

X_a and M_a are exports from nation A and imports into A;
P_d/P_f is the ratio of domestic prices to foreign prices expressed in terms of the domestic currency of A;
z is the rest of the world's price elasticity of demand for A's exports;
u is A's price elasticity of demand for imports;
e_a is A's income elasticity of demand for imports;
e_{rw} is the rest of the world's income elasticity of demand for A's exports;
Y_{rw} is the income of the rest of the world, and
Y_a is the income of nation A.

If z and u are small and/or relative prices do not change significantly, then substitution effects can be ignored. Thirlwall's analysis concentrates on income effects.

Using the natural log form of equations (9.2) and (9.3) and ignoring substitution effects, one obtains Thirlwall's Law of the growth of income that is consistent with an unchanged international payments balance as relating

$$y_a = x/e_a \tag{9.4}$$

where y_a is the rate of growth of nation A's GNP, x is the rate of growth of A's exports, and e_a is A's income elasticity of demand for imports. Since the growth of exports for A depends primarily on the rest of the world's growth in income (y_{rw}) and the world's income elasticity of demand for A's exports (e_{rw}), that is,

$$x = (e_{rw})(y_{rw}), \tag{9.5}$$

then substituting (9.5) into (9.4),

$$y_a = (e_{rw} y_{rw})/e_a. \tag{9.6}$$

If nation A starts from a position of international payments balance, then there is only one rate of growth that this nation can sustain without running into a balance of payments problem. This sustainable growth rate, as shown in equation (9.6) depends on the rest of the world's growth and the relevant income elasticities for imports and exports.[13]

If the growth in the demand for imports is to exactly equal the growth in the demand for exports, then

$$e_{rw} y_{rw} = y_d e_a \qquad (9.7)$$

or

$$(y_d/y_{rw}) = (e_{rw}/e_a). \qquad (9.8)$$

Equation (9.8) is called Thirlwall's Law. This law indicates that if nation A's international payments position is not to deteriorate, then the ratio of the growth of income in nation A to the income growth rate in the rest of the world must be equal to the ratio of rest of the world's income elasticity of demand for A's exports to A's income elasticity of demand for imports. Thus Thirlwall's Law indicates that to get balance in a nation's international payments, the country must adjust its growth in income to its trading pattern as expressed in the ratio of income elasticities for exports and imports. If $e_{rw}/e_a < 1$, and if growth in A is constrained by the need to maintain a balance of payments equilibrium, then nation A is condemned to grow at a slower rate than its trading partners.

For example, if less-developed nations (LDCs) of the world have a comparative advantage in the exports of raw materials and other basic commodities that typically have a low income elasticity of demand, while the LDCs have a high income elasticity of demand (e_{ldc}) for the manufactured products of the developed world, then, for these LDCs:

$$(e_{rw}/e_{ldc}) < 1. \qquad (9.9)$$

Consequently, if LDCs follow the conventional advice of classical economists and continue to develop only their comparative advantage industries and simultaneously try to maintain a position where the market value of exports just equals the market value of imports, then the LDCs are condemned to relative poverty, and the global inequality of income will become larger over time.

Moreover, if the rate of population growth in the LDCs (p_{ldc}) is greater than the rate of population growth in the developed world (p_{dw}), that is, if

$$p_{ldc} > p_{dw}, \qquad (9.10)$$

then the future of the LDCs is even more dismal. The rate of growth of GNP per capita of the LDCs will show a greater relative decline (or slower increase) compared to the standard of living of the developed world, that is,

$$(y_{ldc}/p_{ldc}) \ll (y_{dw}/p_{dw}). \qquad (9.11)$$

In the absence of Keynesian policies to stimulate growth since 1973, the long-term growth rate of the developed world taken as a whole tends to be in the 1 to 2.5 per cent range. As long as the developed world's population growth rate is less than this long-term economic growth rate, these nations will still enjoy a rising living standard.

If reasonable values for the parameters in inequality (9.9) are assumed for the LDCs and the developed nations, then since $(y_{ldc} < y_{dw})$, while $1 < y_{dw} < 2.5$, a dreary prognostication for the global economy emerges. If the free markets are permitted to determine the balance of payments constraints on every nation, then a shrinking proportion of the world's population, mainly those in the developed nations that specialize in high income elasticity of demand for their exports may continue to get richer (or at least hold their own). Nevertheless, a growing proportion of the earth's population in LDCs that remained tied to low income elasticity of demand exports, is likely to become poorer. Furthermore, the slower the rate of growth in income of the rich developed nations, the more rapidly the poor are likely to sink deeper into poverty. In an unfettered global market environment, an improvement in the standard of living of the poor depends on the rich increasing its standard of living faster than any improvement the poor will experience.

Life may not be fair, but surely a civilized global society should not permit such regressive economic laws to operate freely without attempting to change these dismal implications. Surely it is the responsibility of the rich nations to explore the analysis to see if there are policy interventions that can be developed to prevent unfettered market-determined balance of payments constraints from condemning the majority of the world's population to increasing relative – and perhaps even absolute – poverty.[14]

Keynes's *General Theory* was explicitly an analysis of a demand-driven, nonneutral money, closed economy. If Keynes's monetary analysis emphasizing the liquidity motives of firms and households in the operation of an entrepreneur production economy is expanded to analyse an open economy, it should be possible to develop Keynes-like policy proposals to avoid the potential dire outcomes of a free market Thirlwall's Law model.

9.5　THE DEMAND FOR MONEY – DOMESTIC OR INTERNATIONAL

Money has been defined by its two primary functions, namely (a) a medium of contractual settlement, and (b) a liquidity time machine, that is, a store of generalized purchasing power.[15] Keynes's powerful dual-purpose classification of money led to the two essential properties of money (zero or negligible elasticities of production and substitution) which are 'significant attributes' for money in an uncertain world where 'expectations are liable to disappointment and expectations concerning the future affect what we do today'.[16] Using this Keynesian approach, the demand for money (in a closed UMS) via the transactions, precautionary, speculative and financial motives has been developed to a fine edge.[17] The role of money and liquidity relationships in an open NUMS, on the other hand, has not been as similarly developed.

International liquidity problems create perplexing theoretical problems especially for classical analysis where money is a mere numeraire. Classical theory treats international trade as if it were a barter process where goods trade for goods, and monetary theory is just an 'extra complication' (to use Johnson's phrase) in a real or barter analysis. In the real world of open entrepreneurial economies, however, each nation (or currency union region) has its own money for denominating and settling private contracts between the region's residents. Different monies may be used to settle private contracts between residents of one nation and residents of other nations (or currency regions). Central banks may use yet another medium (often not available to the private sector) to settle claims against each other, or against other national banking systems. Financial arrangements and institutions are an essential element in the determination of the level of the international flow of production and exchange of real goods and services. Money really does matter in the determination of real international trade levels and patterns.

What determines the medium of contractual settlement that will be used in international transactions? The money in use, an essential element of all economically developed civilizations, depends upon both law and custom. Arching over all civilizations that use an entrepreneurial form of economic organization is the civil law of contracts. In the absence of law-abiding economic agents committed to obeying this civil law, there can be no significant transactions, freely made, among independent economic agents. In all modern economies the state enforces both law and custom in the case of contractual disputes between residents of the same nation. Thus as long as transactors are law-abiding, the internal medium of contractual settlement is not only whatever is declared to be legal tender by the state, but also anything the state or the central bank undertakes to accept from the public in payment of obligations or in exchange at a fixed rate for legal tender money.[18]

Unfortunately, no such simple chartalist prerogatives exist to determine the money of settlement when contractual disputes occur between residents of different nations (or currency regions). Thus, custom and voluntary cooperation between governments are important factors in encouraging entrepreneurs to engage in international trade. Specifying a particular nation's money as the means of settlement in an international contract immediately determines the nation in whose courts an aggrieved party to an international contract can seek restitution.

In general, local currency cannot be directly used to settle an international obligation denominated in terms of another currency. Thus, the payer of a foreign money contractual commitment will normally have to sell the domestic currency in either a spot or forward exchange market to obtain the means of international contractual settlement.[19] Who organizes and 'makes' the foreign exchange markets will determine the degree of international liquidity that any domestic money is thought to possess. In any UMS among nations that maintain different domestic monies, the nation's central bank operates as a market maker in foreign exchange to guarantee a fixed exchange rate. As long as there is confidence in the ability of the state institutions to maintain the announced fixed exchange rate, the domestic money is a fully liquid international asset capable of being converted immediately into the medium of settlement of any other national currency. In a NUMS, on the other hand, the domestic currency has varying degrees of international liquidity depending on the confidence the public has as to the ability of the market maker(s) of the foreign exchange market to maintain an orderly market. In most NUMS, day-to-day market-making functions are carried out by the domestic commercial banks with the central bank, as long as it has sufficient foreign reserves, acting as a backup provider of foreign exchange to the banks in case the domestic banks cannot provide an orderly market environment.[20] If the central bank refuses (or is unable) to act as the lender of last resort of foreign reserve assets, then each commercial bank that makes the foreign exchange market for its customers will have to hold its own position in foreign reserve assets.

It is essential to comprehend the liquidity motives of economic agents holding cash and other liquid reserve assets in a closed UMS economy facing an uncertain future (Keynes's theory of liquidity preference). A parallel theory of international liquidity and reserve asset holdings for agents operating in an open NUMS must be developed.

9.6   THE NEED FOR RESERVES

When the future is uncertain, the possibility of changing one's mind and altering one's activities as time passes is part of the human condition. In such a world there can be a sequential causality of events. For example, entrepreneurs are continually examining outcomes over time to see if they match previous expectations. Unexpected outcomes at time t_o are inspected for possible evidence of new, different and previously unforeseen trends.

When surprising events are (correctly or incorrectly) perceived to have significantly altered the economic environment, then entrepreneurs will tend to alter their expectations about the future. These revised expectations will induce agents to recast their decisions at time t_1. These changed decisions will affect economic actions and activities at time t_2.

The period between t_0 and t_1 is a data-collecting, processing and identification period. Its calendar length (which cannot be specified in advance) is mainly determined by perceptual and psychological factors. The calendar distance between t_1 and t_2 (between revising expectations and being able to activate different economic actions) is constrained by two economic factors: (a) the length of time each agent is bound by previous forward contractual commitments and (b) the costs of buying oneself out of these contractual commitments. The magnitude of contractual obligations and cost considerations will necessarily limit changes in decisions that could bring t_2 closer in time to t_1. The more uncommitted liquidity one has, or can obtain, to meet new contractual obligations that will be incurred by any new actions undertaken at a point of time, the closer t_2 can be brought to t_1. The possession of sufficient liquidity is freedom in the sense that it permits new actions to be taken quickly, and often shortens the distance between t_1 and t_2 when entrepreneurs perceive past errors and desire to embark on new and different activities.[21] The duration and magnitude of existing contractual commitments (for any given degree of liquidity possessed) forces a posterior calendar time lag on new actions. The holding of liquid reserve assets provides the wherewithal to change spending plans if expectations change. In a nonergodic real world 'liquidity is freedom'.[22]

Hicks invented a taxonomic scheme for classifying asset holdings that decision makers require when making contractual commitments in an uncertain world.[23] *Running assets* are those required for the normal operations of economic processes. In an entrepreneurial economy, contracts are used to organize most production and exchange processes. These contracts lead to a stream of money obligations. The holding of cash balances or other fully liquid assets to meet the contractual obligations coming due in the very near future are the running financial assets necessary to support the normal expenditure activities of buyers.[24]

Reserve assets are assets that are similar in form to running assets but are not normally required for the current level of planned activities. Instead, reserve assets are held for exigencies that can occur during normal economic activities. Precautionary and speculative holdings of money and other liquid assets are financial reserve assets.

The quantity of reserve financial assets the public wishes to hold at any time depends on the magnitude of the future cash-flow problems that the public expects to encounter and the fear that the public has regarding an uncertain future. In a closed economy, the supply (quantity of *available*) reserve assets that are fully liquid at any point of time is determined by the central bank and the organization of the financial markets. In an open international system, since there is no global central bank, the supply of reserve assets is determined by the cooperation of the major central banks and the organization of foreign exchange markets.

In his perceptive analysis of *Reforming the World's Money*, Harrod noted that the management of international financial assets is 'the most important problem confronting those responsible for economic affairs in the free world'.[25] The need to manage and maintain adequate levels of international running assets and reserve assets is essential in promoting economic prosperity in trading nations. Just as for each individual there is a level of transactions and precautionary balances perceived as necessary to meet upcoming contractual obligations, so for each nation there is a level of international asset holding (the foreign reserves of the central bank as running or reserve assets) that are held as a balance to bridge the gap between foreign receipts and upcoming foreign payments liabilities. Individuals and nations face similar cash-flow or running reserve asset liquidity management problems.

If it were possible with perfect certainty to coordinate exactly the time payment of all cash inflows and outflows, individuals or nations would have to hold transaction balances only momentarily, if at all. Since such coordination is, of course, impossible,[26] international liquid assets must be held to bridge significant periods of calendar time. The greater the lack of planned coordination between contractual cash inflows and outflows, *ceteris paribus*, the greater the need to hold stocks of running and reserve liquid assets. In international transactions this need manifests itself in the need for foreign exchange holdings that are positively related to (a) the flow-level of foreign contractual obligations coming due, (b) the lack of coordination between international inflows and outflows, and (c) a need for precautionary or reserve assets to cover possible but unpredictable emergencies in foreign transactions cash flows.

In a closed UMS, an individual's cash holdings can increase at the expense of others, but, in the aggregate, an expansion of liquid cash balance holdings by the public requires an increase in the domestic money supply (that is, the liabilities of the bank and/or the central bank, or in some countries the liabilities of the state). Similarly, each nation can individually increase its foreign exchange holdings at the expense of others, but from a global view all countries cannot on average simultaneously increase their total holdings of running and reserve liquid assets unless new international liquid reserve assets are created.[27]

In a closed economic system every increase in planned expansion of economic activity requires an accommodating (endogenous) increase in the money supply if the increased demand for liquidity to meet the additional contractual obligations per period is to be met[28] and congestion in the money market (which can constrain expansion) is to be avoided. In a similar manner international liquid assets must increase concomitantly with planned international trade expansion.[29]

In domestic money affairs, the central bank is usually given the responsibility of providing for an elastic currency to meet the 'real bills' needs of trade. There is no existing financial mechanism that assures the confluence of the growth in the supply of international reserves and the volume of international trade expands. This, of course, was one of the great disadvantages of the automatic gold standard that, in the nineteenth century, made gold the international money for all contracts enforceable in nations honoring the gold standard. Shortages of gold could limit expansion of global production and trade.[30]

Some have argued that if exports and imports grow at identical rates over a period of time, there is no need to expand the international running reserve base – as if goods exchange for goods in international trade without the intermediation of money. Proponents of this barter view of international trade proclaim that the only time running and reserve financial assets are needed is if a nation's trade balance is unbalanced. This implies that there are no financial constraints to international trade as long as the payments balance of exports minus imports equals zero in each accounting period for each trading partner, with exports and imports growing concomitantly over time.

Once uncertainty and the impossibility of perfect coordination of cash inflows and outflows are recognized as inherent characteristics of all trading relations, it is obvious that an increase in international reserve holdings (liquidity) becomes a necessary condition for expanding trade even in the event that expansion does not increase the size of trade deficits. Even if expansion of trade is balanced over a period of time, and even if cash inflows and outflows are only randomly distributed over time rather than perfectly coordinated, Bernoulli's Law of large numbers suggests that as trade expands, the absolute discrepancy between cash inflows and outflows for each nation at any point of time increases. Larger international reserves would be needed to finance these temporary absolute cash-flow imbalances even if, in the long run and on average, no nation ends up with a trade deficit or surplus.[31]

Increasing the money supply is a necessary prerequisite for expanding economic activity in a closed economy. Similarly, expanding the stock of international running and reserve asset is a necessary (but not sufficient) precondition for the orderly continuous growth of international economic activity. In the days of the automatic gold standard, if world gold supplies entering international asset holdings increased less rapidly than world trade, there was a tendency toward congestion in international financial markets that constrained the growth of trade and typically brought periods of prosperity to an end.

In the period since the Second World War, the US dollar has played the role as the primary international running and reserve asset, with the 'hard currencies' of other major nations and gold playing subsidiary roles. In the 1980s the large US current account deficits helped to provide additional dollar reserve liquidity as the export-led economic growth in Western Europe and the Pacific Rim nations were acclaimed as economic miracles. The world cannot rely on the United States to supply additional international liquid reserves whenever the world needs it. Chapter 14 *infra* proposes a twenty-first-century international payments system that contains a mechanism for expanding international reserves as quickly as enterprise needs these 'real bills'. If Keynes was alive today, he surely would have recommended such a scheme.

First, however, it is necessary to analyse the relationship between international liquidity and stability in the foreign exchange markets.

NOTES

1. H.J. Johnson, 'Money and the balance of payments', *Banca Nazionale Del Lavoro Quarterly Review*, March 1976, p. 5.
2. *The Collected Writings of John Maynard Keynes*, vol. 13, edited by D. Moggridge, Macmillan, London, 1973, pp. 408–9.
3. The specie-flow mechanism involves the sale of a 'perfectly integrated' asset (gold) by residents of A to those in B, with a consequent change in relative production prices and costs (in terms of gold).
4. Johnson, 'Money and the balance of payments', op. cit., p. 16. Emphasis added.
5. A.B. Abel and B.S. Bernanke, *Macroeconomics*, Addison-Wesley, New York, 1992, p. 508.
6. Ibid., p. 508.
7. Ibid., p. 508.
8. Testimony of Professor Paul Davidson, Joint Economic Committee, September 18, 1985.
9. The question of whether the Marshall–Lerner condition will be met for any country has to be made on a case-by-case basis. To the extent that imports of food, raw materials, energy and other manufactured goods are priced in dollars, devaluation significantly lowers the real income of inhabitants of less developed countries and any significant decrease in the nation's demand for imports (in terms of dollars) will be due to a negative income effect.
10. R.F. Harrod, *International Economics*, Cambridge University Press, Cambridge, 1933.
11. The simple foreign trade multiplier formula is $1/[(mps) + (mpm)]$, where mps is the marginal propensity to save.
12. A.P. Thirlwall, 'The balance of payments constraint as an explanation of international growth rate differences', *Banca Nazionale del Lavoro Quarterly Review*, **128**, 1979, pp. 45–53.
13. More generally, equation (9.6) indicates the rate of growth in GNP that will not change

the initial international payments position of exports *vis-à-vis* imports of country A with the rest of the world.

14. If equations (9.9) to (9.11) are permitted to govern outcomes then only if the rich can continue to achieve the historically high real rates of growth experienced during the first 25 years after the Second World War (see Chapter 1 *supra*) can we hope to significantly improve the economic lot of the poorer nations of the world. In that golden age that ended almost three decades ago, Keynes's banking principle policies, rather than liberalized market policies were actively pursued domestically and internationally by the developed world. Both developed nations and LDCs prospered under these policies.

15. In the absence of uncertainty over time, the liquidity functions of money over time would be superfluous as decision makers would be able to insure themselves against all contingencies in an actuarially foreseeable future.

16. J. M. Keynes, *The General Theory of Employment, Interest and Money,* Harcourt, Brace, New York, 1936, pp. 293–4.

17. For example, see P. Davidson, *Money and the Real World*, Macmillan, London, 1972, Chs 6–13.

18. Cf. J.M. Keynes, *A Treatise on Money*, vol. I, Macmillan, London, 1930, reprinted as vol. 5, Macmillan, London, 1971, p. 6. The institutional relationship between the central bank and the national banking system determines which sight drafts for the transfer of ownership of private (bank) facilities the central bank will accept in exchange for legal tender and hence which private debts are the monies of contractual settlement in the domestic economy.

19. Alternatively one can directly sell a liquid asset in a market located in the foreign nation whose currency is needed to settle the contractual commitment. (This assumes that well-organized spot markets exist for the sale of these assets.)

20. If, on the other hand, the market for foreign exchange was completely and instantaneously flexible, as classical theory recommends, there would be no need for anyone to make the market, no one would hold foreign exchange, and any sudden change in expectations about the future (what rational expectation proponents call a change in regime) would call for an instantaneous and disorderly change in the market price for foreign exchange.

21. No wonder that when surprising frightening events shock the market many run for liquidity, for example, the decline in the stock market after the terrorists attacks of September 11, 2001.

22. J.R. Hicks, *Causality in Economics*, Basic Books, New York, 1979, p. 94.

23. J.R. Hicks, *Critical Essays in Monetary Theory*, Oxford University Press, Oxford, 1967, pp. 38–45.

24. Cf. Keynes's income and business motives for demanding money (*The General Theory*, 1936, p. 195).

25. R.F. Harrod, *Reforming the World's Money* Macmillan, London, 1965, p. 1.

26. In modern classical theory, the assumption of the existence of a fictitious Walrasian auctioneer and/or a tâtonnement process, assures such coordination. Classical theory assumes away the liquidity cash-flow problems that decision makers face in the real world.

27. Since the world is essentially on a dollar international standard, the persistent current account deficit that the United States has experienced since 1981 has created the liquid reserves for tremendous growth in international transactions in the last decades of the twentieth century.

28. See Davidson, *Money and the Real World*, op. cit., pp. 159–84, 402–5.

29. Of course, to the extent that payment inflows can be better coordinated with payment outflows, the fewer running assets are needed for any level of international activity. The rising demand for transaction balances as planned spending increases assumes that better coordination cannot be achieved simply because planned spending increases.

30. Moreover, within the inelasticity of total gold reserves, the fact that the flow of specie among trade debtors and creditors failed to provide an easy adjustment mechanism to restore balance, leads to the inevitable abandonment of this form of international money.

31. This, of course, was exactly the problem that Harrod was concerned with.

10. International liquidity and exchange rate stability

10.1 THE FACTS VERSUS THE THEORY OF FLEXIBLE EXCHANGE RATES

Since the breakdown of the Bretton Woods system in 1973, orthodox economists have promoted the conventional view that freely fluctuating exchange rates in a *laissez-faire* market system are efficient. Every well-trained mainstream economist, whose work is logically consistent with classical theory 'knows' that the beneficial effects of a freely flexible exchange rate are:

1. the impossibility of any one country running a persistent balance of payments deficit;
2. that each nation may pursue monetary and fiscal policies for full employment without inflation independent of the economic situation of its trading partners;[1] and
3. that the flow of capital will be from the rich creditor (that is, developed) nations to the poor debtor (that is, less-developed) nations. This international capital flow from rich to poor nations depends on a classical belief in the universal 'law of variable proportions' that determines the real return to both the capital and labor factors of production. Since rich countries have larger capital to labor ratios than poor nations, the law of variable proportions indicates that the real return to capital should be higher in the poor nations where capital is relatively more scarce. Capital, therefore, should flow into the poor nation until the return on capital is equal in each country. The effect of this hypothetical classical international capital flow is to encourage more rapid development of the less-developed countries (LDCs) and, in the long run, a more equitable global distribution of income and wealth.[2]

Since, in classical theory, capital earns a higher return where it is relatively more scarce, investment projects in poor nations financed by this hypothesized free market capital flow from rich to poor nations should generate sufficient sales and foreign earnings for the LDCs to repay the capital loans. If one believes this classical conventional wisdom, then international capital flows are temporary[3] *and self-liquidating.*

The facts since the breakup of Bretton Woods are not consistent with these classical Panglossian promises. First, since the oil shock of 1973 and continuing through the end of the twentieth century, many Latin American nations and African non-oil-producing nations have experienced persistent deficits in their balance of payments. Second, since the late 1970s, the major trading nations of the developed world have been under increasing pressure to coordinate their monetary and fiscal policies. For example, in September 1987 the United States and Germany publicly clashed over incompatible monetary policies. The great October 1987 crash of world financial markets followed. This frightening experience reinforced the idea among the central bankers of the developed nations that if they do not all hang together they will all hang separately. Third, in recent years, flight capital has drained resources from the relatively poor nations toward the richer ones, resulting in a more inequitable redistribution of income and wealth globally as well as within many nations.

10.2   FIXED VERSUS FLEXIBLE EXCHANGE RATES AND ASSET HOLDINGS

In some 'fixed' exchange rate systems, central banks agree to intervene in the exchange market only after the exchange rate moves by a specified (but usually small) per cent. For example, during the 1980s, in the currency arrangement known as the European Monetary System or EMS, France, West Germany, the Netherlands, Ireland, Belgium and Denmark pledged, at least in the short run, to prevent their currencies from rising or falling against each other by more than 2.25 per cent.[4] To maintain the 1980s EMS fixed rate system, the central bank of each member nation entered into an agreement to intervene in the market to limit the movement of the exchange rate.

The success of maintaining a conventional fixed rate system requires that the public be convinced that the central bank that actively intervenes in the market has adequate international reserve assets to 'make' the market price. If the reserve holdings of the intervening bank are perceived as being inadequate, then the market sees that selling the currency that is being defended is a 'one-way' bet to success. The only defense against this situation requires the willingness of foreigners or international agencies such as the International Monetary Fund (IMF) to lend reserves to the besieged central bank.[5] Almost always such loans come with strings attached that depress the domestic real economy.

In most fixed exchange rate systems, there is, of course, a modicum of flexibility within a small range around the fixed rate before any central banks step in to intervene. Even under the gold standard, exchange rates could fluctuate by a few percentage points between the gold export point and the gold import point. In the normal course of events, slight imbalances in trade due to seasonality, random causes, variations in stockpiling, or phases of the business cycle can cause some oscillations in international payment inflows and outflows. These variations will affect the spot market demand and supplies of the currencies of the trading partners leading to some weakening of the exchange rate for nations running a payments deficit. If the public perceives this weakening as a temporary aberration, then a spot rate decline will provide profit opportunities for comptrollers of multinational corporations (and others who engage in international trade and finance). If the weakening is temporary then buying more of the weaker currency to hold and selling some of their holdings of the stronger currency will generate a profit when the temporary aberration is over and the exchange rate reverts back to its 'normal' price. These portfolio transactions create market forces that tend to move the price back toward the original fixed exchange rate after the 'temporary' decline.

The rationale for these profitable portfolio transactions is easily illustrated. Suppose currency A's exchange rate declines by 1 per cent. The comptroller of the XYZ multinational corporation, knowing he/she has a contractual payment in terms of A's currency in the near future, will have to decide whether to buy currency A spot or at the future commitment date. The weaker the exchange rate compared to the 'normal' rate, the greater the incentive to purchase currency A on the spot. This will mean substantial savings compared to the normal exchange rate as long as there is complete confidence in the ability of the central bank to maintain the normal rate.[6]

Whenever an actual exchange rate movement is perceived to be temporary and short-lived, the elasticity of expectations will be approximately zero. Market perturbations that are expected to be temporary and short-lived set loose forces that restore the normal exchange rate with a minimum of central bank direct intervention.

In a flexible exchange rate system, however, if a 3 per cent weakness of currency A occurs, no one can be sure whether the rate will move further away from the original rate or in the reverse direction. If international transactors are on average split evenly (in terms of payment commitments) between those who think the weakness is temporary (inelastic expectations) and those who think it will worsen (elastic expectations), there will be no adjustments in the leads and lags of private trade payments. If the preponderant market view is that the current weakness in the exchange rate is a signal of still larger declines to come, then the elasticity of expectations is elastic. The leads and lags in private sector payments will then tend to reinforce the current decline.

Elastic expectations create instability and induce a process of cumulative exchange rate decline. As Hicks has noted:

> Technically, then, the case where elasticities of expectations are equal to unity marks the dividing line between stability and instability. A slight disturbance will be sufficient to make it pass over to instability. . . . Thus even when elasticities of expectations are equal to unity, the system is liable to break down at the slightest disturbance.[7]

If there is a perception of permanent weakness in an exchange rate in either a fixed or flexible rate system, then the public's uncertainty about the future value of A's currency tends to rise and the elasticity of expectations has a propensity to become more elastic. The public will reduce holdings of transactions and precautionary balances of the weakened currency and substitute either other currencies that are perceived as stronger or other internationally marketable assets (for example, gold) whose value in terms of currencies in which future contractual commitments are denominated is expected to increase. This may induce others, including residents of the country, who are holding positions in assets in that nation with the depreciating currency to fear the future and therefore execute a fast exit strategy to a perceived safe harbor in another country. The resulting 'hot-money' outflow can cascade onto the foreign exchange market and overwhelm the market maker.

The more flexible the exchange rate system is perceived to be, therefore, the more likely an apparent weakness in a currency will induce perceptions of greater uncertainty about the ability of that currency to maintain its value relative to other currencies and the more probable those private sector liquid asset holders will adopt a fast exit strategy and abandon the weakened currency as running and reserve assets.

Individuals often abandon a currency for transaction and precautionary reasons, and not necessarily for the prime purpose of speculation. They may have no idea whether the market is properly evaluating the possibility of a further market decline in the weakened currency, but they will sleep better at night if they transfer more of their precautionary holdings to a safer liquidity time machine. Consequently, these individuals may search out a currency that they think will be a safe harbor if the market for foreign exchange becomes volatile. The resulting movement to other currencies accentuates the weakness of the threatened currency and fosters a fear of further depreciation. This can result in a bandwagon effect until either some event or some official pronouncement encourages individuals to believe that the winds of change are moving in a different direction.[8]

In an uncertain world where unforeseen changes are inevitable, an announced flexible exchange rate system must increase fear of significant exchange rate movements for any given exogenous disturbance. This fear creates disincentives for long-duration international commitments by international traders. It also encourages short-term precautionary and speculative capital movements as expectations about future exchange rates determine today's exchange rate. Our current expectations about the future are anchored only by conventions.

> The essence of this convention – though it does not, of course, work out quite so simply – lies in assuming that the current state of affairs will continue indefinitely, except in so far as we have specific reasons to expect a change. This does not mean that we really believe that the existing state of affairs will continue indefinitely. We know from extensive experience that this is most unlikely.[9]

The existence of credible state-sponsored institutions 'guaranteeing' continuity and orderliness in economic markets will create expectations of stability in the foreign exchange market. Building such institutions affects positively the psychology of participants in financial markets. If dependable stabilizing institutions are absent from a market, expectations can become unhinged even by ephemeral (from hindsight) events. Spot market prices can fluctuate violently, or temporarily and pause at any value until the next agitating event happens. And violent volatility in the spot price of any specific financial asset reduces the liquidity value of that asset and thereby encourages a rush out of that asset and into others such as cash that are perceived as safe harbors.

These psychological aspects of market valuations imply that an unconventional fixed exchange rate system has a better chance of success than a conventional system that requires the central bank with the depreciating currency to intervene by selling its foreign reserves. In an unconventional system, the central bank with the appreciating currency intervenes by buying the money of the nation with the falling exchange rate until the exchange rate returns to its pre-agreed fixed rate range.[10] If for example, nation A's currency rose more than 2.25 per cent against nation B's money, then A's central bank would be pledged to buy nation B's money directly in the market. By selling its own currency without a limit, nation A can assure the exchange rate returned to its agreed-upon fixed rate.

Despite the obvious success of such an unconventional system, it is unlikely to be widely adopted because the nation with the appreciating currency has surrendered national control over its outstanding money supply. Instead, international forces are permitted to determine the amount of domestic money available to the public at home and abroad. Most nations fear giving up their sovereign right to control their domestic money supply.

Consequently this variant of a fixed exchange rate system has rarely been discussed, much less put into operation.

The cooperating nations find it easier to agree on a conventional system where the central bank of any nation with the declining exchange rate steps into the market and actively buys its own money with its foreign reserves. If the central bank's reserves are sufficient, then the exchange rate will be stabilized at the fixed rate zone. If, however, the central bank runs out of reserves, it will be forced to withdraw from the fixed exchange rate system unless the nation obtains reserves from other central banks, usually via 'swaps'.[11]

10.3   THE EFFICIENT MARKET HYPOTHESIS AGAIN

The classical efficient market hypothesis is in direct contrast to Keynes's belief that a freely flexible market price system can generate psychological beliefs creating volatility in market evaluations of financial assets which can then violently depress the real economy. The classical analysis avoids this possibility by presuming that all relevant information about 'economic fundamentals' regarding future demand and supplies currently exists and is available to market participants. This information is embodied in the historical market database and current market price signals and all rational agents make decisions based on this available information. Acting in their own self-interest, rational agents will force the market to establish the 'correct' equilibrium exchange rate. Observed variations around this market equilibrium rate can be attributed to random shocks that will quickly be dampened down by the alert action of informed agents. In this classical explanation it is implicitly assumed that the observed dispersion of prices around the calculated moving average (equilibrium) price does not affect future trends by causing a significant volume of false trades, bankruptcies and other events that can rewrite the future path of the economy.

The widespread acceptance of the efficient market hypothesis has driven Keynes's psychological liquidity preference approach to the formation of spot market evaluations from most academic discussions of financial market performance. Nevertheless, there is mounting empirical evidence of both a short-run and long-run nature that behavior in real world financial markets is incompatible with the efficient market theory. Shiller,[12] for example, has examined the long-run relationship between real stock prices and real dividends in the United States from 1889 to 1981 and concluded that 'the volatility of stock market price indices appears to be too high to accord with the efficient market model'.

If the efficient market theory is not applicable to real world financial markets, then movements in exchange rates can generate their own momentum. Once rapid movements in exchange rates become widely expected, any nation's currency can become subject to a 'flight of capital' – a real world phenomenon without an obvious theoretical counterpart in a classical model. On the other hand, international flight capital is a readily understandable phenomenon if one uses Keynes's psychological liquidity preference approach to financial markets. Flight capital is the open NUMS model equivalent of a bearish surge out of securities because of an expected decline in the spot price in a closed UMS system.

In the absence of credible financial institutions whose explicit function is to maintain orderliness *and* limit the range of movement in financial asset prices, the elasticity of expectations can easily exceed unity as a current unexpected change in exchange rates can induce destabilizing views about the future. With the breakdown in 1973 of the Bretton Woods agreement for maintaining exchange rates, central banks had to increase substantially their holdings of foreign reserves and their active intervention in spot exchange markets to achieve some modicum of stability[13] in repeated attempts to calm the market's possible fears. And if that fails, the IMF is expected to step in to restore stability and orderliness.

10.4 WHO SHOULD 'MAKE' THE EXCHANGE RATE MARKET?

Defenders of freely flexible exchange rates implicitly assume that a *laissez-faire* market system must possess an equilibrium price vector that clears all markets simultaneously. Proponents of flexible rates argue that if only central banks would remove themselves as 'makers' of the foreign exchange market, then private sector entrepreneurs – presumably international bankers – would move in and immediately move the exchange rate to its predetermined stable equilibrium value.

Market-maker international bankers are motivated solely by the profit motive (as opposed to nationalist pride or political myopia that, it is sometimes claimed, motivates central bankers). These entrepreneurs 'know' the exchange rate that maintains a general equilibrium among all trading partners. If the original private sector market-maker banker-entrepreneurs in the exchange market fail to find the 'correct' exchange rate that eliminates persistent international payment imbalances, then they will face bankruptcy. Other international bankers, it is suggested, will spring up and do a better job in identifying the correct equilibrium prices over time.

Of course, this orthodox view assumes that there exists a stable equilibrium set of exchange rates over time. Unexpected changes and the potential for bankruptcy by private sector international bankers who make the foreign exchange markets are incompatible with this assumption. The possibility of bankruptcy of the original international bankers-cum-market makers or their customers would create discontinuities which endanger all existence proofs of there being any stable general equilibrium set of exchange rates. If bankruptcy occurs, it can be shown that no general equilibrium may exist[14] and hence there is no 'correct' equilibrium exchange rate for the market maker to identify.

Only if private sector international bankers who make the spot exchange market can correctly and fully anticipate a stable future can the threat of bankruptcies and the ensuing discontinuities that threaten the existence of a general equilibrium solution be avoided. In an uncertain world, there is no reason to believe that private bankers are able to forecast future economic and political events with fewer persistent errors than central bankers and central government. Moreover only the latter, with cooperative efforts among nations, can create sufficient liquidity to quell almost any private sector liquidity shifts.

Even if a long-run equilibrium exchange rate could exist, why should profit-maximizing private sector bankers attempt to identify it? If these bankers believe that in the short run the expectation elasticities of others are elastic, there is more money to be made by swimming before the tide. For a private sector financial market participant, the lure of making short-term capital gains by anticipating even ephemeral fluctuations becomes paramount. As Keynes noted: 'life is not long enough; – human nature desires quick results, there is a peculiar zest in making money quickly . . . Furthermore, an investor who proposes to ignore near-term market fluctuations needs greater resources for safety'.[15]

If there are private sector foreign exchange market makers who attempt to maintain the long-run exchange rate in the face of short-term disturbances, then these agents will need more liquid assets as reserves than central bankers require under a fixed exchange system.[16] Yet it is unlikely that, in the aggregate, private foreign exchange dealers would find it either possible or profitable to hold more reserve assets than central banks do.

If there is a private banker who has sufficient reserves to swim against the short-term tide and take a position in defending an exchange rate, and by so doing promote the public interest, such a banker would be considered idiosyncratic or eccentric by the public and his/her professional colleagues. As Keynes pointed out, the long-term investor, that is, the person who is not in and out for a quick turn of profit, is the person

who most promotes the public interest [by providing stability to an otherwise potentially volatile system], who will in practice come in for the most criticism, whenever investment funds are managed by committees or boards or banks. For it is in the essence of his behavior that he should be eccentric, unconventional and rash in the eyes of average opinion [otherwise, he would not be swimming against the tide of public opinion]. If he is successful, that will only confirm the general belief in his rashness; and if in the short run he is unsuccessful, which is most likely, he will not receive much mercy. Worldly wisdom teaches that it is better for reputation to fail conventionally, than to succeed unconventionally.[17]

Private sector international bankers and multinational company (MNC) comptrollers are required each day to demonstrate publicly their ability to augment the 'bottom line' in *each* accounting period. When private sector bankers are entrusted with the making of foreign exchange markets and MNC comptrollers committed to park corporate funds in currencies that are expected to appreciate or at least be a safe harbor in the current accounting period, then these dedicated entrepreneurs will find it easier to achieve success by swimming in the lead of the tide of public opinion rather than trying to buck the short-term currents.[18] Under such circumstances instability rather than stability is likely to be the rule under any but the most stationary of economic environments. A truly flexible exchange rate will not have any private or central bank market maker to limit short-term exchange rate movements in the face of intermittent dashes toward fast exits and safe harbors whenever a storm is expected. A flexible rate system therefore is unlikely to inspire confidence in the stability of the current exchange rate.

A fixed, or at least very stable, exchange rate whose movements are tightly constrained is a necessary condition encouraging entrepreneurs to engage more freely in international production, investment and trading transactions. In such a constrained exchange rate system, those entrepreneurs who engage in many foreign transactions know that they can store liquidity in either domestic or foreign assets with the full confidence that at any moment they can, without suffering a considerable capital loss, convert a marketable asset into the standard in which their expected international liabilities are falling due. Without the presence of a foreign exchange market maker who is willing to swim against volatile short-run tides even if it means incurring significant short-run losses on occasion, orderly markets for foreign exchange cannot long exist except for a coincidence of short-term factors that offset each other and create temporary stability.

The trick of the entrepreneurial money economy game lies in the need to hold assets whose expected liquidity value is relatively stable in terms of the same units as future liabilities and future money costs of production. 'The convenience of holding assets in the same standard as that in which future liabilities may fall due and in a standard in terms of which the future money cost of output is expected to be relatively stable, is obvious'.[19] In a world of uncertainty and unpredictable changes, there can be no store of value over a period of calendar time in an entrepreneurial economy, unless contractual obligations are fixed in some nominal unit. Whatever the nominal unit of contractual obligation is, it has a unique role to play in an entrepreneur system.[20]

In an entrepreneurial economy, 'the firm is dealing throughout in terms of sums of money. It has no object in the world except to end up with more money than it started with. *That is the essential characteristic of an entrepreneur economy*'.[21] In an open NUMS entrepreneurial economy where multinational firms daily deal in production contracts denominated in different money units, the object of an ongoing business enterprise engaging in these international transactions will be to end up with more money than it started with – in terms of those monies in which most of its future liabilities and production costs are expected to be denominated. Thus expected stickiness of exchange rates over the life of the production period is a necessary condition to encourage entrepreneurs to engage in long-term production and investment commitments that cross national boundaries.

The more flexible exchange rates, the greater the incentives to make 'more money' through financial currency speculation rather than through real production processes. Flexibility *per se* tends to encourage expanding international capital flows relative to production and trading payment flows. It is not therefore surprising to find that exchange rate values are normally dominated by capital movements rather than purchasing power parities since the breakdown of the Bretton Woods agreement. If a fixed exchange rate system could be reinstituted and if the publicly announced rules convinced people that central banks are immutably committed to defend the preannounced exchange rate, then it would not be surprising to find purchasing power parities become more important in exchange rate determination in the twenty-first century.

NOTES

1. In 1968, Professor Harry Johnson wrote (in *The Times* of London, 9 December) 'the basic argument for floating exchange rates is so simple that most people have considerable difficulty in understanding it . . . a floating exchange rate would save a country from having to reverse its full employment policies because they lead to inflation and deficit'.
2. The Thirlwall's Law analysis of Chapter 9 suggested a tendency towards a more inequitable income and wealth distribution. The facts support Thirlwall's Law rather than classical theory.
3. Apparently, classical economists do not conceive of 'flight capital' as an economic problem. Indeed naive classicists claim that those with wealth have the right in any circumstance to choose when and where they move their reserves independent of the damage such moves may inflict on the national and international economy. But all the rights of the individual always are, and should be, constrained by the potential impacts

on society that the exercise of these rights can have in particular circumstance. For example, no one would defend someone shouting 'Fire' in a crowded auditorium as indisputably protected under an individual's right of free speech. In many circumstances, flight capital can cause more damage then yelling fire in an auditorium.

4. In the late 1980s, the United Kingdom joined the EMS but in 1993, a speculative attack on the British pound forced the United Kingdom to abandon the system.

5. In an unconventional system when the central bank with the appreciating currency intervenes, since the central bank can expand its own currency as much as it desires, it is not too difficult to convince the public that the central bank will sell whatever quantities are necessary to preserve the fixed exchange rate.

6. Those holding currency A and having a forward contractual commitment in terms of B will at the same time be trying to revise their financial arrangements in order to avoid selling currency A for as long as the exchange rate is weak. Those holding currency B and having a forward contractual commitment in currency B will purchase money of A to resell for B at the commitment date if the transaction costs of the foreign exchange market are less than the difference between the current spot price of A and the normal price, as long as the normal price is expected to prevail at the commitment date.

7. Cf. J.R. Hicks, *Value and Capital*, 2nd edn, Oxford University Press, Oxford, 1946, p. 255. Also see pp. 205–6, 250–52, 264–6.

8. In September 1992, doubts about the ability of the UK to remain in the EMS led to huge movements out of the pound sterling which the Bank of England was unable to unilaterally stop until the UK abandoned the EMS and let the pound float. Later in the year when similar doubts were raised about the French franc, the outflow was stopped by cooperative and decisive actions to support the franc by both the German Bundesbank and the Bank of France. This cooperative effort alleviated fears and kept the exchange rate between the franc and the German mark fixed.

9. J.M. Keynes, *The General Theory of Employment, Interest and Money,* Harcourt, Brace, New York, 1936, p. 152.

10. Since each nation can always create additional amounts of its own money, the central bank with the appreciating currency can aggressively continue to sell until the exchange rate falls back to its preagreed upon fixed rate. Very often this is done via 'swaps' between the central banks in the surplus and deficit nations. In other words, the surplus nation creates its domestic currency which it 'swaps' with a sum of foreign 'money' created by the deficit nation's central bank that is deposited in the surplus nation's central bank. The deficit nation can then use the swap to intervene in the market.

11. Often the ability to borrow is tied to the government's commitment to depress the economy (in real terms) to reduce imports and expand exports (in the hope that the Marshall–Lerner condition is applicable).

12. R.J. Shiller, 'Financial markets and macroeconomic fluctuations', mimeo, 1984.

13. See S. Weintraub, 'flexible exchange rates', *Journal of Post Keynesian Economics*, **3**, Summer 1981, pp. 467–78.

14. See K. Arrow and F. Hahn, *General Competitive Analysis*, Holden-Day, San Francisco, 1971, pp. 355–61.

15. Keynes, *The General Theory*, p. 157.

16. See Weintraub, 'Flexible exchange rates', op. cit.

17. Keynes, *The General Theory*, pp. 157–8.

18. Those who place their beach blankets at the edge of the surf during mid-tide in order to have easy access to the sea must surely know they will have to retreat in front of the advancing tide if they are not to be inundated – even if they know that more than half the time they will remain high and dry.

19. Keynes, *The General Theory*, pp. 236–7.

20. Since the money-wage contract is the most ubiquitous domestic forward contract in non-slave societies, the money-wage plays a predominant and persistent role in the determination of employment and the domestic market prices of producible goods.

21. *The Collected Writings of John Maynard Keynes*, vol. 29, edited by D. Moggridge, Macmillan, London, 1979, p. 89. Italics added.

11. If markets are efficient why has there been so much volatility in financial markets?

In the decades of the 1980s and 1990s the world witnessed increasing volatility in many financial markets around the world. Why is there so much volatility? Are financial markets *inherently* destabilizing and fragile or is today's financial fragility the result of market 'liberalization' policy decisions taken since the 1970s? We are again being haunted by Minsky's frightening financial fragility question 'Can it happen again?'[1] where 'it' is a replay of the Great Depression.

11.1 EFFICIENCY VERSUS LIQUIDITY

Peter L. Bernstein is the author of the best-selling book *Against the Gods*,[2] a treatise on risk management, probability theory and financial markets. Bernstein noted that since the Second World War 'the number of stock markets around the world has grown from 50 to just over 125 – even the Chinese, nominally still socialists have seen fit to establish stock markets on their territory'.[3] Accordingly, one might ask, if financial markets are, as Minsky suggests, so fragile and destabilizing, why are so many emerging economies using them?

How one responds to these queries depends on the underlying economic theory that one explicitly, or implicitly, utilizes to explain the role of financial markets in an entrepreneurial economy. The efficient market theory assumes that financial markets can reliably forecast the future and therefore market values accurately reflect the present value of the 'known' future stream of money receipts that will accrue to the asset holder.

Efficient market theory is the backbone of conventional economic wisdom whose mantra is 'the market knows best' how to optimally allocate scarce capital resources and promote maximum economic growth. This efficient market theory view is succinctly epitomized in former US Treasury Secretary Lawrence Summers's statement: 'the ultimate social functions [of financial markets are] spreading risks, guiding the investment of scarce capital, and processing and disseminating the information possessed by diverse traders . . . prices will always reflect fundamental values . . . The logic of efficient markets is compelling'.[4] Proponents of efficient market theory typically urge the liberalization of all financial markets where there is government regulation of financial flows.

In contrast, those economists favoring liquidity preference theory suggest the need for vigilant regulation of financial markets with institutions and rules constraining and affecting the behavior of market participants. The logic of Keynes's *liquidity preference theory* is that the primary function of financial markets is to provide liquidity for asset holders. Since a liquid market must be an *orderly* one, rules and institutions must be developed to guarantee orderliness. If Keynes's liquidity preference theory of orderly financial markets is relevant, then financial markets can never deliver, in either the short or long run, the efficiency promised of efficient market theory. *In the real world, efficient markets are not liquid and liquid markets are not efficient.*

Bernstein argues that efficient market theory is *not* the relevant theory for the world in which we live. Bernstein states: 'The fatal flaw in the efficient market hypothesis is *that there is no such thing as an [efficient] equilibrium price . . .* [and] a market can never be efficient unless equilibrium prices exist and are known'.[5] If the future is uncertain (nonergodic) then efficient prices cannot be 'known' by market participants. Bernstein endorses Keynes's liquidity preference theory as the relevant explanation for the global growth of financial markets when he argues that 'a stock market without liquidity ceases to be a market'.[6]

11.2 TAXING VOLATILITY: THEORY VERSUS THE FACTS

New Keynesians Joseph Stiglitz[7] and Lawrence Summers, following the lead of Old Keynesian James Tobin,[8] have argued that an *ad valorem* tax on all financial market transactions is socially desirable in that it will reduce the observed volatility in our 'super-efficient financial markets'. They indicate that Keynes initiated the recommendation for a universal financial transactions tax as a socially desirable policy.

In *The General Theory*, Keynes argued that speculation can have adverse effects on real economic outcomes. He suggested that public access to financial markets should be, like access to Casinos, inaccessible and expensive. Indeed, after the collapse of the Wall Street stock market in the 1930s, Keynes suggested that the 'introduction of a *substantial* Government transfer tax on all transactions might prove the most serviceable reform available, with a view to mitigating the dominance of speculation over enterprise in the United States'.[9]

A recent study by Jones and Seguin,[10] however, appears to conflict with this 'Keynesian' claim that transaction taxes reduce volatility. This study notes that on May 1, 1975 fixed commissions on the New York Stock Exchange (NYSE) and American Stock Exchange (AMEX) were uniformly changed (lowered[11]) to negotiated commissions, while the commission structure on all over-the-counter (OTC) transactions in the United States was unchanged. Using daily data for one year before and one year after the change in commission basis, Jones and Seguin examined daily volatility in five sample portfolios sorted by size.[12] A total of 1872 securities traded on NYSE and AMEX and the OTC were studied and the OTC portfolios were used as a 'control sample'. Jones and Seguin calculated cross-sectional mean market values for each portfolio and daily return standard deviations (their measure of volatility).[13] They concluded that the 'empirical evidence uniformly reject the hypothesis that the abolition of [higher] fixed commissions increase volatility . . . we find a reduction in transactions costs is associated with a decline in . . . volatility'.[14]

We may ask 'How can such eminent economic theorists as Tobin, Stiglitz and Summers, and even the old, original Keynesian, J.M. Keynes, apparently, be so wrong?'. The apparent difference between Jones and Seguin's empirical results and the claims that transaction taxes reduce volatility requires an investigation into how economists explain the existence of speculative activity on financial markets. The existence of speculative activity depends on the axioms invoked to explain how agents make decisions involving outcomes that will occur in the uncertain future. Significantly different explanations regarding the effects of speculation and the efficiency of financial markets depend on whether one accepts or rejects the ergodic axiom.

11.3   ERGODICITY, EFFICIENT MARKETS AND NOISE TRADERS

Efficient market theory claims that agents analyse past and present market data (that is, price signals that are presumed to provide 'information' about future events) in forming rational expectations as a basis for making utility-maximizing decisions. If agents take actions based on these rational expectations, then markets are efficient in that the resulting set of spot and forward prices result in a welfare optimum. Logical consistency requires any observed volatility to be explained as due to random shocks that push the system away from its welfare optimum and long-term growth rate. The ergodic axiom is a necessary foundation for efficient market theorists to claim that (a) there exists real 'market fundamentals' that are immutable in the sense that they cannot be changed by human action and (b) these fundamentals determine the conditional probabilities of future outcomes (or a menu of all possible states of the world and possible contingencies) that are reflected in today's financial market prices.

In efficient market theory, agents gather information about fundamentals to calculate statistically reliable conditional probabilities regarding the predetermined future path of the economy. If gathering this information is very costly, then there can be private return incentives for each market participant to outrace all others in calculating the actuarially reliable future and thereby beat the rest of the market participants by having information that others have not yet obtained. In developing his theory of financial markets, Stiglitz states that beating the market 'affects how the pie is divided, but does not affect the size of the pie'.[15] The size of the market payoff 'pie' is fixed and determined by 'real' immutable parameters, the so-called market 'fundamentals'. Future real returns of the underlying real assets are the inevitable outcomes predetermined by today's fundamentals and unalterable by human activity. Of course, this information will inevitably reveal itself (at least in the long run) in determining the secular trend of financial market prices. By asserting that 'production, in every state of nature, in every contingency is precisely what it would have been had the information not been available',[16] Stiglitz is arguing that the future is immutably determined by market 'fundamentals'. Stiglitz's argument that some market participants obtain information about the preprogrammed future before others (the theory of asymmetric information) requires that the system be ergodic if the information is to be statistically reliable.

Old and New Keynesians as well as classical economists all accept the efficient market hypothesis as the applicable description of real world financial markets and therefore they are invoking the ergodic axiom. One logically inevitable conclusion of the efficient market hypothesis is that, as Stiglitz states, the most 'important social function' of financial markets is to *correctly* allocate real capital among industries in accordance with *reliable* information about future rates of return determined by fundamentals.[17]

Stiglitz claims that a small transactions tax has a strong deterrent effect primarily on short-term speculators.[18] The tax will not be a deterrent to long-term asset holders who are rational[19] market participants who 'base their trading on fundamentals . . . and are willing to wait a long time to realize a return'.[20] Long-term asset holders are displaying optimal behavior.

Short-term traders consist of essentially two groups: 'the noise traders and those who live off them'.[21] Observed volatile financial market prices are movements – *away* from fundamental-determined values. This volatility is attributed primarily to the existence of 'noise traders', that is, speculators who mistakenly believe they know how the stock market works and therefore do not have to acquire the correct information regarding future outcomes from the fundamentals. Other rational short-term traders feed on these foolish noise traders and thereby ultimately return the market to its fundamental trend value. Stiglitz's explanation of the horrendous speculative volatility that we observe in our world is the 'mistaken belief of all speculators' that they can do better than the market by ignoring fundamentals.[22] Since 'the turnover tax primarily affects the short-term [noise trader] speculator'[23] who is the creator of excessive volatility, a tax on such foolish speculators will save them from their own folly and save resources for society and is therefore socially desirable.

If markets are efficient, then market forces should economically eliminate all those noise traders who persistently make errors in financial markets. How then can Stiglitz explain the centuries-long persistence of speculation observed in real world financial markets? If error-making noise traders are the cause of market volatility, then for volatility to persist over more than a single generation requires Stiglitz's analysis to assume that there is a stream of new short-term traders who constantly replace those old noise traders who are killed off. Both the dead old noise traders and their new replacements 'are betting that they can do better than the market . . . based on the mistaken belief that (all!) speculators can do better than the average'.[24]

In developing his noise-trader-as-fool argument, Stiglitz has cornered himself into a logical inconsistency that requires him to use a contradiction to try to extricate himself. Implicit in Stiglitz's model is the notion that there is something strange and different about financial markets *vis-à-vis* product markets. Stiglitz accepts the argument that the imposition of a transaction tax in any product market will *distort* the Pareto-efficient price structure. He argues that a similar tax in the financial markets, however, does not have such a deleterious effect but rather 'such a tax may be beneficial'.[25] Short-run speculation trading is attributed primarily to the action of fools (noise traders) who interfere with the efficient capital allocation function of financial markets. A transaction tax, by making it more costly for fools to engage in short-run financial market activity, therefore improves the efficiency of financial markets.

If financial markets are efficient and immutable market fundamentals are the determinants of the future returns, then those irrational noise traders who make persistent errors will either become extinct via some Darwinian economic process, or they will survive only by learning how not to make persistent mistakes.[26] Nevertheless, the pragmatist Stiglitz recognizes that after several centuries of significant volume of daily trades on financial markets – and daily trading volume has increased dramatically in the last two decades – speculation continues to exist and even increase. But how can persistently mistaken 'noise traders' continue to exist in an efficient market system where rational traders can feed off these fools?

To resolve this dilemma of the centuries-old existence of speculation in financial markets, Stiglitz appeals to authority – the ultimate free market authority and successful circus impresario, P.T. Barnum. Stiglitz misquotes Barnum's dictum 'There's a sucker born every minute'[27] as 'There is a fool born every moment'[28] and even incorrectly attributes this homily to one G.T. Barnum. Nevertheless, Stiglitz's appeal to Barnum's authority implies that society continues to produce, even in the long run, fools who irrationally believe they can beat the market.

Faced with the contradiction between the implications of the efficient market hypothesis where those who make persistent errors are eradicated and his attribution of volatile financial markets to the persistent existence of foolish market participants, Stiglitz has done the only 'rational' thing that he can do. He ignores this logical inconsistency. Instead, Stiglitz buttresses his argument that 'irrationality is pervasive' by appealing to the facts that this ubiquitous, persistent irrationality exists even among Stiglitz's brightest economics students.[29] If students at our most prestigious universities are such irrational dolts, then what can one expect of the average financial market participant bereft of exposure to any efficient market analysis?

Stiglitz either does not realize, or else he ignores the idea, that if centuries-long 'pervasive irrationality' is necessary for his explanation of financial market volatility, then logical consistency requires him to admit that irrationality can persist and be pervasive in all product markets.[30] If Barnum's homily that there is a sucker born every minute is a necessary condition for one's market model, then one must reject the orthodox argument that all markets involve efficient Darwinian processes that, at least in the long run, eradicate persistent error-making fools. If Barnum is correct (and he certainly understood the circus market), then orthodox theory cannot claim that *laissez-faire* markets will maximize the welfare of the community, even in the long run. Pareto efficiency becomes a tale on a par with Aesop's fables. To provide an analysis of speculation and volatility, Stiglitz is throwing away both the classical bath water and the classical baby.[31] Stiglitz's problem is that he has confused the logic of efficient financial market behavior in a presumed ergodic system with real world financial market behavior when agents know they are dealing with an uncertain (nonergodic) future.[32]

11.4   SUMMERS, TOBIN AND SUPER-EFFICIENT MARKETS

Lawrence Summers and his wife Victoria Summers advocate a financial transaction tax to reduce financial market volatility.[33] Using the same microfoundations as Stiglitz to explain financial market volatility, Summers and Summers attribute volatility to the persistence of foolish noise traders who are 'trading on the basis of something other than information about fundamental values'.[34]

Exacerbating this impact of fools on market values, Summers and Summers add a 'positive feedback' trading strategy by rational traders who know about fundamentals and therefore know that noise traders are fools. These positive feedback traders, however, see that their self-interest is to go with the flow. They trade often in the short term (using strategies like stop-loss orders) to ensure themselves of short-term gains rather than swimming against the tide to make the inevitable long-run arbitrage profit resulting when spot prices move away from 'fundamental values.[35]

Summers and Summers claim that:

> [T]here are strong economic efficiency arguments in support of some kind of [transactions tax] . . . that throws 'sand into the gears' to use Tobin's phrase, of our excessive well-functioning [super-efficient?] financial markets. The efficiency benefits from curbing speculation are likely to exceed any costs of reduced liquidity or increased costs of capital. . . . Excessive speculation that increases volatility . . . create[s] rather than reduce[s] risk, distort[s] the allocation of investment, and limit[s] information contents of asset prices.[36]

Finally, since 1974, perhaps the best-known advocate of financial transaction taxes is James Tobin.[37] In 1995, Eichengreen, Tobin and Wyplosz forcefully argued that short-term volatility in foreign exchange markets due to speculation can have 'real economic consequences devastating for particular sectors and whole economies'.[38] To constrain speculative behavior they propose a global transaction tax to discourage short-term round tripping thereby putting 'grains of sand' into the operation of what they called 'super *efficient* financial markets'.[39] We shall discuss this Tobin tax proposal in Chapter 12 *infra*.

11.5   KEYNES, SPECULATION AND LIQUID FINANCIAL MARKETS

Keynes's explanation of the existence of speculative activity requires rejecting the restrictive ergodic axiom. At any point of time, the future is uncertain in the sense that the actuarial profit or a reliable mathematically based expectation of gain calculated in accordance with existing probabilities cannot be obtained from any existing data set.[40] In 1937, Keynes emphasized the difference between his 'general theory' and classical orthodoxy. In classical theory,

> [f]acts and expectations were assumed to be given in a definite form; and risks . . . were supposed to be capable of an exact actuarial computation. The calculus of probability . . . was supposed capable of reducing uncertainty to the same calculable state as that of certainty itself . . . I accuse the classical economic theory of being itself one of these pretty, polite techniques which tries to deal with the present by abstracting from the fact that we know very little about the future . . . [a classical economist] has overlooked the precise nature of the difference which his abstraction makes between theory and practice, and the character of the fallacies into which he is likely to be led.[41]

In other words, even if 'fundamentals' exist today and even if a data set permits one to estimate today's (presumed to exist) objective conditional probability distribution, such calculations do not form a *reliable* base for forecasting the future. Today's conditional objective probabilities are not reliable actuarial guides to the future.

As we have already noted, Keynes's description of uncertainty matches technically what mathematical statisticians call a nonergodic stochastic system. In a nonergodic system, one can never expect whatever data set exists today to provide a *reliable* guide to future outcomes. In such a world, markets cannot be efficient. Instead *the primary function of financial markets is to provide liquidity*. This liquidity function involves the ability to buy and resell assets in a well-organized, orderly market in order to obtain the medium of contractual settlement to meet one's future nominal contractual liabilities when they come due.

The ability to maintain one's liquidity may be important to individuals in the real world, but it is not an important social function *if markets are efficient*.[42] Logical consistency for those claiming financial market efficiency requires the presumption that people can also plan their future spending on goods and services efficiently by buying financial assets whose maturity date matches the individual's life-cycle spending pattern stream (for example, as assumed in overlapping generation models). Sudden liquidity needs to meet uncertain, unpredictable future contractual obligations when they come due, or cases where issuers of financial assets cannot meet their contractual obligation to pay interest or redeem the security at its maturity date, have no role to play in efficient market theory.

If, however, agents in one's model believe their world is uncertain (nonergodic), as Keynes and later Hicks[43] claim, then decision makers 'know' that what others call today's 'fundamentals' do not provide a statistically reliable guide to the future. In such a world, protecting the value of one's liquid portfolio against unforeseen and unforeseeable changes in financial market values becomes an important economic activity. Accordingly, portfolio fund managers must, in an instant, conjecture how other market players will interpret a news event occurring anywhere in the world.

In a nonergodic system, one is always uncertain about future market valuations:

> [A] practical theory of the future [market valuation is] . . . based on a flimsy foundation. It is subject to sudden and violent changes. The practice of calmness and immobility, of certainty and security, suddenly breaks down. New fears and hopes will, without warning, take charge of human conduct. The forces of disillusion may suddenly impose a new conventional basis of valuation.[44]

In a world of instant communication, any event occurring in the world can set off rapid changes in subjective evaluation of the market value of one's portfolio. Speculation about the psychology of other market players can result in lemming-like behavior which can become self-reinforcing and self-justifying. In a nonergodic system, if enough agents possess the same 'incorrect' expectations (to use Stiglitz's phrase), the result can be that these faulty expectations actually create future outcomes. The first 'irrational' lemmings to hit the ocean of liquidity may not drown. They may survive and even thrive to have more irrational expectations and lead more lemming-leaps into liquidity in the future.

11.6   KEYNES, LIQUID FINANCIAL MARKETS AND THE EMPIRICAL FINDINGS

In a nonergodic world, the primary function of financial markets is to furnish liquidity by providing an orderly, well-organized environment where financial assets can be readily resold for cash while the essential properties of the underlying real capital assets prevent them from producing the attribute of liquidity.[45] In so doing, financial markets promote the separation of ownership and management.[46] In the absence of a liquid financial market '[t]here is no object in frequently attempting to revalue an investment to which we are committed'.[47] If capital markets were completely illiquid, then there would be no separation of ownership and control. Once some volume of real investment was committed, the owners would have an incentive to use the existing facilities in the best possible way no matter what unforeseen circumstances might arise over the life of plant and equipment. Perhaps then capital markets might behave more like the efficient markets of mainstream theory.

Keynes's analysis of the operations of an entrepreneur money-using market system presumes an uncertain (nonergodic) environment, therefore in his *General Theory* the primary function of financial markets is to provide liquidity. Under circumstances where bullish sentiment dominates liquid financial markets, savers can be encouraged to readily provide the funding that induces entrepreneurial-investors to spend sums on new investment projects that far exceed their current incomes. Under other circumstances where the bear position is overriding, an excessive desire to maintain one's fully liquid position can develop that may impede the production of new investment capital even when real resources are idle and therefore readily available to produce new real capital goods. Too great a demand for liquidity can prevent 'saved' (that is, unutilized) real resources from being employed in the production of investment goods.

Keynes explicitly recognized that the introduction of sand in the wheels of liquidity- providing financial markets via a transactions tax is a double-edged sword. He noted that a financial transactions tax 'brings us up against a dilemma, and shows us how the liquidity of investment markets often facilitates, though it sometimes impedes, the course of new investment'.[48]

Keynes explained the circumstances that create price stability in financial markets when he noted that:

> [It] is interesting that [asset price] stability . . . and its sensitiveness . . . should be so dependent on the existence of a variety of opinion about what is uncertain. Best of all that we should know the future. But if not, then, if we are to control the activity of the economic system . . . it is important that opinions differ.[49]

In other words, the 'best of all' possible worlds for financial market stability would be an ergodic system where the future can be known with statistical reliability. Then the future can be reduced to actuarial certainty, that is, 'we should know the future' and market efficiency would be assured as long as agents operated in their 'known' self-interest.

The ergodic axiom is required to justify Summers's claim that financial markets encourage probabilistic risk spreading based on actuarial certainty calculations. If the system is nonergodic then rational risk spreading is impossible. Instead, the best reason for financial markets in a nonergodic world is to provide liquidity. One desirable attribute of a liquid financial market is to have a substantial number of market participants who hold continuously differing expectations about the future so that any small upward change in the market price brings about a significant bear reaction, while any slight downturn induces a bullish reaction. The result will be spot financial market (resale) price trend stability over time while the market maintains a high degree of liquidity. In a nonergodic environment, the expectations of either the bulls or the bears cannot be described as either rational (in the Lucas sense) or *ex ante* correct. Accordingly, market stability requires a continuous (and dense) spectrum of both bull and bear expectations simultaneously. The more participants in this spectrum, the less, *ceteris paribus*, volatility. Supporting this dense spectrum of bull and bear expectations requires a credible market maker who assures the public that no matter what happens, orderliness will be maintained.

As the next section of this chapter explains, Tobin and his followers conflate the concept of volume with that of volatility when they argue that a transaction tax will lower market volume by reducing the number of market participants (especially the short-term traders). This reduction in volume, Tobin argues, assures less volatility. It is this confusion of volume with volatility that makes these 'Keynesian' claims inconsistent with the empirical findings that transaction taxes and volatility are positively related. The Jones and Seguin empirical findings, however, are consistent with Keynes's *General Theory* analysis where the larger the number of market participants with differing opinions, at any point of time, *ceteris paribus*, the more stable the market price of traded liquid assets. The more stable the price in financial markets the greater the degree of liquidity of the asset.[50]

11.7   ERGODICITY, EFFICIENT MARKETS AND THE EMPIRICAL FINDINGS

For those who proclaim the efficiency of financial markets, logical consistency requires them to claim that the 'observed' secular trend of financial market prices (typically measured by a moving average) is determined by immutable (ergodic) real sector fundamentals.[51] Presumably these fundamentals are 'dynamic' in the sense of Sargent that the probability 'of how likely it is' to have a future regime change, that is, a change in the fundamentals, must be already encapsulated in the information existing at the initial instant for rational expectations to be formed.[52] If one does not presume that every possible future regime change is already nested in existing probabilistic information about every contingency in every state of the world, then financial markets cannot be claimed to be efficient as today's real capital allocations can result in future possible egregious costly errors.[53]

By claiming that financial markets are not only efficient but are superefficient, Tobin and the New Keynesians are accepting the ergodic axiom in spades. Consequently, the measured daily variance around the statistical time-series (moving) average that is determined by fundamentals, can only be attributed to random 'white noise' (and hence the name 'noise traders'). But in an ergodic stochastic system, anything that increases the number of participants increases the size of the sample at each point of time and therefore must decrease the measured 'white noise' variance around the daily mean. It is not surprising that Jones and Seguin found that a reduction in transaction costs on the NYSE and AMEX increased volume and therefore the size of the sample compared to the pre-transactions cost reduction period. If the sample increases, the variance, which Jones and Seguin used as the measure of volatility, must decline. This is a statistical property of sampling from a homogeneous population and has nothing to do with the behavior of participants in the financial market.

The only exception to this statistical property where calculated variance depends on sample size and is independent of people's liquidity preference would be if the additional sample observations were being drawn from a different statistical universe, for example, if a significant proportion of additional participants entering the financial markets behave in a different manner from those observed in the original sample. Any observed increased volume might then be associated with a plethora of similar thinking 'irrational' participants who suddenly enter the market previously dominated by 'rational' beings. Then the market might exhibit what central banker Alan Greenspan, in a widely quoted speech given in 1996, labeled 'irrational exuberance'.

But in an efficient market, the larger the number of homogeneous participants, the smaller the variance, since variance has the property of being inversely related to the size of a random unbiased sample. In the long run as irrational traders are made extinct by an efficient market, the remaining sample will be unbiased and volume and variance will be inversely related. Only rational traders can survive.

Reducing transaction costs is equivalent to lowering the admission price for participation. If the system is ergodic then the entry of more traders, by definition, increases the breadth of the market. In statistical terms, this implies that as the size of the sample drawn each day from a given universe increases, the variance declines. Tobin, Summers and Stiglitz are excellent econometricians and should have recognized that their acceptance of the logic of efficient market theory and the use of a white noise analogy implies that raising transaction costs must, *ceteris paribus*, increase variance by reducing the size of the sample (volume) at any point of time.

If fundamentals *determine* the future secular trend in the financial asset prices, then it logically follows that speculators who have 'the object of securing profit from knowing better than the market what the future will bring forth'[54] are irrational fools who in the long run must lose their shirts. Every (rational?) decision maker 'knows' that financial price movements (that is, volatility around the fundamental value) is merely a random walk. There is, therefore, no rational role for the speculative motive in any model that presumes 'rational' self-interest financial behavior. And that is why Stiglitz and Summers and Summers must rely on the continuous new generations of pervasive and persistent irrational fools to explain secular excessive volatility.

11.8 ARE REAL CAPITAL ALLOCATION DECISIONS EFFICIENT?

Keynes defines enterprise as 'the activity of forecasting the prospective yield of assets over their whole life'[55] and the marginal efficiency of capital as a 'series of annuities given by the returns expected from the capital-asset during its life'.[56] Do these definitions imply that entrepreneurs make decisions 'as if' they are in an ergodic system?

Not really. Using terms such as 'forecasting' and 'the expectation of yield' in his discussion of entrepreneurial investment decisions, Keynes warns the reader that:

> Our knowledge of the factors which will govern the yield of an investment some years hence is usually very slight and often negligible . . . In fact, those who seriously attempt to make any such estimate are often so much in the minority that their behaviour does not govern the market . . . if human nature felt no temptation to take a chance, no satisfaction (profit apart) in constructing a factory, a railway, a mine or a farm, there might not be much investment merely as the result of cold calculation.[57]

Moreover, an entrepreneurial 'decision to do something positive can only be taken as a result of animal spirits . . . and not of the outcome of the weighted average of quantitative benefits multiplied by quantitative probabilities'.[58] In other words, the expectations embodied in entrepreneurs' investment allocation decisions cannot be the rational expectations that result in the efficient allocation of capital decisions described by New Classical and New Keynesian economists. Enterprise, in the real world we inhabit, is unlikely to mimic the allocation of capital implied in an ergodic system.

Neither real world financial markets nor capital goods markets are, in classical terms, efficient.[59] Keynes clearly and completely rejected the special and restrictive ergodic axiom as a basis of explaining behavior by investors in long-lived real capital goods formation as well as saver-participants in financial markets who are making liquid portfolio allocation choices. In rejecting the need for the restrictive ergodic axiom, Keynes placed the burden on those who make use of such a highly special assumption to justify it, while those who reject any special restrictive axiom are not required to prove the general negative.[60]

Despite their willingness to accept the presumption of efficient financial markets and its underlying ergodic axiom as an unquestioned universal truth, the commonsense of Tobin and his followers regarding real world financial markets cannot help but break into their logical models – with injury to their logical consistency. Old and New Classical economists do not suffer from such logical problems. Like 'Ricardo [Friedman and Lucas] offer us the supreme intellectual achievement, unattainable by weaker [mainstream Keynesian] spirits, of adopting a hypothetical world remote from experience as though it was the world of experience and then living in it consistently'.[61]

When Tobin and others advocate a universal transactions tax to impede disruptive speculation, they are recognizing that the expectations that drive spot financial market prices are not rational. Rather real world financial market prices involve, as Keynes noted, a conventional valuation based on the psychological confidence we have of forecasts that we 'know' cannot be statistically reliable.[62] Valuations based on forecasting market psychology can, at times, create speculative whirlpools.

11.9 SPECULATIVE WHIRLPOOLS AND BANDWAGONS

Although Keynes did not use the ergodic–nonergodic terminology, he utilized this concept when he claimed that Jan Tinbergen's (econometric) Method 'was invalid [because] . . . the economic environment is not homogeneous over a period of time (perhaps because non statistical factors are relevant)',[63] that is, economic time series are nonstationary. Since nonstationarity is a sufficient condition for nonergodicity, Keynes's concept of financial and economic uncertainty implies nonergodicity. More recently, Robert Solow has endorsed Keynes's position. Solow wrote that 'much of what we observe cannot be treated as the realization of a stationary stochastic process without straining credulity'.[64] Since nonstationarity is a sufficient condition for a nonergodic environment, Solow's statement is a recognition that important economic data, which some call the fundamentals, cannot be generated by ergodic systems. Consequently these 'fundamentals' provide no guide to the 'correct' equilibrium price of financial assets over time.

With his emphasis on uncertainty as the major force explaining the speculative demand for liquidity, Keynes had to reject the classical ergodic axiom of efficient market theory to explain market behavior. Consequently, using efficient market theory to explain speculation is, to Keynes and Post Keynesians, equivalent to relying on the axiom of parallel lines in a nonEuclidean world to explain why 'in experience, straight lines apparently parallel often meet'.[65] Rebuking these lines for crashing into each other is similar to relying on persistent irrational behavior of noise traders to explain market volatility. Both are useless homilies.

Asset liquidity requires market broadness to permit each individual to sleep easily, assured that savings vehicles are good stores of general purchasing power. The empirical results of Jones and Seguin demonstrate that by reducing transaction costs one enhances daily liquidity and stability provided that certain conditions are met.[66] These conditions are (a) both the bulls and bears are widely represented among the additional participants and (b) within each of these categories there are a continuum of divergent views among individuals as to when to change from the bull to bear position and vice versa. To the extent that a reduction in transaction costs increases the number of participants in both the bull and bear positions, then, *ceteris paribus*, there is more likely to be a denser continuum and therefore less moment by moment or daily variability. In such circumstances, as Keynes noted, speculation can become mere bubbles on the steady stream of enterprise.

If, at any point of time, however, there is a sudden swing to a bandwagon consensus, that is, there is an abrupt lack of broad market participants with differing (not rational) expectations about the future, then there can be a rapid swing in market prices. A bandwagon effect occurs when a consensus view suddenly congeals regarding the possibility of a severe change in the future spot market price of financial assets. The bandwagon concept implies that suddenly a preponderance of participants appear only on one side of the market (whether it be in the bull or bear position). What is required is a market maker institution with sufficient resources to assure some measure of market price stability to prevent this volatility due to private sector bandwagon actions. The market maker must announce that it will swim against any developing consensus view regarding a change in market psychology. This announcement by the market maker must be deemed credible by market participants.

In the absence of a market maker with sufficient financial asset resources to stem the bandwagon tide, 'enterprise becomes the bubble on a whirlpool of speculation'.[67] It is 'bandwagon' movements in financial markets and not daily white noise variance that causes problems in financial markets. The resultant change in the secular trend of financial market prices due to bandwagons can have 'real economic consequences devastating for particular sectors and whole economies'.[68]

Keynes's whirlpool of speculation analogy is not a description of a daily (or hourly?) volatility around a long-term stable secular trend as measured by Jones and Seguin in terms of daily return standard deviation. Rather, disruptive speculation involves unpredictable sharp and profound changes in the *ex post* moving average secular trend due to anticipating market psychological swings. Even if there had been 'bandwagon' changes in expectations during the year following May 1, 1975, we should expect that the Jones and Seguin empirical results would show less daily variance (volatility) in the NYSE and AMEX market portfolios *vis-à-vis* the 'control' OTC portfolios. Before May 1, 1975, the NYSE and AMEX markets were broader and deeper markets than the OTC market. The post-May 1, 1975 reduction in NYSE and AMEX transaction costs merely increased the broadness and depth of the NYSE and AMEX markets, and therefore reduced their daily variance more than in the OTC market.

11.10   A POLICY IMPLICATION: BUFFERING CONVENTIONAL WISDOM

In a nonergodic world, Keynes insisted the conventional wisdom is that market participants believe that the existing market valuation is correct. The market 'knows'

> [t]hat the existing state of affairs will continue indefinitely, except in so far as we have specific reasons to expect a change . . . We are assuming, in effect, that the existing market valuation, however arrived at, is uniquely correct in relation to our existing knowledge . . . though, philosophically speaking, it cannot be uniquely correct, since our existing knowledge does not provide a sufficient basis for a calculated mathematical expectation.[69]

In the world of experience, the conventional wisdom is that as long as it is expected that the psychology of the market is not changing there will be an inertia in market valuations. It then follows that any policy that involves reducing if not eliminating the possibility of disruptive speculation in financial markets must involve building institutions that assure market participants that the 'correct' market psychology is a belief in a persistent, stable (moving average) trend in market prices over time.[70]

If, for example, the market participants believe that there exists a market maker who can guarantee an unchanging spot market price (or changing only within very small boundaries) over time under preannounced and readily understood rules of the game in an orderly and well-organized market, then the existence of this creditable market maker will provide an anchor for 'market psychology'. For participants to believe in the market maker's ability to maintain the target spot (resale) price, however, the market maker must have a 'sufficient' inventory of money and that item that is being sold in the relevant market. In our current foreign exchange market system, for example, this implies that the domestic monetary authority[71] has credibility (and a sufficient inventory of foreign reserves or easy access to additional reserves) and has announced that it will use its reserves to maintain an orderly market at the 'proper' exchange rate.[72]

To prevent disruptive speculation in any specific market, therefore, requires a buffer stock policy[73] practiced by a market maker. If the majority of market participants believe in the market maker's buffer stock approach, the only speculators that could exist would then be fools, that is, a small group of offsetting bulls and bears, who disagree with the vast majority of market participants but whose actions cannot affect market movements. Provided there is an effective buffer stock market maker, there should be no disruptive speculation and enterprise can continue at its current steady stream toward an unknown future.

NOTES

1. H.P. Minsky, *Can 'It' Happen Again?*, M.E. Sharpe, Armonk, 1982.
2. P.L. Bernstein, *Against the Gods*, Wiley, New York, 1996.
3. P.L. Bernstein, 'Stock market risk in a Post Keynesian world', *Journal of Post Keynesian Economics*, **21**, 1998, p. 16.
4. L.H. Summers and V.P. Summers, 'When financial markets work too well: a cautious case for a securities transaction tax', *Journal of Financial Services*, **3**, 1989, p. 166. In an efficient market theory world, economic fundamentals such as price/earnings ratios determine stock market prices.
5. P.L. Bernstein, 'Why the efficient market offers hope to active management', *Journal of Applied Corporate Finance*, **12**, Summer 1999, p. 132.
6. Ibid., p. 132.
7. J. Stiglitz, 'Using tax policy to curb speculative short-term trading', *Journal of Financial Services*, **3**, 1989, pp. 101–13.
8. J. Tobin, 'The new economics one decade older', *The Janeway Lectures on Historical Economics*, Princeton University Press, Princeton, NJ, 1974. Also B. Eichengreen, J. Tobin and C. Wyplosz, 'The case for sand in the wheels of international finance', *Economic Journal*, **105**, pp. 162–72.
9. J.M. Keynes, *The General Theory of Employment, Interest and Money*, Harcourt, Brace, New York, 1936, p. 160. Emphasis added. See also p. 159.
10. C.M. Jones and P.J. Seguin, 'Transactions costs and price variability: evidence from commission deregulation', *American Economic Review*, **87**, pp. 728–37.
11. The introduction of negotiated commissions on the NYSE and AMEX 'instigated a permanent decline in commissions – regardless of the metric used, commissions on institutions fell between 31% and 42% . . . [and for individuals] between 2% and 47%' while volume increased substantially (Jones and Seguin, op. cit., p. 750).
12. Each sample portfolio was based on outstanding market value of common equity (size) with sample 1 being the largest size stocks and sample 5 being the smallest size.
13. Jones and Sequin, op. cit., p. 729.
14. Ibid., p. 729. Using Swedish data, S.P. Umlauf ('Transaction taxes and the behavior of

the Swedish stock market', *Journal of Financial Economics*, **23**, pp. 227–40) also demonstrated that variance increased as a financial transactions tax rate increased.

15. Stiglitz, op. cit., p. 103.
16. Ibid., p. 103.
17. Ibid., pp. 102–3. The underlying Walrasian equations ground out a secular trend of financial market prices that are Pareto efficient.
18. Ibid., pp. 105–7. If asset holders are presumed to be wealth maximizers, then, as demonstrated in Chapter 12, this claimed differential impact of a transactions tax on short-term holders *vis-à-vis* long-term asset holders can be demonstrated to be mathematically incorrect. Also see J.R. Hicks 'A suggestion for simplifying the theory of money', *Economica*, **2**, 1935, pp. 1–19, and R. Kahn 'Some notes on liquidity preference', Manchester School, **22**, 1954, pp. 227–45, who demonstrate that the effects of any change in transaction costs is independent of the holding time of an asset.
19. Note that the term rational only makes sense in an ergodic world.
20. Stiglitz, op. cit., p. 105.
21. Ibid., p. 106.
22. Ibid., p. 106.
23. Ibid., p. 105.
24. Ibid., p. 106. In most empirical studies the *ex post* moving average of what actually happens in the markets is presumed to be the best estimate of the statistical average (over time) that the fundamentals of an ergodic world has predetermined. The fact that econometric analysis of time-series market data always reveals a reversion to the mean is merely, as Basil Moore often says, an arithmetic necessity of calculation of time-series moving averages.
25. Ibid., p. 102.
26. Moreover, there is no reason to have a public policy to rescue specific individual market participants from the error of their ways.
27. See *The Oxford Dictionary of Quotations*, Oxford University Press, Oxford, 2nd edn, 1959, p. 35.
28. Stiglitz, op. cit., p. 106.
29. 'This kind of irrationality is pervasive. Three-fourths of my students believe they are in the top half of the class' (Stiglitz, ibid., p. 106).
30. Especially durable goods where the expected stream of utility will be yielded at many dates far into the future.
31. Finally, it should be noted that Stiglitz initially argued that it is the rush to be the first to obtain reliable information in a world of asymmetric information that wastes society resources. Nevertheless in laying the blame for volatility on 'noise traders' who do not try to find *reliable* information about fundamentals (Stiglitz, op. cit., p. 105), Stiglitz's argument that a transactions tax will reduce the waste of resources seeking to beat the crowd by obtaining reliable information first is irrelevant. A transaction tax, according to Stiglitz, will not affect rational traders seeking reliable information. Rational information seekers in a world of asymmetric information will still have an incentive to beat the rest of the crowd of rational traders in a feeding frenzy on noise traders as long as the tax is less than the hypothesized social return.
32. In associating financial markets with gambling casinos, Stiglitz has failed to realize that casino gambling activities always involve an ergodic system where there are fixed and known time-immutable probability distributions, while in the financial market no such immutable probability distribution need exist.
33. Summers and Summers, op. cit., p. 216.
34. Ibid., p. 170.
35. Ibid., p. 171.
36. Ibid., pp. 165–6.
37. Tobin, op. cit.
38. Eichengreen et al., op. cit., p. 164.
39. Ibid., p. 164.
40. Keynes, *The General Theory*, pp. 161–3.

41. J.M. Keynes, 'The General Theory', *Quarterly Journal of Economics* (1937) reprinted in *The Collected Writings of John Maynard Keynes*, vol. 14, edited by D. Moggridge, Macmillan, London, 1973, pp. 112–15. All page references are to the reprint.

42. Stiglitz recognizes that market participants may want liquidity, that is, may want to exchange money for securities or vice versa, and that such financial market exchanges (free of tax) are Pareto efficient (Stiglitz, op. cit., p. 104). With asymmetric information, however, those possessing less information about the future are (by definition) trading 'based on *incorrect expectations*'. Consequently, Stiglitz suggests, it is not obvious that a transactions tax that will make trading on incorrect expectations more expensive lowers social welfare.

43. J.R. Hicks, *Causality in Economics*, Basic Books, New York, 1979, p. vii.

44. Keynes, 1937, op. cit., pp. 114–15.

45. Keynes (*The General Theory*, p. 241n) argues attribute of '[t]he "liquidity" is by no means independent of the presence of' two essential properties, namely that the asset is not reproducible via the employment of labor and it is not substitutable for the producible output of industry.

46. Keynes, *The General Theory*, pp. 150–51; P. Davidson, *Money and The Real World*, Macmillan, London, 1972, pp. 61–9; P.L. Bernstein, 'Stock market risk in a post Keynesian world', *Journal of Post Keynesian Economics*, **21**, 1998, pp. 17–18.

47. Keynes, *The General Theory*, p. 151.

48. Ibid., p. 160.

49. Ibid., p. 172.

50. Only in the nonergodic world that is our entrepreneurial economic system is it sensible to organize complex and lengthy production and exchange processes via the use of nominal contracts (P. Davidson, *Post Keynesian Macroeconomic Theory*, Edward Elgar, Cheltenham, 1994). In such a world, the primary function of organized financial markets is to provide liquidity by permitting the resale of assets in an orderly market. Only secondarily do modern super-efficient financial markets affect the allocation of new capital among industries and to the extent that it apportions capital, this distribution is not predetermined by some long-run immutable real economic fundamentals.

51. Or as Sargent suggests 'Rational expectations . . . imputes to the people inside the model much more knowledge about the system they are operating in than is available to the economist or econometrician who is using the model to try to understand their behavior. In particular, an econometrician faces the problem of estimating probability distributions and laws of motion that the agents in the model are assumed to know. Further, the formal estimation and inference procedures of rational expectations econometrics assumes that the agents in the model already know many of the objects the econometrician is estimating'. (T.J. Sargent, *Bounded Rationality in Macroeconomics*, Oxford: Oxford University Press, 1993, p. 21).

52. Ibid., pp. 26–7.

53. In the neoclassical Walrasian microfoundations that Samuelson synthesized with Keynes's macroeconomics, all producible goods are readily resalable at the equilibrium price vector that encompasses all spot and forward prices determined at the initial instant for all future times. In such an equational system, there is no separation of the market value of underlying real asset and market value of corresponding financial assets – for money and hence nominal financial asset prices are presumed neutral. Liquidity therefore is not a primary function of only financial markets. The $n+m-1$ markets for all new and pre-existing goods provide every good in every time period with liquidity as anyone can be either a buyer or a seller in any of these myriad of markets. In an ergodic world, therefore, it is not possible to experience any drastic reevaluations of the price of assets that are predetermined by real fundamentals.

54. Keynes, *The General Theory*, p. 170.

55. Ibid., p. 170.

56. Ibid., p. 135.

57. Ibid., pp. 149–50.

58. Ibid., p. 161.

59. As anyone who observes empty shops, office buildings, excess capacity in the auto industry, and so on should readily recognize.

60. Keynes, 1937, op. cit., p. 109.

61. Keynes, *The General Theory*, p. 192.

62. Ibid., p. 148. G.L.S. Shackle (*Epistemics and Economics*, Cambridge University Press, Cambridge, 1972) has pursued the nonergodic basis for asset market valuations to the extreme. Shackle maintained that conventional theory is schizophrenic in that it assumes that there is a stable rate of interest (at least in the long run as a fundamental) while recognizing that an active spot market for bonds requires bull and bear participant interactions where all the participants think the interest rate will change. In essence Shackle is asking how can there be so much volume in the securities market each day if all participants know that the existing market price reflects the best available valuation of some long-run immutable fundamental.

63. J.M. Keynes, 'On Mr. Tinbergen's method', *Economic Journal*, **47**, 1937 reprinted in *The Collected Writings of John Maynard Keynes*, vol. 14, 1973, p. 308. All references are to the reprint.

64. R.M. Solow, 'Economic history and economics,' *American Economic Review Papers and Proceedings*, **75**, 1985, p. 328.

65. Keynes, *The General Theory*, p. 16.

66. Jones and Seguin, op. cit., p. 736.

67. Keynes, *The General Theory*, p. 159.

68. Eichengreen et al., op. cit., p. 164.

69. Keynes, *The General Theory*, p. 152.

70. In fact, all markets in liquid assets require the institution of one or more credible 'market makers' who follow some preannounced rules of the game to assure orderliness in the market. The more orderly the market maker keeps the market, the less the moment-to-moment volatility. It is only when market makers fail in their responsibility to maintain orderly markets that volatility becomes disorderly and speculation can have real disruptive effects.

71. In the global economy of the twenty-first century, however, no national monetary authority is likely to always have sufficient credibility under all circumstances. Accordingly, we shall require a cooperative international monetary payments system, an international monetary clearing unit system, which has specific rules for a buffer stock policy that assure exchange rate stability (see Chapter 14).

72. That is the explanation of why currency boards with reserves equal to the domestic money supply can fix the exchange rate (often at the expense of the domestic credit market).

73. Use of buffer stocks as a public policy solution to stabilize prices over time is as old as the biblical story of Joseph and the Pharaoh's dream of seven fat cows followed by seven lean cows. Joseph – the economic forecaster of his day – interpreted the Pharaoh's dream as portending seven good harvests where production would be much above normal followed by seven lean harvests where annual production would not provide enough food to go around. Joseph's civilized policy proposal was for the government to store up a *buffer stock* of grain during the good years and release the grain to market, without profit, during the bad years. This would maintain a stable price over the 14 harvests and avoiding sky-rocketing prices and speculative hoarding in the bad years and depressing prices and dumping inventories in the good years. The Bible records that this civilized buffer stock policy was a resounding economic success.

12. Exchange rates and the Tobin tax

Eichengreen, Tobin and Wyplosz have argued that volatility in foreign exchange markets due to speculation can have 'real economic consequences devastating for particular sectors and whole economies'.[1] To constrain speculative behavior in exchange rate markets, Eichengreen et al. propose a very small tax on all foreign exchange transactions. At the same time that this proposal appeared in print in the winter of 1994–95, the Mexican peso crisis spilled over into the dollar problem. In international financial markets where image is often more important than reality, the dollar was initially dragged down by the peso while the German mark and Japanese yen appeared to be the only safe harbors for portfolio fund managers. Only after the Clinton administration bailed out the Mexican peso by providing a long-term dollar loan did the dollar recover on international foreign exchange markets. In April 1995, Federal Reserve Chairman Alan Greenspan testified before Congress that 'Mexico became the first casualty ... of the new international financial system' where electronic global communication permits hot portfolio money to slosh around the world 'much more quickly'.

Keynes had likened the battle of wits among portfolio fund managers to find financial assets whose price would rise, to a beauty contest where

> [I]t is not a case of choosing those which, to the best of one's judgement are really the prettiest, nor even those which average opinion genuinely think the prettiest. We have reached the third degree where we devote our intelligence to anticipating what average opinion expects average opinion to be. And there are some who practise [sic] the fourth, fifth and higher degrees.[2]

In the 1990s the proportion of foreign assets, especially from 'emerging markets', bulked large in many fund portfolios. Keynes's 'beauty contest' analogy became an appropriate description of international portfolio fund manager's behavior with respect to the foreign exchange market. To manage one of the more profitable funds, managers must, in an instant, conjecture how other market players will interpret a news event occurring anywhere in the world. Even in the absence of reliable information, rapid evaluations of the potential effects of any event on exchange rates and hence on portfolio values are essential as rival market participants can move funds from one country to another in nanoseconds with a few clicks on the computer keyboard or a quick telephone call to some international market at any time of the day or night.

In today's global economy any news event that fund managers even suspect that others will interpret as a whiff of currency weakness can quickly become a conflagration spread along the information highway. This results in lemming-like behavior that can be self-reinforcing and self-justifying. If the major central banks or an international agency such as the International Monetary Fund (IMF) does not dispatch sufficient resources immediately to intervene effectively to extinguish speculative currency fires, then the resultant publicity is equivalent to shouting 'fire' in a theater. The consequent panic worsens the situation and central banks whose currencies are seen as safe havens may lose any interest in a coordinated response to the increasing inferno. The more uncertain, that is, not statistically reliably predictable the future appears, the more fund managers may admit that they cannot anticipate what will happen in the near future. Consequently the greater the impending speculative storm, the more desirable it will be to store savings in a 'safe harbor'. This possession of safe liquid assets soothes our fears of becoming illiquid if anything unpredictable occurs during the stormy period.[3]

Essentially pragmatists such as Eichengreen, Tobin and Wyplosz are arguing that hot-money flows produce obvious disruptive real effects and therefore the social costs of an unfettered exchange rate system far exceed any social benefits. In contrast, logically consistent mainstream economic theorists presume that government intervention in the form of taxes or regulations impose significant social costs while there are only social benefits produced by *laissez-faire* foreign exchange markets that permit individual free choice.[4]

If the pragmatists are correct that the social costs of free exchange markets exceed benefits, then what is required is not a system of *ad hoc* central bank or IMF interventions while what Federal Reserve Chairman Greenspan called the 'new international financial system' burns the real economy. What is necessary is to build permanent fireproofing rules and structures that prevent 'beauty contest' induced currency fires. Crisis prevention rather than crisis rescues must be the primary long-term objective. If the developed nations do not hang together on a currency-fire prevention system, then they may all hang separately in a replay of the international financial market crisis of the Great Depression.

12.1   IS SOCIAL CONTROL OF EXCHANGE MARKETS BAD?

Reasonable people do not think it is a violation of civil liberties to prohibit people from boarding an airplane with a gun. Moreover, no one would think we are impinging on individual rights, if the society prohibits anyone from entering a theater with a Molotov cocktail in one hand and a book of matches in the other – even if the person indicates no desire to burn down the theater. Yet, in the name of free markets, we permit the 'Soros effect'[5] where one or more fund managers anticipate the possibility of an exploding Molotov cocktail and therefore yell 'fire' in the crowded international financial markets any time the 'image' of a possible profitable fire moves them.

Fifty years ago, Keynes recognized that 'there is not a country which can . . . safely allow the flight of funds [hot money] . . . Equally there is no country that can safely receive . . . [these portfolio] funds which cannot safely be used for fixed investment'.[6] Eichengreen et al. have taken up this Keynesian theme and argued for fire prevention in the form of a permanent small (less than 0.5 per cent) tax on exchange transactions to put 'sand in the wheels of super-efficient [international] financial markets'.[7] (This is equivalent to levying a small admission tax, rather than banning the Molotov cocktail member of the theater audience.)

Academic discussions of the so-called 'Tobin tax' usually do not focus on the theoretical rational for such taxes. Rather the emphasis is on the institutional feasibility or the impracticality of imposing capital controls at this time.[8] Little discussion of the theoretical rationale for imposing any controls or costs on foreign exchange transactions is provided.

Keynes on the other hand, provided a rationale for governmental regulation and control of international financial flows. As long as the social convention is maintained that assumes the existing state of affairs will continue until there is some reason to expect change, portfolio managers 'need not lose sleep'[9] for they know that only an unforseen 'change in the news *over the near future*' can affect the value of their portfolio.[10] Each fund manager believes his/her portfolio is a safe store of liquidity for any short period, while the underlying real investments and trade flows are fixed and illiquid for the community. This distinction between what was apparently liquid for the individual but fixed for the community can impose severe real costs especially when savers fearing the future all try to exit quickly from their position in holding liquid financial assets.

In the 1940s, Keynes specifically analysed this problem in an open economy context and concluded that a system of outright prohibition of international hot-money (liquidity-seeking) flows would be required. What is needed is governmental controls (putting boulders in the way) of international hot-money flows, rather than levying a small transaction tax (putting grains of sand in the wheels of international finance).

12.2 CAPITAL UNCERTAINTY, SPECULATIVE FLOWS AND THE TOBIN TAX

Chapter 5 developed an algebraic analysis of the behavior of bulls and bears in financial markets. This analysis can be used to analyse the possible effects of a Tobin tax. The market price of any liquid asset in a well-organized, orderly but otherwise free market can change over time. Savers who are storing claims on resources must contemplate the possibility of an appreciation or depreciation in the market price of any liquid asset at any future date affecting the market value of their portfolio. This potential capital gain or loss is obtained by subtracting today's spot price (p_s^{t0}) from the expected spot price at a future date (p_s^{t1}). When ($p_s^{t1} - p_s^{t0}$)>0, a capital gain is expected from holding the asset until $t1$; if ($p_s^{t1} - p_s^{t0}$)<0, a capital loss will be expected.

Let q be the future expected income to be received from holding a financial security and c be its carrying costs where both q and c are denominated in terms of a specific currency. Offsetting the possible capital loss on choosing any liquid asset is the value of earnings ($q-c$) over the time interval the asset is held. There are also transaction costs (T_s) incurred in both buying and reselling any liquid asset. Measured in absolute monetary values q and c tend to increase with the length of the time interval the asset is held. On the other hand, T_s is independent of the time interval and normally increases at a decreasing rate as the transaction value of the asset increases. Consequently, as Hicks argued, since transaction costs 'are independent of time . . . it will not pay to invest money for less than a certain period'.[11] In other words, if there are no expected capital gains (or losses) then for any given expected flow of $q-c$, T_s sets a minimum time interval that the asset must be held to prefer it to cash.

Orthodox literature tends to adopt the convention that q and c are evaluated as annual rates of return rather than as the absolute sums suggested by Hicks. This annual rate of return evaluation approach often encourages the analyst to treat T_s as negligible. But as Kahn has noted, if transactions were costless, maximizing the value of one's portfolio would be determined entirely by what is expected to happen between the initial instant and the immediate next instant 'and expectations about later dates do not become directly relevant until tomorrow, when behavior is decided afresh'.[12] In other words, if T_s is negligible while the spot price is expected to change from moment to moment, then no rational fund manager should worry about the long-run earnings $(q-c)$ of any portfolio investment. Every expected small change in the next moment's spot market price will provide sufficient capital gains or losses to induce significant changes in one's portfolio holdings. It therefore follows that given an unchanging expectation of the future earnings stream and potential capital gains or losses, when the magnitude of transaction costs (in absolute value terms) increases, then the minimum time interval until one can expect a positive return from holding an asset increases. There is, however, always some possible larger absolute value of a capital gain that permits the holder to sell the asset earlier than this minimum period and still obtain a positive return.

Tobin and his colleagues give the impression that because their proposed small grains of sand (that is, a very low tax rate) converts to larger negative annual rates the shorter the time interval of a speculative round trip, therefore, the greater the disincentive, the shorter the time interval. For example, Eichengreen et al. note that: '[A 0.5 per cent] tax translates into an annual rate of 4% on a three-month round trip . . . more for shorter trips'.[13] (Of course a 0.5 per cent Tobin tax also translates into a 12 per cent annual rate on a one-month trip or a 365 per cent tax on a one-day round trip.) By evoking higher annual rates of return on shorter and shorter holding periods, the impression is conveyed that a small 'grains of sand' Tobin tax rate will be an overwhelmingly large deterrent for daily or even monthly speculative flows, while the 'grains of sand' tax is 'a negligible deterrent consideration in a long term portfolio'.[14]

In truth, however, the Tobin tax, like all transaction costs, is independent of the holding time between the hypothetical speculative round, and therefore its deterrent capability is not a function of the time period. Comparing annualized rates for different time intervals obscures rather than clarifies the question of how big a deterrent is any given magnitude of a Tobin tax on a speculative round trip. This issue can be clarified by measuring capital gains or losses, q, c and T_s as absolute values in the formulas developed below. The resulting analysis demonstrates that an expected increase in the spot exchange rate of anything in excess of 1.1 per cent is sufficient to more than offset the deterrent effect of a negative 365 per cent annual rate on a daily round trip, or a 12 per cent return on a monthly trip and so on imposed by a 0.5 per cent Tobin tax. Using absolute magnitudes provides a clearer guide to policy than annualized rates.[15]

If, for a specific liquid asset the portfolio manager (without any risk aversion[16]) expects

$$(q - c) + (p_s^{t1} - p_s^{t0}) - T_s > 0, \qquad (12.1)$$

then the manager is a 'bull'. If it is expected that

$$(q - c) + (p_s^{t\,1} - p_s^{t\,0}) - T_s < 0, \qquad (12.2)$$

then the fund manager is a 'bear'. A portfolio manager will choose to move his/her money into those assets that are expected to yield the highest positive values[17] and sell those assets that have negative perspective yields.

In the simplest case, if $(q-c)$ minus T_s equals zero, then if

$$(p_s^{t\,1}/p_s^{t\,0}) > 1, \qquad (12.3)$$

the person is a bull, while if

$$(p_s^{t\,1}/p_s^{t\,0}) < 1, \qquad (12.4)$$

the person is a bear. In a closed economy, if one holds money as a liquid store of value, then there is no future net income[18] $((q - c) = 0)$, no capital gain or loss $((p_s^{t\,1} - p_s^{t\,0}) = 0)$, and no transaction costs $(T_s = 0)$.

In an open economy, flexible exchange rate system, fund managers will not only have to anticipate the expected future income (net of carrying costs), transaction costs of buying and reselling, and capital gain or loss on all tradable domestic *and* foreign liquid securities that can be held in one's portfolio. For international liquid assets they must also factor in possible changes in exchange rates to decide what, if any, international liquid assets to buy, hold or sell at any moment of time.

Whenever some event, whether ephemeral or not, induces one or more managers of large portfolios to suddenly change their expectations regarding future spot exchange rates, then there can be a significant movement of funds from one country to another. Even the mere suspicion that an event will encourage others to undertake a significant international flow can encourage lemming-like behavior in fund managers to change their expectations of $p_s^{t\,1} - p_s^{t\,0}$ and act promptly to try to beat the crowd.

In today's floating exchange rate system, nations must hold significant foreign reserves as a buffer stock to encourage and support orderly, organized exchange markets. Orderliness can be maintained in the face of lemming-like speculative portfolio flows until either:

1. the foreign reserves of the nation suffering the outflow of hot money are nearly exhausted. Then the nation cannot maintain an orderly exchange rate market and fund managers who are latecomers cannot readily convert their holdings into foreign assets if at all,[19] or
2. the country being drained of reserves increases its interest rate (that is,

the $q - c$ term) sufficiently to offset the expected potential capital loss from holding liquid assets denominated in its currency, or

3. central banks (singly or cooperatively) actively intervene in the exchange market in an attempt to change private sector expectations regarding $p_s^{t1} - p_s^{t0}$, or

4. some form of taxation is added to increase the value of the T_s term to offset the expected capital gain from an exchange rate change, or

5. some forms of outright prohibition of hot-money portfolio flows are successfully introduced.

The Tobin tax falls under item (4) where governments use taxation in an attempt to stop speculative flows of hot money.[20] By modifying inequalities (12.1) to (12.4) to account for a Tobin tax, we can estimate the magnitude of the effects of the tax on portfolio decisions. We want to focus attention on a comparison of the effect of an expected change in the exchange rate on the fund manager's behavior with and without a Tobin tax. To do so, let us include the fund manager's expected capital gains (or losses) for each security (in terms of the currency the security is denominated in) in the magnitude of $q - c$. This will permit us to reserve the term $p_s^{t1} - p_s^{t0}$ for analysing the effect of a manager altering his/her view of the spot exchange rate in the near future. Thus the relationship for determining one's bullishness (or bearishness) requires evaluating the following terms:

$$(q - c) + (p_s^{t1} - p_s^{t0}) - (x)(p_s^{t1} + p_s^{t0}) - T_s$$

where (x) equals the magnitude of the Tobin tax rate. If

$$(q - c) + (p_s^{t1} - p_s^{t0}) - (x)(p_s^{t1} + p_s^{t0}) - T_s > 0 \qquad (12.5)$$

the person is a bull, while if

$$(q - c) + (p_s^{t1} - p_s^{t0}) - (x)(p_s^{t1} + p_s^{t0}) - T_s < 0 \qquad (12.6)$$

the portfolio manager is bearish.[21] By comparing inequalities (12.5) and (12.6) with inequalities (12.1) and (12.2) it is obvious that given the values of $(q-c)$ and T_s, a small Tobin tax increases slightly the differential between changes in expected future spot price and current spot price (for any given time interval) before speculative bull or bear responses are induced *vis-à-vis* the no Tobin tax situation. Consequently a small 'grains of sand' Tobin tax, like any other small transaction cost, can stop speculation on small movements in the exchange rate. As the following inequalities demonstrate, any significant change in the exchange rate in the short run will quickly swamp any 'grains of sand' Tobin tax disincentive. Moreover, as suggested below, the Tobin tax can have a significantly larger impact on stemming international trade and arbitrage activities than its impact on a simple speculative round trip.

For comparison with the no tax situation where we assumed $(q-c)-T_s = 0$, when there is a Tobin tax, if

$$(p_s^{t\,1}/p_s^{t\,0}) > (1 + x/1 - x), \tag{12.7}$$

then the person is a bull. Moreover, there will still be bearish sentiment, even if the current spot price is expected to rise as long as

$$(p_s^{t\,1}/p_s^{t\,0}) < (1 + x/1 - x). \tag{12.8}$$

Comparing inequalities (12.7) and (12.8) with inequalities (12.3) and (12.4) provides us with a measure of the magnitude of the minimum expected changes in the exchange rate that must occur to induce bullishness or bearishness in the presence of a Tobin tax compared to the no tax case. For example, if the magnitude of the Tobin tax is 0.5 per cent, then the expected future spot price must increase only by more than 1.1 per cent more than it would have had to increase in the absence of the tax to induce a bullish sentiment. In other words, even though the negative annual rate of return on a one- day round trip is 365 per cent when there is a 0.5 per cent Tobin tax, any increase in the spot price of more than an additional 1.1 per cent compared to the no tax situation can still spawn significant speculative flows. Consequently, the imposition of a Tobin Tax *per se* will not significantly stifle even very short-run speculation if there is any whiff of a weak currency in the market. In fact, any Tobin tax significantly less than 100 per cent of the expected capital gain (on a round trip) is unlikely to stop the sloshing around of hot money.

All that is required to set off speculative flows is an expected change in the exchange rate that is $(1 + x)/(1 - x)$ greater than what would set off speculation regarding the exchange rate in the absence of the Tobin tax. Obviously, then, if an institution can be developed that can control hot-money flows and assure portfolio managers that exchange rates will be stable over time, this will do more to inhibit speculative short-term round tripping than any small Tobin tax.

Almost by definition during a speculative run on a currency, one expects significantly large changes in the exchange rate over a very short period of time. For example, the Mexican peso fell by approximately 60 per cent in the winter of 1994–95. A Tobin tax of more than 23 per cent would have been required to stop the speculative surge of the peso crisis. At best then a 'grains of sand' small Tobin tax might slow down the speculative fever when 'grains of sand' small exchange rate changes are expected. When dealing with small differentials in exchange rates, however, one is likely to be discussing the question of arbitrage rather than speculation. Accordingly, the Tobin tax is more likely to be a constraint on arbitrage flows rather than on speculative flows. The former usually involves small differences in spot prices, while the latter term should be reserved for larger differences in prices.

The grains of sand Tobin tax might be the straw that breaks the speculative back of very small portfolio managers, since normal transaction costs (T_s) of foreign transactions are essentially regressive.[22] An additional proportional (Tobin) tax on top of a large regressive transaction cost can keep small speculators out of the market. For movements of larger sums, however, the normal transaction costs quickly shrink to a negligible proportion of the total transaction. Since in today's freewheeling financial markets, individuals with even small portfolio sums can join mutual funds that can speculate on foreign currencies, a Tobin tax is unlikely to constrain even small investors – who can always join a large mutual fund to reduce the impact of total transaction costs sufficiently to reduce the remaining Tobin tax to relative insignificance whenever speculative fever runs high.

Finally, there is a rule of thumb that suggests that under the current flexible exchange rate system, there may be four or more normal hedging financial transactions involved in any single arm's-length international trade transaction. This exceeds the two financial transactions implicit in Eichengreen's et al. proverbial short-term speculative (nonhedged) roundtrip.[23] If this 2:1 ratio is anywhere near correct, a 0.5 per cent Tobin tax could be equivalent to instituting an additional 2 per cent universal tariff on all goods and services traded in the global economy. It would appear then that a Tobin transaction tax might throw larger grains of sand into the wheels of international real commerce than it does into speculative hot-money flows.

Whether this 2:1 ratio is accurate or not, the important principle involved here is that as long as some hedging transactions are required on arm's-length real trade flows occurring in a flexible exchange rate system, the impact of the Tobin tax is likely to be at least as large and probably larger on international trade than on international portfolio flows.[24] Independent of questions of the political and economic feasibility of instituting a ubiquitous Tobin tax, therefore, proposals to increase marginally transaction costs for foreign exchange by either a Tobin tax or a small feasible opportunity cost tax on capital is unlikely to prevent speculative feeding frenzies that lead to attacks on major currencies while it may inflict greater damage on international trading in goods and services and arbitrage activities.

Keynes provided a clear outline of what is needed when he wrote:

> We need an instrument of international currency having general acceptability between nations . . . We need an orderly and agreed upon method of determining the relative exchange values of national currency units . . . We need a quantum of international currency . . . [which] is governed by the actual current [liquidity] requirements of world commerce, and is capable of deliberate expansion . . . We need a method by which the surplus credit balances arising from international trade, which the recipient does not wish to employ can be set to work . . . without detriment to the liquidity of these balances.[25]

Such considerations led Keynes to suggest an outright prohibition of all significant international portfolio flows through the creation of a supranational central bank and his 'bancor' plan. At this stage of economic development and global economic integration, however, a supranational central bank is not politically feasible. Accordingly what should be aimed for is a more modest goal of obtaining an international agreement among the major trading nations. To be economically effective and politically feasible, this agreement, while incorporating the economic principles that Keynes laid down in his bancor plan, should not require any nation to surrender control of local banking systems and fiscal policies.

Keynes introduced an ingenious method of direct prohibition of hot-money flows by a 'bancor' system with fixed (but adjustable) exchange rates and a trigger mechanism to put more of the onus of resolving current account deficits on surplus nations. It is possible to update Keynes's prohibition proposal to meet twenty-first-century circumstances. In Chapter 14, an updated system will be proposed. The eight provisions of the system suggested in Chapter 14 meet the criteria laid down by Keynes. The proposed system is designed

1. to prevent a lack of global effective demand[26] due to any nation(s) either holding excessive idle reserves or draining reserves from the system,
2. to provide an automatic mechanism for placing a major burden of payments adjustments on the surplus nations,
3. to provide each nation with the ability to monitor and, if necessary, to put boulders into the movement of international portfolio funds in order to control movements of flight capital,[27] and finally
4. to expand the quantity of the liquid asset of ultimate international redemption as global capacity warrants.

Moreover, this system will be in the best interests of all nations for it will make it easier to achieve global full employment without the danger of importing inflationary pressures from one's trading partners.

Before developing this twenty-first-century analysis of a plan to reform the international payments' system, the many suggested alternatives to a Tobin tax that have been proposed for preventing the fires of currency speculation will be analysed in Chapter 13. It will be explained why these alternatives are not any better designed than the Tobin tax to do the job that is required.

The grains of sand of a Tobin tax may prick the small bubbles of speculation, but the sand is more likely to significantly restrict the flow of real trade and international arbitrage activities. On the other hand, the sands of the Tobin tax will be merely swept away in whirlpools of speculation. Boulders are needed to stop the destructive currency speculation from destroying global enterprise patterns, for 'it is enterprise which builds and improves the world's possessions.'

Eichengreen et al. should be praised for forcing economists to focus their attention on the problem of excessive speculative volatility in the exchange rate markets. This problem is not easily resolved. If we start with the defeatist attitude that it is too difficult to change the awkward system in which we are enmeshed, then no progress will be made. We must reject such defeatism at this exploratory stage and merely inquire whether particular proposals for improving the operations of the international payments system to promote global growth will be effective without creating more difficulties than those inherent in the current system. The health of the world economic system will not permit us to muddle through.

NOTES

1. B. Eichengreen, J. Tobin and C. Wyplosz, 'The case for sand in the wheels of international finance', *Economic Journal*, **105**, 1995, p. 164.
2. J.M. Keynes, *The General Theory of Employment, Interest and Money*, Harcourt, Brace, New York, 1936, p. 151.
3. Transactions costs (of holding alternative liquid assets) in the broadest sense – that is including the fear of rapid unpredictable changes in spot prices, or operating in a thin spot market where no financial institution will act as a residual buyer and seller – are basic to determining the magnitude of transactions, precautionary and speculative demands for money in the current income period. If all assets were instantaneously resalable without any costs, there would never be a need to hold 'barren money' rather than a productive asset, except for the necessary nanosecond before it was necessary to meet a contractual commitment that came due. In the real world, the magnitude of actual costs of moving between liquid assets and the medium of contractual settlement is related to the degree of spot market organization and the existence of financial institutions that 'make' spot markets and that thereby assure reasonable moment-to-moment stickiness in spot prices.

4. Some orthodox theorists will consider *ad hoc* central bank intervention in exchange markets an acceptable short-run palliative if disruptive 'shocks' create disorderly market conditions. Purists will deny the need for any intervention. Orthodox purist theorists reach this conclusion by conflating the concept of speculation with that of arbitrage. Since the latter is always a stabilizing force, orthodox purists insist that the former is also always stabilizing.

5. In a single day in September 1992, fund manager George Soros not only made millions by speculating against the English pound but he also forced the Bank of England to abandon any attempt to maintain an orderly exchange market while staying within the European Monetary System (EMS).

6. *The Collected Writings of John Maynard Keynes*, vol. 25, edited by D. Moggridge, Macmillan, London, 1980, p. 25.

7. Eichengreen et al., op. cit., p. 164. Eichengreen et al. have also explored the possibility of imposing compulsory interest-free deposits or other capital requirements (therefore creating an opportunity cost tax) to discourage short-term round tripping, but not long-term investment.

8. See P. Garber and M.P. Taylor, 'Sand in the wheels of international finance', *Economic Journal*, **105**, 1995, pp. 162–72 and P. Kenen, 'Capital controls: the EMS and EMU', *Economic Journal*, **105**, 1995, pp. 181–92.

9. In Keynes's day, major international financial markets did not operate around the globe and hence permit trading 24 hours a day. In today's global financial system, sleep is more of a luxury for international portfolio managers.

10. Keynes, *The General Theory*, p. 153. Each manager believes him/herself equally capable as his/her rivals to interpret quickly the effects of any changes as they occur.

11. J.R. Hicks, 'A suggestion for simplifying the theory of money', *Economica*, 2, 1935, pp. 1–19. Reprinted in J.R. Hicks, *Critical Essays in Monetary Theory*, Clarendon, Oxford, 1967. All references are to the reprint.

12. R.F. Kahn, 'Some notes on liquidity preference', *Manchester School*, **22**, 1952. Reprinted in R.F. Kahn, *Selected Essays on Employment and Growth*, Cambridge University Press, Cambridge, 1972, p. 91. All references are to the reprint.

13. Eichengreen et al., op. cit., p. 164.

14. Ibid., p. 165.

15. In recent statements, Tobin has stated that a tax rate of only 0.2 per cent is needed. In that case any expected small capital gain in excess of 0.4 per cent is sufficient to induce speculative round tripping.

16. Mainstream theorists often assume that the fund manager requires a risk premium evaluated in terms of a probability. Thus if we were to analyse the problem in terms of probabilistic risk, equation (12.1) would be rewritten as:

$$(q - c) + P[(p_s^{t1} - p_s^{t0})] - T_s > 0, \qquad (12.1a)$$

where P (<1) is the probability risk or decision weight. On the other hand, Keynes (*The General Theory*, p. 148) and others (for example, P. Davidson, 'Is probability theory relevant for uncertainty? A different perspective', *Journal of Economic Perspectives*, 5, 1991 pp. 29–43) have argued that uncertainty is different from probabilistic risk. In a world of uncertainty no reliable probability ratio can be assigned. Consequently, in what follows, the equations in the text will not be weighted by any probability ratio. This implies that fund managers must rely upon their 'animal spirits' in deciding whether to act on their conjectures about the future.

17. If we permit unlimited borrowing to finance asset holdings, then since the cost of borrowing is included in computing c, the portfolio manager will buy all available assets as long as they meet inequality (12.1). If fund managers are limited in their ability to borrow, then they will choose those assets with the highest values for inequality (12.1).

18. If bank demand deposit money provides some positive interest income each day that it is held, then the q in our equations would have to be redefined as daily income in excess

of what could be earned by holding demand deposit (Cf. Keynes, *The General Theory*, p. 167n). In principle nothing is lost by ignoring this complication.

19. The fear of this occurrence can, in itself, induce a panic among fund managers similar to what occurs when someone yells fire in a theater.

20. In his *A Treatise on Money*, Keynes (Macmillan, London, 1930, vol. 2, pp. 313–14) proposed 'punitive taxation' on the floating of foreign issues in the domestic securities market and an additional 10 per cent income tax on income earned by domestic residents on foreign loans in order to constrain foreign domestic portfolio investment primarily for income earning purposes. In this *Treatise* proposal, Keynes was not dealing with speculative activities.

21. If one prefers to introduce risk aversion via a probabilistic risk factor P, where $P<1$, then the relevant inequalities are: if

$$(q - c) + P[(p_s^{t1} - p_s^{t0}) - (x)(p_s^{t1} + p_s^{t0})] - T_s > 0, \qquad (12.5a)$$

the person is a bull, while if

$$(q - c) + P[(p_s^{t1} - p_s^{t0}) - (x)(p_s^{t1} + p_s^{t0})] - T_s < 0, \qquad (12.6a)$$

the portfolio manager is bearish.

22. Cf. Hicks, op. cit., p. 67.

23. Although there is very little direct evidence of this multiple for arm's-length real international trade flows, there are logical reasons why a multiple should exist. First any bank that provides a forward transaction to a customer without having a client who needs an identical opposite trade will hedge the risk via engaging in spot and swap transactions. Such bank behavior implies a multiple of the original customer transaction. Second, the growth of swap and forward transactions *via-à-vis* spot transactions is consistent with the view that more hedging per trade transactions are occurring compared to the past. (I am indebted to Jan Kregel for this suggestion.)

24. Many politicians favor a Tobin tax as a 'cash cow' rather than for its alleged effect on slowing international speculation. A Tobin tax is seen as a rich source of tax revenue. R. Kelly ('A framework for European exchange rates in the 1990's', in J.G. Smith and J. Michie (eds), *Unemployment in Europe*, Academic Press, London, 1994) has estimated that a 0.5 per cent Tobin tax would yield one billion pounds sterling per day for the UK government.

25. *The Collected Writings*, vol. 25, p. 168.

26. J. Williamson ('Exchange rate management: the role of target zones', *American Economic Review Papers and Proceedings*, **87**,1987, p. 200) recognizes that when balance of payments 'disequilibrium is due purely to excess or deficient demand', flexible exchange rates *per se* cannot facilitate international payments adjustments.

27. This provides an added bonus by making tax avoidance and profits from illegal trade more difficult to conceal.

13. The plumbers' solution to destabilizing international capital flows

A consistent theme throughout this book has been that the logic of classical economic theory assumes away the fundamental economic problems of a market-oriented, money-using entrepreneurial economy. These aspects neglected by classical theory are particularly relevant for understanding the international payments questions involving liquidity, persistent and growing debt obligations, and the importance of instituting stable exchange rates and avoiding a freely flexible exchange rate system.

An example of the sanguine classical response to those arguing against freely flexible prices and exchange rates is Professor Milton Friedman's reply to me in our 'debate' in the economic literature. Friedman stated: 'A price may be flexible . . . yet be relatively stable, because demand and supply are relatively stable *over time* . . . [Of course] violent instability of prices in terms of a specific money would greatly reduce the usefulness of that money'.[1] It is nice to know that as long as prices or exchange rates remain relatively stable, or 'sticky' over time, then there is no harm in permitting them to be flexible.

The problem arises when there are volatile movements in exchange rates. Should there be a deliberate policy to intervene in the market to maintain relative stability or should a *laissez-faire* market be permitted to determine the price? Keynes helped design the Bretton Woods agreement to foster action and intervention to fix exchange rates and control international payment flows. Friedman sold the public on the beneficence of government inaction and the free market determination of exchange rates.

Nowhere is the difference between the Keynes–Post Keynesian view and the view of those who favor *laissez-faire* more evident than when concerned with questions of international capital movements and payment mechanisms; the desirability of a flexible exchange rate system; and the importance of the international debt problem. We explore these differences in the remainder of this book.

13.1　CAPITAL MOVEMENTS

Large speculative and precautionary international capital flows can create serious international payments problems for most nations – even those whose economic record has been exemplary. Unfortunately, in a *laissez-faire* system of capital markets, there is no way of distinguishing between the movement of funds being used to promote genuine real investment for developing the world's resources and funds that take refuge in one nation's money after another in the continuous search for either speculative gains, hiding from the tax collector, laundering illegal earnings, or funding terrorist operations.

The international movement of significant amounts of speculative, pre-cautionary, or even illegal funds can be so disruptive as to impoverish most, if not all, nations who organize production and exchange processes on an entrepreneurial basis. Keynes warned that 'Loose funds may sweep round the world disorganizing all steady business. Nothing is more certain than that the movement of capital funds must be regulated'.[2]

Even in these days of global electronic communication, governments can monitor and control international capital flows if they have the will and the necessary cooperation of other governments. As long as governments have the power to tax and central bankers have the power to audit and regulate their respective domestic banking systems, large international capital flows can be observed and controlled provided there is international cooperation in this matter. As long as currency is issued only in small denominations, the physical bulkiness of moving large sums secretly across borders cannot be a major threat to any capital controls policy.

In recent years, governments' desire to avoid capital controls has made it easy to hide not only legally earned income and wealth from tax collectors but also profits from drug and other illegal transactions from law enforcement agencies. This encourages uncivilized behavior by self-interested economic agents – and thereby imposes an important, if often neglected, real cost on society.[3] What is more important, flight capital has often drained resources from the relatively poor nations toward the richer ones, resulting in a global inequitable redistribution of income and wealth, thereby increasing the immiseration of a majority of the people on this planet.

Cooperation between nations[4] in detecting, reporting and controlling disruptive capital funds movements among nations can be readily accomplished through the international payment's mechanism described in Chapter 14. Moreover, the successful implementation of this proposed international payments scheme assures inelastic expectation elasticities regarding the rates of exchange among various nations' monies; therefore, this new payments system will create stabilizing expectational forces. Within a very short span of calendar time after a new payments scheme like the one proposed in Chapter 14 is implemented, problems of speculative and precautionary 'hot-money' flows, as well as the international movements of income and wealth to avoid the tax collector or law enforcement officers could quickly shrink to relative insignificance.

Since 1973, when the world embarked on its great classical experiment of floating rates, there have been periodic bouts of great inflation, increasing rates of unemployment, a persistent growth of international debt, and an increasingly inequitable international distribution of global income – as many of the rich nations got richer, while most of the poor nations got poorer on a per capita basis and suffered huge 'flight capital' losses to the wealthy.

Since 1982, one nation – the United States – appears to have been able to take advantage of the existing international payments system to obtain a 'free lunch', that is, to run massive persistent international payments deficits. Although residents of most other nations may resent the ability of the United States to use the present system to obtain this 'free lunch', they are hesitant to change a system that is heralded by classical economists as the only mechanism that permits the freedom to choose through free markets. To be against the existing system is considered to be anti-free markets. To be for some government constraints on market actions is an unpopular position in these days when planning has failed so spectacularly in Eastern Europe. In the absence of a complete collapse of the international monetary payments system, the very unstable status quo will remain unless development of an attractive feasible alternative for reforming the current international payments system is put on the public agenda. It is an old adage in political science that 'you can't beat somebody with nobody!'.

Any suggestion for reforming the international payments mechanism should build on whatever advantages the current system possesses, while providing rules to prevent any nation from enjoying a free lunch – unless a free lunch is available to all. It is possible to provide all with a free lunch if a new payments system has a built-in expansionary bias that encourages nations to operate closer to full employment than the existing system does.

Before developing our suggestion for an international payments scheme which provides this expansionary bias, it is necessary to explain why the existing flexible exchange rate system tends to encourage national policy that imparts a slow growth, depressionary bias.

13.2   FLEXIBLE EXCHANGE RATES AND EXPORT-LED GROWTH

Between the end of the Second World War and the mid-1960s the success of Keynes's revolution in encouraging domestic full employment policies created an endemic problem of wage-cost inflation for most of the developed countries of the world. Without the persistent threat of large-scale unemployment, workers in the developed nations, and labor unions in particular, became more aggressive in their wage demands. By the late 1960s most developed nations began to pursue 'stop–go' policies that generated small planned recessions to reduce the market power of workers to demand inflationary wage increases. These temporary recessions were followed by expansionary Keynesian policies to move the economy back toward full employment until the next round of inflationary wage demands was tabled by workers.

With the breakdown of the Bretton Woods fixed exchange rate system and the movement toward a *laissez-faire* flexible exchange rate environment, some nations found that by pursuing an export-led growth policy, rather than a Keynesian policy of deliberately stimulating some component of internal effective demand, the nation could move toward higher employment levels without unleashing domestic inflationary wage demands. If a nation runs an export surplus, its exchange rate tends to appreciate thereby reducing the price of imported consumer goods in terms of domestic money. Wage earners find their real income increasing without having to demand higher money-wage rates. With export-led growth and flexible exchange rates, any latent inflationary forces in the surplus nation can be exported to one's trading partners who run trade deficits and suffer a depreciation of the exchange rate. The resulting higher domestic prices for imports reduce the purchasing power of the domestic money-wage rate. Unless threatened by significant increases in unemployment, workers in these deficit nations will demand an increase in the money-wage, at least to offset the increased cost of living, and thereby increase inflationary pressures.

Unfortunately, all countries cannot achieve export-led growth simultaneously. If all nations attempt to adopt this method of fostering economic growth by encouraging export expansion while constraining import demand, either all will fail to expand (with the result of global stagnation), or for each successful nation there must be one or more other nations that fail to achieve satisfactory growth while experiencing growing international debt and higher inflation rates.[5]

A flexible exchange rate regime guarantees that for every 'successful' economy that pursues a mercantilist trade surplus policy for expansionary purposes, there must be offsetting failure nations plagued with persistent trade deficits and the problem of importing inflation. For every winner on the flexible rate system, there must be one or more losers. In a fixed exchange rate system, on the other hand, export-led growth does not provide a nation with an advantage by permitting more employment and growth with less inflation compared with Keynesian policies that stimulate internally generated demand. A fixed exchange rate regime operating in tandem with intelligent internal aggregate demand and income management policies will create an environment where all nations simultaneously can be winners as economic growth increases globally without any nation necessarily running into a balance of payments constraint. A fixed exchange rate system combined with intelligent international cooperative Keynesian policies, therefore, holds out the promise that all nations can be winners of a free lunch.

Since the breakdown of the Bretton Woods agreement, it has become increasingly unpopular for a government to use fiscal policy to directly stimulate increases in the domestic components of aggregate demand. Any nation foolish enough to attempt, on its own, to engage in Keynesian fiscal (and/or monetary) policies aimed at deliberately stimulating internal effective demand to lift its industries out of a recessionary or slow growth mode will become enmeshed in a balance of payments problem as imports rise relative to exports.[6] Simultaneously, any resulting stronger domestic markets that significantly reduce unemployment might encourage inflationary wage and profit demands by domestic workers and firms.

In the 1980s and early 1990s, nations such as Japan and the East Asian tigers of Thailand, Singapore, Taiwan, Hong Kong and South Korea were proclaimed 'successful', or even 'economic miracles' by mainstream academics and the financial media. These nations achieved such accolades because they were able to expand output and employment through export-led growth without causing significant domestic inflation. Of course if exports exceed imports and continue to grow more rapidly than imports, then a nation's foreign reserves increase, enhancing its international creditor status. This success encourages the inflows of more foreign capital funds thereby putting pressure on the exchange rate to rise. Domestic prices of imports decline thereby (more than?) offsetting any inflationary tendency in domestically produced goods.

Because of the requirements of double-entry bookkeeping, however, successful export-led growth economies force trade deficits, loss of international reserves, and increased international indebtedness on their trading partners. These export-led growth policies pursued by successful nations are nothing more than a late twentieth-century form of 'beggar thy [trading] neighbor' activities that must ultimately backfire as other nations adopt the same strategy.

In a world operated according to classical axioms, export-led growth should be no more desirable in terms of generating employment without inflation than internally generated demand growth. Despite Adam Smith's claim that increasing exports were the initiating force underlying the growth of the wealth of nations, classical economic theory assumes that the economy will track the long-run full employment growth trend no matter what the primary source of demand growth.

Until the 1990s, the facts seemed to demonstrate that miraculously successful economies tend to pursue export-led growth rather than domestic demand-induced expansions. During the decade of the 1980s and into the early 1990s, nations such as West Germany, Japan, Taiwan, Singapore, Hong Kong and South Korea were not only applauded for their economic miracles by leading Monetarist and classical Keynesian scholars, but they were proclaimed to be shining examples of the proper functioning of a classical capitalist economy operating free from oppressive government intervention. Yet there is nothing in modern classical theory that justifies relying primarily on export-led growth. And the collapse of these economic miracle cases in the 1990s suggests that export-led growth, in the current international payments system, may not be the key to perpetual prosperity.

13.3   EXPLAINING THE FACTS

The Bretton Woods agreement formed the basis of the initial post-Second World War international payments system. In large measure this system was shaped by Keynes's 'incompatibility thesis', which argued that flexible exchange rates and free international capital mobility conditions are incompatible with global full employment and rapid economic growth in an era of multilateral free trade. Until 1973 the Bretton Woods international payments system accommodated Keynes's 'incompatibility thesis'. This accommodation occurred when a fixed exchange rate system with widespread international capital-flow regulations was combined with a civilizing principle that Keynes had emphasized, namely that creditor nations must accept a major responsibility for solving persistent international payments imbalances.

Unfortunately the essence of Keynes's *General Theory* analysis of a money-using, market-oriented, entrepreneur economy was never incorporated into orthodox economic theory. Accordingly, by the 1960s, mainstream classical economists were developing closed and open economy models based on the three classical axioms that Keynes had overthrown.[7] Once these classical axioms were reintroduced into mainstream theory, models again incorporated some form of Say's Law and aggregate supply was the determinant of aggregate demand. The resulting classical (supply-side) models 'demonstrated' that Keynes's incompatibility thesis was wrong. Instead these classical models 'proved' that free trade and optimum global economic growth required freely flexible exchange rates, free international capital mobility and flexible domestic labor markets. In these classical models, regulations to limit financial flows (whether cross-border capital flows or within a nation) imposed huge costs on society. Free the banking system and financial markets from 'onerous' government oversight and regulation, permit unregulated offshore banking and, policy makers were assured, a world of heavenly economic bliss would envelop the planet. Only the supply-side limitation of available resources and the level of technical progress would prevent the immediate achievement of a Garden of Eden on Earth.

As we have already noted, Samuelson's 1947 formalization of the *Foundations of Economic Analysis*[8] hamstrung the 'Keynesian' response to this classical counter revolution. Samuelson's book, which provided the microfoundations for Neoclassical Synthesis Keynesianism, imposed on all economic theorizing the three classical axioms that Keynes had rejected. This theoretical model offspring from this unfortunate marriage of classical axioms with Keynesian macro policies was dubbed 'Bastard Keynesianism' by Joan Robinson. The logical inconsistency between their micro and macroeconomic models made these Old Keynesians easy prey for the academic classical counterrevolution of the late 1960s and 1970s. Nevertheless, this successful academic resurrection of the classical system would have not been sufficient to alter the policy mix if it were not for the events of the 1970s.

The 1973 oil price shock created huge international payments imbalances and unleashed inflationary forces in oil-consuming nations. Politicians found irresistible the allure of the Panglossian siren song that 'all is for the best in the best of all possible worlds provided we let well enough alone'. Without having to admit that they did not know what to do, policy makers used the conclusions of the 1960s classical counterrevolutionary theories to justify their abandonment of Keynes's international policy prescriptions to constrain 'hot-money' international capital flows and to maintain fixed, but adjustable, exchange rates. Instead, a 'leave it to the efficient marketplace' philosophy was adopted. Then, if anything went wrong, policy makers could suggest that they could not be blamed – for, after all, the market 'knows best', as Nobel Laureates Milton Friedman[9], Robert Lucas, Robert Merton and Myron Scholes continually assured us.

The resulting new international world of finance made the exchange rate itself an object of speculation. Utilizing new computer technology, financial capital could move around the globe at the speed of light. In the last quarter of the twentieth century, international financial transactions grew thirty times as fast as the growth in international trade. International financial flows dominated trade payments. Exchange rate movements reflected changes in speculative portfolio positions rather than changes in patterns of trade.

Significant exchange rate movements affect the international competitive position of domestic *vis-à-vis* foreign industries and therefore tend to depress the inducement to invest in large projects with irreversible sunk costs.[10] In an uncertain (nonergodic) world where the future cannot be reliably predicted from past and present price signals, volatile exchange rates undermine entrepreneurs' confidence in their ability to appraise the potential profitability of any large investment project. Every exchange rate increase threatens domestic industries not only with significant loss of export-market share but also loss of home-market share as imports become less expensive. Managers realize that any upward blip in the exchange rate during the lifetime of any contemplated real investment project can saddle their enterprises with irreversible costly idle capacity. Consequently, the marginal efficiency of investment is reduced. The greater the uncertainty regarding future exchange rates, the less investment globally – just as Keynes's liquidity preference and investment theory predicted. As a result, trade and real investment spending in open economies have become the tail wagged by the international speculative exchange rate dog.

Instead of producing the utopian promises of greater stability, more rapid economic growth and full employment claimed by classical economists, liberalization of capital-flow regulations has been associated with exchange rate instability, slower global economic growth and higher global unemployment. Liberalization drove the final nail into the coffin of the postwar golden age of economic development. The post-1973 international payments system has not served the emerging global economy well. *The Financial Times* of London and *The Economist*, both early strong advocates of the post-1973 floating rate system, acknowledged that this system was a failure and was sold to the public and the politicians under false advertising claims.[11] In its 26 September 1998 (p. 80) issue, *The Economist* concluded that either a pure floating rate or a dirty (semi-fixed) floating exchange rates were of 'no use'.

The issues of trade, debt and currency exchange rates are intertwined and today's liberalized international financial system is on a course that can lead to an economic calamity.[12] Yet no governmental policy maker, IMF and/or World Bank official wants to speak out and be accused of setting off a panic. The most sober judgment of these officials is that the best thing that can be done is to buy more time by making plumbing adjustments to head off a crash and hope for the global economy to right itself in the long run as the efficient market theory predicts. Apparently, decision makers in power do not undertake fundamental reform measures until they are forced to by crisis.

When the 1997 Asian financial crisis and the 1998 Russian debt default paralysed financial markets in the autumn of 1998, it appeared that these events forced political leaders to recognize the need for major international monetary institutional reforms. Even the advisors to President Bill Clinton were perturbed enough to encourage the president to speak out for the need for a new international financial architecture.

But the global economy stepped back too quickly from the brink in 1999. The crisis receded and no reforms were launched. Instead, Keynes's aphorism 'Worldly wisdom teaches that it is better for reputation to fail conventionally than succeed unconventionally'[13] again seemed to rule the day. There was no national leader willing to challenge conventional economic analysis and call for a *complete* and *thorough* overhaul of an international payments system that is far worse than the one abandoned in 1973. Instead there were calls for plumbing patches on the current payments system in terms of a marginal transaction tax here and/or a marginally larger lender of last resort there, and/or marginally higher capital adequacy ratios for banks as part of a package for more 'transparency', and even inconsistent calls for Keynesian spending in Japan while lauding fiscal budget surpluses in the United States and reducing government deficits in the European Union. There was, and still is, no one with significant media visibility who has the courage to speak out in public forums and suggest that the classical economic philosophy that has rationalized our domestic and international macroeconomic affairs in recent decades is a formula for potential economic disaster at worst and modest global economic growth at best.

Until there is a fundamental reform of the architecture of the world's international payments system it will be impossible for any individual nation, except perhaps the United States, to undertake national macro policies to maintain high levels of aggregate demand internally without fear of a balance of payments constraint. As long as the US dollar is the main form of foreign reserves, the United States does not have to worry about a balance of payments constraint. Since 1981, the United States has run large trade deficits with impunity. Because of the large US trade deficit in 2000, the effective demand of the global economy was some $400 + billion higher and the global economy was better off than it would have been if the United States was constrained by its huge current account deficit.[14] When the US import demand faltered in 2001, most of the rest of the world slipped into recession, and even rapidly growing economies, for example, China, found their growth rates were significantly lower.

The introduction of the euro in 1999 has created another potential international payments problem. If international liquidity holders ever reveal a strong preference for the euro over the dollar as reserve asset, then Gresham's Law will come into play. Any global stimulus coming from the United States could readily disappear in the early years of the twenty-first century. The result will be an additional deflationary force unleashed on the global economy. And yet, it is only through a significant stimulus to global effective demand that we can restore a golden age of economic growth for the twenty-first century similar to that experienced by the global economy between 1950 and 1973.

This Post Keynesian message is contrary to the conventional wisdom of mainstream economic theory where the latter attributes the cause of persistently high unemployment to labor market rigidities (in closed economic models) and, in an open economy context, government interference in exchange rates, capital flows and investments (via crony capitalism). Since the late 1960s, the conventional wisdom of economists has been to advocate micro policies to free up both labor and capital markets.

This belief in a policy to loosen labor and international capital movements, can be called 'the laxative theory to economic bliss.' If any one country, using such purgative capital and labor market medicines, succeeds in increasing its employment and growth, it does so only by exporting some of its unemployment to its trading partners. The pursuit of these purgatory prescriptions by several core nations simultaneously will invoke a negative sum game that unleashes deflationary forces around the globe.

13.4   A LESSON FROM THE GOLD STANDARD ERA

It is said: 'Those who do not study history are doomed to repeat its errors'. The gold standard provided the world with a fixed and credible exchange rate system. From 1880 to 1914, however, there were many banking crises 'but they rarely turned into currency crises, except at the Latin American periphery . . . despite very large international capital flows'.[15] Even though defaults occurred, global investment continued, as London, acting as the clearinghouse for international trade, made 'sterling the main vehicle currency in both international payments and investments. *It was the absence of alternative currencies to hold that reduced the speculative element in short-term money flows*'.[16]

In this gold standard era, bouts of inflation, unstable political conditions, revolution, or a collapse of export (commodity) prices led to recurrent currency crises in the Latin American periphery. But 'debt collectors moved in, with rescheduling and fresh loans . . . as soon as service on the bonds was resumed, the investors came back . . . The crucial point in all this was that the gold standard was stable at the centre, unstable at its Latin American periphery . . . As a rule, currency crisis hit second class countries, not first class ones'.[17]

This changed in the period between the world wars when international capital-flow crises struck the core countries as well as the periphery. In the

1920s, even as core countries attempted to return to the gold standard, the resulting exchange rate peg was not credible. Competition between financial centers in London, Paris and New York made multilateral clearing cumbersome and difficult, especially when there were persistent imbalances in international payments. Only the continual recycling of the US current account surplus by American banks in most of the 1920s prevented the collapse of the world economy. Meanwhile the United States adopted tariffs that made it very difficult for Europeans to run a balanced trade position or to earn dollars to repay postwar dollar loans.

In 1928 when US funds were diverted from international loans to Wall Street speculation, the international payments system started to crumble. Money began flowing from deficit to surplus countries as reserves were liquidated to service debts to the United States. When commodity prices collapsed, the periphery defaulted on these loans – but this time 'the contagion spread to Europe' as Germany tried to balance its international payments by severely depressing its economy. As unemployment rose drastically, a German default occurred in 1931. 'A deflationary hurricane swept over the world, as investors scrambled for liquidity'.[18] Huge speculative waves attacked the core currencies. Interbank credits could not stem these assaults. The result was to end private foreign investment flows for decades.

Can this happen again as the euro and the yen compete with the US dollar as an international reserve currency, especially if the United States as the world's largest debtor slips into recession and the world relies on liberalized financial markets to finance payments imbalances?

13.5 PLUMBING SOLUTIONS TO END FINANCIAL MARKET VOLATILITY

Despite their willingness to accept the 'compelling logic' of efficient market theory, any nonideolog mainstream economist can recognize that the recurring international financial market crises of the 1990s, and the persistent long recession that has plagued Japan since the Bank of Japan deliberately set out to burst Japan's 1980s financial asset price bubble, demonstrates that liberalized financial markets cannot provide a strong defense against 'it'[19] happening again. The commonsense of Tobin and his New Keynesian followers regarding volatility in international financial markets cannot help but break into their logical models of super-efficient markets – with injury to their logical consistency. To constrain today's international financial market volatility, we have noted that these 'Keynesians' advocate a Tobin tax. Unfortunately although Tobin's assessment of the problem is correct, as we noted in Chapter 12, the empirical evidence is that any increase in the transaction costs significantly increases rather than decreases measured market volatility. Moreover, as we have already explained, a Tobin tax does not create a greater disincentive for short-term speculators as Tobin has claimed. The 'Tobin tax' solution is the wrong tool to solve the growing international financial speculative market problem.

Other mainstream economists have proposed different solutions to this problem of international market volatility. These proposals include an international lender-of-last-resort facility, a currency board, and the complete liberalization of all markets.

Since the Mexican peso crisis of 1994, some pragmatic policy makers have advocated a lender-of-last-resort to stop international financial market liquidity hemorrhaging and to buy time to encourage international investors to reschedule existing debts and make fresh loans.[20] In 1994, US Treasury Secretary Robert Rubin encouraged President Clinton to play this lender-of-last-resort role. The IMF stepped into this lender role when the 1997 Asian crisis and 1998 Russian default occurred. When it appeared that the IMF might approach the end of its liquidity rope in 1999, Stanley Fischer, then the Associate Director of the IMF, suggested that the G7 nations provide additional funding for an international lender of last resort.[21] Fischer's cry for a G7 collaborative funding is equivalent to recruiting a volunteer fire department to douse the flames after someone has cried fire in a crowded theater. Even if the fire is ultimately extinguished there will be many innocent casualties. Moreover, every new currency fire requires the lender of last resort to pour more liquidity into the market to put out the flames. The goal should be to produce a permanent fire-prevention solution, not to rely on organizing larger and larger volunteer fire-fighting companies after each new currency fire breaks out.

The man who 'broke the Bank of England', George Soros, as well as some academic economists, have recommended a currency board solution. A currency board fixes the exchange rate so that the domestic currency supply does not exceed the amount of foreign reserves a nation possesses. Thus, if and when investors panic and rush to exit from a nation, the currency board maintains the exchange rate by selling foreign reserves and reducing the domestic money supply by an equivalent sum. A currency board solution, therefore, is equivalent to the blood letting prescribed by seventeenth-century doctors to cure a fever. Enough blood loss can, of course, always reduce the fever but often at a terrible cost to the body of the patient. Similarly, a currency board may douse the flames of a currency crisis but the result can be a moribund economy. The effect of Argentina's currency board on its domestic economy is clear evidence of this effect.

Friedman[22] and many others have suggested a return to completely flexible exchange rates without any nation's central bank in the background holding foreign reserves to assure that it might decide to step in if the foreign exchange market becomes disorderly. Unfortunately whenever there is a persistent international payments imbalance, free market exchange rate flexibility can make the situation worse. For example, if a nation is suffering a tendency toward international current account deficits due to imports exceeding exports, then free market advocates argue that a decline in the market price will end the trade deficit. If, as we have noted previously, the Marshall–Lerner condition does not apply, then a declining market exchange rate worsens the situation by increasing the magnitude of the payments deficit.

If, the payments imbalance is due to capital flows, there is a similar perverse effect. If, for example, country A is attracting a rapid net inflow of capital because investors in the rest of the world think the profit rate is higher in A, then the exchange rate will rise. This rising exchange rate creates even higher profits for foreign investors in terms of their domestic currency and contrarily will encourage others to rush in with additional capital flows, pushing the exchange rate even higher. If then there is a sudden change in sentiment (often touched off by some ephemeral event), then a fast exit bandwagon will ensue, pushing the exchange rate perversely down.

13.6 THE BRETTON WOODS EXPERIENCE AND THE MARSHALL PLAN

Too often economic discussions on the requirements for a good international payments system to eliminate payment imbalances have been limited to the question of the advantages and disadvantages of fixed versus flexible exchange rates. Although this issue is very important, the facts of experience since the end of the Second World War plus Keynes's revolutionary liquidity analysis indicate that more is required than simply choosing between fixed and flexible exchange rates if a mechanism is to be designed to resolve persistent international payment imbalances while simultaneously promoting full employment economic growth and a long-run stable international standard of value.

The postwar world has conducted several experiments with the international payments system. For a quarter of a century after the war, there was a fixed, but adjustable, exchange rate system (1947–73) set up under the Bretton Woods agreement. Since 1973, we have operated under a flexible exchange rate system.

The 1947–73 period was, as we have already noted in the first chapter, an era of unprecedented sustained economic growth in both developed and developing countries. During the Bretton Woods epoch, free economies experienced unprecedented real economic growth. Moreover, during this period, there was 'a much better overall record of price level stability' *vis-à-vis* either the post-1973 period or the previous era of fixed exchange rates under the gold standard (1879–1914).[23] The free world's economic performance in terms of both real growth *and* price level stability during the Bretton Woods period was unprecedented. Moreover, even the economic record during the earlier gold standard fixed exchange rate period was better than the world's economies have experienced during the 1973–2001 period of flexible exchange rates. The dismal post-1973 experience of recurrent unemployment and inflationary crises, slow growth in Organization for Economic Cooperation and Development (OECD) countries, and debt-burdened growth and/or stagnation (and even falling real GNP per capita) in developing countries contrasts sharply with the experience during the Bretton Woods period.

What can we surmise from these facts? First, several hundred years of experience support the thesis that a fixed exchange rate system provides an international environment that is more compatible with greater real economic growth and price stability compared to what was experienced under a flexible exchange rate regime. Second, the significantly superior performance of the free world economies during the Bretton Woods fixed rate period compared to the earlier gold standard fixed rate period suggests that there must have been an additional condition besides exchange rate fixity that contributed to the unprecedented growth during the 1947–73 period. That additional condition had been spelled out by Keynes in the 1940s, in developing his proposals for an international payments scheme. To reduce entrepreneurial uncertainties and the possibility of massive currency misalignments Keynes recommended the adoption of a fixed, but adjustable, exchange rate system. What is more important, Keynes argued that the main cause of failure of any traditional payments system, whether based on fixed or flexible rates, is its inability to actively foster continuous global economic expansion when persistent current account imbalances among trading partners occurred. This failure

> can be traced to a single characteristic. I ask close attention to this, because I shall argue that this provides a clue to the nature of any alternative which is to be successful. . . . It is characteristic of a freely convertible international standard that it throws the main burden of adjustment on the country which is the *debtor* position on the international balance of payments – that is, on the country which is (in this context) by hypothesis the *weaker* and above all the *smaller* in comparison with the other side of the scales which (for this purpose) is the rest of the world.[24]

Keynes concluded that an essential improvement in designing any international payments system requires transferring 'the *onus* of adjustment from the debtor to the creditor position', and aiming 'at the substitution of an expansionist, in place of a contractionist, pressure on world trade'.[25] In other words, to achieve a golden era of economic development requires combining a fixed, but adjustable, rate system with a mechanism for requiring the surplus trading nation(s) to initiate most of the efforts necessary to adjust a payments imbalance, without removing all discipline from the deficit trading partner.

During the first half of the Bretton Woods era, the world's major creditor nation, almost accidentally, accepted responsibility for curing global current account imbalances via the Marshall Plan and other forms of foreign and military aid. It was the failure of the Bretton Woods system to perpetuate this creditor nation action in the 1960s that led to its ultimate abandonment and the end to the golden era of economic development.

After the Second World War, the economic recovery of the free capitalist world required the European nations to run huge import surpluses to feed their populations and rebuild their stock of capital. Under the orthodox rules of free market economies, this implied that the United States would have to provide enormous credits to finance the required export surplus to Europe. The resulting European indebtedness would be so burdensome that it was unlikely that, even in the long run, the European nations could ever service this debt. Moreover, US policy makers were mindful that reparation payments after the First World War were financed by US investors lending Germany foreign exchange and Germany never repaid these loans. Given this history and existing circumstances it was obvious that private lending facilities could not be expected to provide the credits necessary for European recovery.

The only mechanism available to international debtor nations for redressing this potentially lopsided global import export trade flow was for them to accept the main burden of adjustment by 'tightening their belt' and reduce their demand for imports to what they could earn from exports.[26] Even if the debtor nations had abandoned the fixed exchange rate mechanism and opted for a depreciating currency under a flexible exchange rate system to force the European residents to 'tighten their belts,' the result would have reduced the European standard of living to a starvation level. Any conventional free market solution available to the European nations after the Second World War would so depress the standard of living as to possibly inducing political revolutions in most of Western Europe.

Instead the United States produced the Marshall Plan and other foreign grants and aid programs. The Marshall Plan provided $5 billion in aid in

18 months and a total of $13 billion in four years. (Adjusted for inflation, in 2000 this is equivalent to approximately $130 billion.) Marshall Plan transfers represented approximately 2 per cent per annum of the GNP of the United States. Yet no US resident felt deprived of goods and services. Real GNP per capita in the United States during the first year of the Marshall Plan was still 25 per cent larger than in the last peacetime year of 1940. Per capita GNP continued to grow throughout the 1950s.[27] There was no real sacrifice associated with this export surplus. These exports were produced by employing what otherwise would have been idle (involuntarily unemployed) resources. For the first time in its history, the United States did not suffer from a severe recession immediately after the cessation of a major war. The world experienced an economic 'free lunch' as both the potential debtors and the creditor nation gained from this 'give away'.

By 1958, however, although the United States still had an annual goods and services export surplus of more than $5 billion, US governmental and military transfers exceeded $6 billion, while there was a net private capital outflow of $1.6 billion.[28] The postwar US surplus position on current account was at an end. As the US current account swung into deficit other nations began to experience current account surpluses. These nations converted a portion of their dollar current account surplus into gold. For example, in 1958, the United States lost more than $2 billion in gold reserves. These trends accelerated in the 1960s, partly as a result of increased US military and financial aid responses to the construction of the Berlin Wall in 1961 and later because of the increasing US involvement in Vietnam. At the same time, a rebuilt Europe and Japan became important producers of exports so that the rest of the world became less dependent on US exports.

The United States maintained a positive merchandise trade balance until the first oil price shock in 1973. More than offsetting this trade surplus during most of the 1960s, however, were foreign and military unilateral transfers plus net capital outflows. The Bretton Woods system had no way of automatically forcing the emerging surplus nations to step into the adjustment role that the United States had been playing since 1947. Instead they continued to convert some portion of their annual dollar surplus into calls on US gold reserves. The seeds of the destruction of the Bretton Woods system and the golden age of economic development were sown as surplus nations drained gold reserves from the United States.

When the United States closed the gold window and unilaterally withdrew from Bretton Woods in 1972, the last vestige of Keynes's enlightened international monetary approach was lost – apparently without regret or regard as to how well it had served the global economy.

NOTES

1. M. Friedman, 'A response to his critics', in *Milton Friedman's Monetary Framework: A Debate With is Critics*, edited by R.J. Gordon, University of Chicago Press, Chicago, 1974, p. 151.
2. *The Collected Writings of John Maynard Keynes,* vol. 25, edited by D. Moggridge, Macmillan, London, 1980, p. 25.
3. Nations with banking institutions which make it difficult for foreign authorities to obtain information regarding bank accounts held by depositors are likely to encourage the influx of funds from terrorist organizations, tax evaders, drug money and hot-money flows. Thus, it is not surprising that exchange rates often reflect speculative and flight capital flows rather than purchasing power parities.
4. To argue, from the outset, that international cooperation in sharing records and helping enforce capital flows cannot be achieved, is unduly pessimistic. It paints a picture of the human condition where nations are willing to cooperate in military wars at a cost of the lives of a large portion of their youth, but unwilling to cooperate even if it costs the recipient nations a 'fast buck'.
5. The one practical exception to this generalization is when a small, unimportant, nation pursues export-led growth. If a nation is so insignificant, then its trade surpluses are unlikely to inflict significant deficits or inflationary tendencies on any of the other trading nations. Thus the importance of being unimportant for export-led growth.
6. Since the world is on a US dollar standard, the one exception to this rule is the United States. It can run payment deficits with impunity, as long as other nations perceive the US dollar as the liquid asset *par excellence* for meeting all international contractual liabilities.
7. These classical axioms are the neutrality of money axiom, the gross substitution axiom and the ergodic axiom. See Davidson (P. Davidson, 'Reviving Keynes's Revolution', *Journal of Post Keynesian Economics*, 7, 1984, pp. 561–75).
8. P.A. Samuelson, *Foundations of Economic Analysis*, MIT Press, Cambridge, MA, 1947.
9. In an article in the October 12, 1998 edition of the *Wall Street Journal*, Milton Friedman argued that with market-determined exchange rates, exchange rate pressures will always be dissipated, despite the long-known argument that in the absence of the Marshall–Lerner condition, market forces would exacerbate exchange rate problems. For a further discussion see Section 13.5 *infra*.
10. While, at the same time vastly increasing the liquidity demands of entrepreneurs, bankers and ultimately central bankers in terms of foreign reserve holdings. The results are episodes of international liquidity crises.
11. *The Economist* magazine (January 6, 1990) indicated that the decade of the 1980s will be noted as one in which 'the experiment with floating currencies failed'. Almost two years earlier (February 17, 1987), *The Financial Times* admitted that 'floating exchange rates, it is now clear, were sold on a false prospectus . . . they held out a quite illusory promise of greater national autonomy . . . [but] when macro policies are inconsistent and when capital is globally mobile, floating rates cannot be relied upon to keep the current accounts roughly in balance'.
12. In the summer of 1999, Russia's latest de facto default on its international debt was avoided only by the IMF and the 'Paris Club' creditors lending Russia sufficient funds in a blocked account to permit the servicing of this 'old' debt.
13. J.M. Keynes, *The General Theory of Employment, Interest and Money,* Harcourt, Brace, New York, 1936, p. 158.
14. Without recognizing that, under the current system, nations have an incentive to pursue export-led economic growth policies, the *New York Times* (August 20, 1999, p. C1) appeared to be surprised that Asia's and Europe's recovery from the economic turmoil of 1998 occurred while there was a sharp growth in US imports from Asia and Western Europe. The growth in US imports, however, is the other side of the coin necessary for the recovery of Asia and Western Europe.

15. R. Skidelsky, *Capital Regulation: For and Against*, Social Market Foundation, London, 1999, p. 3.
16. Ibid., p. 5, emphasis added.
17. Ibid., pp. 8–9. Does not this experience appear to have some similarities to events in the post-1973 era when the world was on a dollar standard?
18. Ibid., p. 13.
19. H.P. Minsky, *Can It Happen Again?*, M.E. Sharpe, Armonk, 1978.
20. Compare 'A lesson from the gold standard era', Section 13.4 *supra*.
21. S. Fischer, 'On the need for an international lender of last resort', paper presented at a joint session of the American Economics Association and the American Finance Association, New York, January 1999.
22. M. Friedman, 'Markets to the rescue', *Wall Street Journal*, October 12, 1998, p. A22.
23. R.I. McKinnon, 'Interest rate volatility and exchange rate risk: new rules for a common monetary standard', *Contemporary Policy Studies*, **8**, April 1990, p. 10.
24. *The Collected Writings*, vol. 25, p. 27.
25. Ibid., p. 176.
26. The 'scarce currency' clause of the Bretton Woods agreement would permit European nations to discriminate against American imports. But this would not resolve the problem since there was no other major source of the goods necessary to feed and rebuild Europe.
27. Only in the small recessions of 1949 and 1957 did per capita GNP stop growing. But even during these brief periods, it never declined.
28. Figures obtained from *Statistical Abstract of the United States 1959*, US Bureau of Census, Washington, DC, 1959, p. 870.

14. The architectural solution: reforming the world's money

The 1950–73 global golden age of economic development required international institutions and policies that operated on principles inherent in Keynes's 1940s proposals for a new international payments system. The analysis of the last five chapters of this volume has provided the theoretical foundations for comprehending the need for (a) reforming the world's money in the twenty-first century and (b) updating Keynes's original proposal for a postwar international monetary scheme

14.1 REFORMING THE INTERNATIONAL PAYMENTS SYSTEM

In the twenty-first century interdependent world economy, a substantial degree of economic cooperation among trading nations is essential. Keynes's original 'bancor' plan for reforming the international payments system required the creation of a single supranational central bank. At this stage of the evolution of world politics, however, a global supranational central bank is politically neither feasible[1] nor necessary. The following Post Keynesian proposal does not require the establishment of a supranational central bank even if this is believed desirable on other grounds. The clearing union institution suggested in this chapter is a more modest proposal aimed at obtaining an international agreement that does not require surrendering national control of either local banking systems or domestic monetary and fiscal policies. Each nation will still be able to determine the economic destiny that is best for its citizens without fear of importing deflationary repercussions from their trading partners. Nor will each nation be able to export domestic inflationary forces to their international neighbors.

What is required is a closed, double-entry bookkeeping clearing institution to keep the payments 'score' among the various trading nations plus some mutually agreed-upon rules to create and reflux liquidity while maintaining the purchasing power of the international currency. There are eight major provisions in a proposal that will meet the needs of the global economy in the twenty-first century. They are detailed below.

First, the unit of account and ultimate reserve asset for international liquidity is the International Money Clearing Unit (IMCU). All IMCUs can be held *only* by the central banks of nations that abide by the rules of the clearing union system. IMCUs are not available to be held by the public.

Second, each nation's central bank or, in the case of a common currency (for example, the euro) a currency union's central bank, is committed to guarantee one-way convertibility from IMCU deposits at the clearing union to its domestic money. Each central bank will set its own rules regarding making available foreign monies (through IMCU clearing transactions) to its own bankers and private sector residents.[2]

Since central banks agree to sell their own liabilities (one-way convertibility) against the IMCU only to other central bankers and the International Clearing Union while they simultaneously hold only IMCUs as liquid reserve assets for international financial transactions, there can be no draining of reserves from the international payments system. Ultimately, all major private international transactions clear between central bank accounts in the books of the international clearing institution.

The guarantee of only one-way convertibility permits each nation to institute controls and regulations on international capital fund flows if necessary. The primary economic function of these international capital-flow controls and regulations is to prevent rapid changes in the bull–bear sentiment from overwhelming the market maker and inducing dramatic changes in international financial market price trends that can have devastating real consequences.

There is a spectrum of different capital controls available. At one end of the spectrum are controls that primarily impose administrative constraints either on a case-by-case basis or an expenditure category basis. Such controls may include administrative oversight and control of individual transactions for payments to foreign residents (or banks) often via oversight of international transactions by banks or their customers.

Mayer has argued that the 1997 East Asian currency contagion problem was due to the interbank market that created the whirlpool of speculation and that what was needed was 'a system for identifying . . . and policing interbank lending'[3] including banks' contingent liabilities resulting from dealing in derivatives. Echoing our nonergodic theme, Mayer declares 'The mathematical models of price movements and covariance underlying the construction of these [contingent] liabilities simply collapsed as actual prices departed so far from "normal" probabilities'.[4]

Other capital controls include (a) policies that make foreign exchange available but at different exchange rates for different types of transactions and (b) the imposition of taxes (or other opportunity costs) on *specific* international financial transactions, for example, the 1960s US interest equalization tax.

Finally there can be many forms of monetary policy decisions undertaken to affect net international financial flows, for example, raising the interest rate to slow capital outflows, raising bank reserve ratios, limiting the ability of banks to finance purchases of foreign securities, and regulating interbank activity as suggested by Mayer.

The IMF, as lender of last resort during the 1997 East Asian contagion crisis, imposed the same conditions on all nations requiring loans for international liquidity purposes. The resulting worsening of the situation should have taught us that in policy prescriptions one size does *not* fit all situations. Accordingly, the type of capital regulation a nation should choose from the spectrum of tools available at any time will differ depending on the specific circumstances involved. It would be presumptuous to attempt to catalog what capital regulations should be imposed for any nation under any given circumstances. Nevertheless, it should be stressed that regulating capital movements is a necessary *but not a sufficient* condition for promoting global prosperity. Much more is required.

If any government objects to the idea that the IMCU proviso No. 2 provides governments with the ability to limit the free movement of 'capital' funds, then this nation is free to join other nations of similar attitude in forming a regional currency union (UMS) and thereby assuring a free flow of funds among the residents of the currency union.

Third, contracts between private individuals in different nations will continue to be denominated into whatever domestic currency permitted by local laws and agreed upon by the contracting parties. Contracts to be settled in terms of a foreign currency will therefore require some publicly announced commitment from the central bank (through private sector bankers) of the availability of foreign funds to meet such private contractual obligations.

Fourth, the exchange rate between the domestic currency and the IMCU is set initially by each nation or currency union's central bank – just as it would be if one instituted an international gold standard. Since private enterprises that are already engaged in trade have international contractual commitments that would span the changeover interval from the current system, then, as a practical matter, one would expect, but not demand, that the existing exchange rate structure (with perhaps minor modifications) would provide the basis for initial rate setting.

Provisos No. 7 and No. 8 below indicate when and how this nominal exchange rate between the national currency and the IMCU would be changed in the future.

Fifth, an overdraft system should be built into the clearing union rules.

Overdrafts should make available short-term unused creditor balances at the clearing house to finance the productive international transactions of others who need short-term credit. The terms will be determined by the *pro bono publico* clearing union managers.

Sixth, a trigger mechanism to encourage any creditor nation to spend what is deemed (in advance) by agreement of the international community to be 'excessive' credit balances accumulated by running current account surpluses. These excessive credits can be spent in three ways: (a) on the products of any other member of the clearing union, (b) on new direct foreign investment projects, and/or (c) to provide unilateral transfers (foreign aid) to deficit members. Spending via (a) forces the surplus nation to make the adjustment directly by way of the balance on goods and services. Spending by way of (c) permits adjustment directly by the current account balance, while (b) provides adjustment by the capital accounts (without setting up a contractual debt that will require reverse current account flows in the future).

These three spending alternatives force the surplus nation to accept a major responsibility for correcting the payments imbalance. Nevertheless this provision gives the surplus country considerable discretion in deciding how to accept the 'onus' of adjustment in the way it believes is in its residents best interests. It does not permit the surplus nation to shift the burden to the deficit nation(s) via contractual requirements for debt service charges independent of what the deficit nation can afford.[5] The important thing is to make sure that continual oversaving[6] by the surplus nation in the form of international liquid reserves is not permitted to unleash depressionary forces and/or a building up of international debts so encumbering as to impoverish the global economy of the twenty-first century.

In the unlikely event that the surplus nation does not spend or give away these credits within a specified time, then the clearing agency would confiscate (and redistribute to debtor members) the portion of credits deemed excessive.[7] This last resort confiscatory action (a 100 per cent tax on excessive liquidity holdings) would make a payments adjustment via unilateral transfer payments in the current accounts.

Under either a fixed or a flexible rate system with each nation free to decide on how much it will import, some nations will, at times, experience persistent trade deficits merely because their trading partners are not living up to their means – that is because other nations are continually hoarding a portion of their foreign export earnings (plus net unilateral transfers). By so doing, these oversavers are creating a lack of global effective demand. Under provision No. 6, deficit countries would no longer have to deflate their real economy in an attempt to reduce imports and thereby reduce their payments imbalance because others are excessively oversaving. Instead, the system would seek to remedy the payments deficit by increasing opportunities for deficit nations to sell abroad and thereby work their way out of their deteriorating debtor position.

Seventh, a system to stabilize the long-term purchasing power of the IMCU (in terms of each member nation's domestically produced market basket of goods) can be developed. This requires a system of fixed exchange rates between the local currency and the IMCU that changes only to reflect permanent increases in efficiency wages.[8] This assures each central bank that its holdings of IMCUs as the nation's foreign reserves will never lose purchasing power in terms of foreign-produced goods. If a foreign government permits wage-price inflation to occur within its borders, then, the exchange rate between the local currency and the IMCU will be devalued to reflect the inflation in the local money price of the domestic commodity basket.

If, on the other hand, increases in productivity lead to declining production costs in terms of the domestic money, then the nation with this decline in efficiency wages (say of 5 per cent) would have the option of choosing either (a) to permit the IMCU to buy (up to 5 per cent) less units of domestic currency, thereby capturing all (or most of) the gains from productivity for its residents while maintaining the purchasing power of the IMCU, or (b) to keep the nominal exchange rate constant. In the latter case, the gain in productivity is shared with all trading partners. In exchange, the export industries in this productive nation will receive an increasing relative share of the world market.

By devaluing the exchange rate between local monies and the IMCU to offset the rate of domestic inflation, the IMCU's purchasing power is stabilized. By restricting use of IMCUs to central banks, private speculation regarding IMCUs as a hedge against inflation is avoided. Each nation's rate of inflation of the goods and services it produces is determined solely by (a) the local government's policy toward the level of domestic money-wages and profit margins *vis-à-vis* productivity gains, that is, the nation's efficiency wage. Each nation is therefore free to experiment with policies for stabilizing its efficiency wage to prevent inflation as long as these policies do not lead to a lack of global effective demand. Whether the nation is successful or not in preventing domestic goods price inflation, the IMCU will never lose its international purchasing power in terms of any domestic money. Moreover, the IMCU has the promise of gaining in purchasing power over time, if productivity grows more than money-wages and each nation is willing to share any reduction in real production costs with its trading partners.

Proviso No. 7 produces a system designed to, at least, maintain the relative efficiency wage parities among nations. In such a system, the adjustability of nominal exchange rates will be primarily (but not always, see

proviso No. 8) to offset changes in efficiency wages among trading partners. A beneficial effect that follows from this proviso is that it eliminates
the possibility that a specific industry in any nation can be put at a competitive disadvantage (or secure a competitive advantage) against foreign
producers solely because the nominal exchange rate changed indepen-
dently of changes in efficiency wages and the real costs of production in
each nation.

Consequently, nominal exchange rate variability can no longer create the
problem of a loss of competitiveness due solely to the overvaluing of a currency as, for example, experienced by the industries in the American 'rust
belt' during the 1982–85 period. Even if temporary, currency appreciation
independent of changes in efficiency wages can have significant permanent
real costs as domestic industries abandon export markets and lose domestic market business to foreign firms and the resultant existing excess plant
and equipment is cast aside as too costly to maintain.

Proviso No. 7 also prevents any nation from engaging in a beggar-thy-
neighbor, export-thy-unemployment policy by pursuing a real exchange
rate devaluation that does not reflect changes in efficiency wages. Once the
initial exchange rates are chosen and relative efficiency wages are locked in,
reduction in real production costs which are associated with a relative
decline in efficiency wages is the main factor (with the exception of proviso No. 8) justifying an adjustment in the real exchange rate.

Although proviso No. 6 prevents any country from piling up persistent
excessive surpluses, this does not mean that it is impossible for one or more
nations to run persistent deficits. Consequently proposal No. 8 below provides a program for addressing the problem of persistent international
payment deficits in any one nation.

Eighth, if a country is at full employment and still has a tendency toward
persistent international deficits on its current account, then this is *prima
facie* evidence that it does not possess the productive capacity to maintain
its current standard of living. If the deficit nation is a poor one, then surely
there is a case for the richer nations who are in surplus to transfer some of
their excess credit balances to support the poor nation.[9] If the deficit nation
is a relatively rich country, then the deficit nation must alter its standard of
living by reducing its relative terms of trade with its major trading partners.
Rules, agreed upon in advance, would require the trade-deficit rich nation
to devalue its exchange rate by stipulated increments per period until evidence becomes available to indicate that the export–import imbalance is
eliminated without unleashing significant recessionary forces.

If, on the other hand, the payment deficit persists despite a continuous
positive balance of trade in goods and services, then there is evidence that
the deficit nation might be carrying too heavy an international debt service

obligation. The *pro bono* officials of the clearing union should bring the debtor and creditors into negotiations to reduce annual debt service payments by (a) lengthening the payments period, (b) reducing the interest charges, and/or (c) debt forgiveness.[10]

It should be noted that proviso No. 6 embodies Keynes's innovative idea that whenever there is a persistent (and/or large) imbalance in current account flows, whether due to capital flight or a persistent trade imbalance, there must be a built-in mechanism that induces the surplus nation(s) to bear a major responsibility for eliminating the imbalance. The surplus nation must accept this burden for it has the wherewithal to resolve the problem.

In the absence of proviso No. 6, under any conventional system, whether it has fixed or flexible exchange rates and/or capital controls, there will ultimately be an international liquidity crisis (as any persistent current account deficit can deplete a nation's foreign reserves) that unleashes global depressionary forces. Thus, proviso No. 6 is necessary to assure that the international payments system will not have a built-in depressionary bias. Ultimately then it is in the self-interest of the surplus nation to accept this responsibility, for its actions will create conditions for global economic expansion some of which must redound to its own residents. Failure to act, on the other hand, will promote global depressionary forces which will have some negative impact on its own residents.

14.2 ALTERNATIVE FINANCIAL ARCHITECTURAL PROPOSALS

Two other major alternative architectural proposals for an international payments system have been discussed in the economics literature. In the 1980s, Williamson introduced his target zone fixed equilibrium (real) exchange rate (FEER) system while McKinnon suggested a fixed nominal purchasing power parity (PPP) exchange rate system.[11] Both Williamson and McKinnon accept the argument that the existing flexible rate system is fundamentally flawed and therefore advocate a fixed exchange rate system. McKinnon notes the tremendous 'dissatisfaction with wildly fluctuating relative currency values, euphemistically called "floating" or "flexible" exchange rates'.[12] Williamson argues that the post-Bretton Woods flexible exchange rate system 'has proved unsatisfactory' for two major reasons. First, it has led to 'recurring, and at times massive, currency misalignments . . . [where a] misalignment is defined as a persistent deviation of the real exchange rate from the "fundamental equilibrium exchange rate" [or FEER], the level that can be expected in the medium term to reconcile internal and external balance'.[13] Second, according to Williamson, the flexible rate system fails to pressure nations 'to coordinate their economic policies'.[14]

Williamson and McKinnon offer different bases for determining what is the proper price at which to fix the exchange rate in their respective proposals. Williamson's FEER proposal recommends a 'target zone system' where 'a limited number of major countries negotiate a set of mutually consistent targets' for fixing the exchange rate (the FEER target) to maintain internal and external balance in the 'medium term'. Williamson defined internal balance as 'the lowest unemployment rate consistent with the control of inflation', without specifying what inflation rate and what unemployment rate is acceptable under this internal equilibrium concept. An internal balance implies that this unspecified 'acceptably low rate of inflation' should be associated 'with unemployment at the NAIRU' (non-accelerating inflation rate of unemployment).[15] External balance is defined as 'a current account balance that is sustainable and appropriate in light of thrift and productivity'.[16] Market exchange rates are permitted to fluctuate within a broad zone of plus or minus 10 per cent around the target FEER rate.[17] The zone around FEER is explicitly defined in terms of a 'soft buffer' where 'a country would not have an absolute obligation to prevent rates from straying outside the [±10%] zone under strong market pressures'.[18]

McKinnon recommends a system where the major central banks announce targeted fixed nominal exchange rates (within a narrow band) 'set at approximately sustainable purchasing power parities'. Once set, McKinnon claims that all that would be necessary would be for the major central banks to 'adjust their domestic money supplies to maintain these nominal exchange rate parities and, concomitantly, maintain the same rates of domestic price inflation in internationally tradeable goods'.[19]

14.3   CRITICISM OF WILLIAMSON'S FEER PROPOSAL

Williamson indicated that the target rate of growth of nominal income that is relevant for 'internal balance' is the inflation rate 'plus the growth of potential output'. A nation should either increase or decrease the target nominal output growth rate until the said internal balance is achieved. The target growth in nominal demand is endogenized to secure a 'soft landing' onto the presumed exogenous NAIRU and acceptable inflation rate for each nation. Unfortunately the inflation–unemployment rate experience of the United States since 1992 has, even in mainstream academic circles, discredited the notion of an exogenous NAIRU. Yet, Williamson has not proposed any alternative to NAIRU as part of his internal balance criteria. Accordingly, his internal balance criteria cannot be met.

Despite the obvious faults in the current flexible rate system, Williamson argues that flexible exchange rates have four distinct and important 'social functions' that are not possessed by a fixed rate system. These alleged advantages are (a) a *facilitating payments adjustment function* whenever export–import imbalances occur; (b) *a speculative pressures absorbing function* which prevents 'every change in speculative sentiment to lead to a change in international reserves and/or interest rates' which might harm the economy; (c) *a liberating monetary policy function* which permits nations to pursue different interest rate targets and (d) *a reconciling function* which harmonizes inflation rates among nations. The flexible market rate zone of plus or minus 10 per cent around the fixed FEER rate permits the Williamson proposal to capture the four social functions of a flexible system while providing the stability of a fixed exchange rate system.[20]

Unfortunately Williamson fails to provide any empirical evidence to demonstrate that these claimed 'social function' advantages of flexible rates have ever actually been achieved in the real world. Chapter 1's comparison of the historical experience of both the gold standard era and the Bretton Woods period *vis-à-vis* the existing flexible system indicates that

1. a flexible rate system has not made payment adjustments easier as the division between the international debtors and creditors has worsened since the 1970s;
2. to the extent that a flexible exchange rate system 'reconciles' differential rates of inflation it typically results in higher (correlated) rates of inflation in all nations compared to the experience under the gold standard and the Bretton Woods periods;
3. the post-1973 flexible rate system has forced the major G7 nations to deliberately and explicitly coordinate monetary and interest rate policy rather than being able to run independent monetary policies; and
4. at times the existing system has been unable to absorb speculative pressures. Instead, massive, coordinated action by major nations' central banks and the IMF to alleviate the speculative pressures on the exchange rate has often been required.

In other words, an objective reading of the empirical evidence does not support Williamson's assertion that a large zone around FEER is justified on the basis of the operative usefulness of these alleged social functions due to exchange rate flexibility.

Moreover, by quietly introducing two exceptions, Williamson surreptitiously admits the possibility that these alleged social functions of a flexible exchange rate system cannot be achieved in the real world. The first exception is that flexibility facilitates payments adjustment '*except* where disequilibrium [between exports and imports] is due purely to excess or deficient demand'.[21] In other words, Williamson's FEER proposal promotes a socially desirable payments adjustment only if all trading partners are already at a stable full employment equilibrium position. If, however, Williamson's target zones are chosen to induce sufficient unemployment to control inflation (as suggested in his use of the NAIRU concept in providing one criteria for internal equilibrium), then Williamson's proposed FEER system will always require a long-run deficiency in effective demand to assure that the nation's unemployment rate does not fall permanently below the presumed-to-exist NAIRU. In defining the target for internal equilibrium in terms of an acceptable NAIRU that requires significant domestic unemployment, Williamson introduces the exception that prevents the facilitating payments function that he claims is a benefit of flexibility in his broad 20 per cent FEER target exchange rate zone from being operative.

Williamson's second exception occurs in his warning that the alleged 'absorbing speculative pressures' function of a broad flexible exchange rate zone is applicable to the real world provided speculative '*changes do not lead to the prolonged and substantial movements away from equilibrium that constitutes misalignments*'.[22] It is gratifying to know that if speculative pressures are not prolonged and do not lead to substantial misalignments, then large flexible zones can absorb the resulting relatively insignificant problems thrown up by speculation. But, as McKinnon has demonstrated and Williamson has admitted, persistent and sometimes significant misalignments appear to be in the nature of the flexible system. Hence, one cannot expect Williamson's large target zones to serve a speculative absorbing function at those times when such a speculative absorbing facility is most needed.

Williamson's proposal by itself can generate significant disruptive speculative pressures since (a) targets are 'regularly updated in the light of new data on differential rates of inflation' and (b) each nation 'need not accept an absolute obligation to keep its exchange rate within the target zone'.[23] Finally Williamson admits that the wide zones are justified in part by 'skepticism as to our ability to calculate sensible exchange rate targets with any degree of accuracy'.[24] If Williamson and Miller as authors of a FEER zone cannot 'calculate sensible target zones with any degree of accuracy', how are policy makers to decide on the correct FEER zone?

Given these reservations regarding the correctness of any calculated

FEER target, McKinnon has noted Williamson's proposal 'which keeps open the option for occasional official adjustments in par values . . . remain[s] vulnerable to speculative attacks'.[25]

14.4   CRITICISM OF MCKINNON'S PPP PROPOSAL

McKinnon claims that his proposal for setting nominal targets at approximate sustainable purchasing power parities would force central banks to gear their monetary policies to produce 'roughly the same rates of domestic price inflation in internationally tradable goods'.[26] Underlying McKinnon's analysis is the belief in that the quantity theory of money is applicable to real entrepreneurial economies. Milton Friedman has stated that

> [T]he quantity theory presumption . . . [is] that changes in the quantity of money as such *in the long run* have a negligible effect on real income, so that nonmonetary forces are 'all that matter' for changes in real income over decades and 'money does not matter'. On the other hand, we have regarded the quantity of money . . . as essentially 'all that matters' for the long run of nominal income.[27]

In other words, the quantity theory, and therefore McKinnon's proposal, requires the acceptance of the neutral money axiom as an article of faith. If money is neutral, then the price level of producible goods is a joint outcome of the monetary forces which solely determine nominal income and the real forces which are presumed to be the only determinants of real income. McKinnon's analysis and recommendations are conditional on the money neutrality presumption that changes in the quantity of money have *no effect* on real output, employment, or economic growth for the 'indefinite future'. It is only because of this neutral money assumption that McKinnon can argue that once these PPP rates are fixed there would be no need ever to change them as long as each nation followed the rules, even if short-run real disturbances were to occur. Monetary policy to maintain the PPP nominal rate, McKinnon assures us, will prevent any real shock from altering the full employment level of real output.[28] This claimed result of the PPP system preventing any real shock from affecting the full employment output is nothing more than a reflection of McKinnon's unquestioned acceptance of the neutral money axiom. In other words, McKinnon is really assuming what he claims to be proving.

If, however, money is not neutral, as Keynes argued and most macro economists including Friedman admit (at least in the short run),[29] then McKinnon's proposals would not provide the smooth adjusting mechanism that he describes, except perhaps in the long run, when 'we are all dead'.

14.5   A COMPARISON OF THE THREE ARCHITECTURAL PROPOSALS

The Williamson, McKinnon and Post Keynesian proposals all recommend fixing exchange rates, but the basis of the fix differs.

Williamson would have central bankers negotiate a set of *real* exchange rates based on the amorphous idea of maintaining simultaneous internal and external equilibrium. But even Williamson admits such equilibrium notions 'involve an element of subjective judgment and will therefore permit obfuscation'.[30] Nevertheless, the target exchange rate (FEER) is defined with apparent concreteness as that 'rate which is expected to generate a current account surplus or deficit equal to the underlying capital flow over the cycle'.[31] Despite this apparent specificity, the target is still idiosyncratic since the calculated FEER depends upon what the authorities believe is the current account surplus or deficit that financial free markets are willing to fund over some nonspecific future calendar time labeled either the 'cycle' or the 'medium run'. Each year (and perhaps sooner) the FEER might be updated upon the fancy of the authorities[32] in the light of unspecified 'major changes' in expected international net capital flows. Moreover, Williamson admits that there needs to be sufficient flexibility 'to allow for derogation from normal rules when circumstances warrant'.[33] Anytime enough speculators believe they can beat the authorities in recognizing 'the light of major changes' or circumstances warrant 'a derogation from normal rules', excessive speculation will occur.

McKinnon would have the initial *nominal* rates 'set to approximate sustainable purchasing power parities' and announced to be 'fixed into the indefinite future'.[34] Unless money is neutral in both the short and the long runs, however, the claimed benefits of McKinnon's PPP architectural proposal cannot be shown to occur.

In contrast to both Williamson and McKinnon, the Keynes–Post Keynesian proposal would start by searching for neither the Holy Grail of FEER, nor the correct PPP. Instead, the system would start with the existing nominal exchange rate parities in order not to disrupt existing trade relations (for example, money contracts, ongoing real investments) merely to start up a new system. Since both the Williamson and McKinnon proposals envision significant changes in the existing exchange rate at the date of conversion to the new system,[35] both proposals involve potentially large real start-up costs. Since the Keynes–Post Keynesian proposal accepts the existing rate structure, no additional start-up costs would be incurred.

Under what conditions should the fixed rate target be changed? In essence, Williamson indicates that the FEER rates would not change as long as the authorities used coordinated interest rate policy to 'manage the exchange rate'. The targets, however, 'should be regularly updated in the light of new data on differential inflation between countries . . . [and] real shocks or new information'.[36] Accordingly, changes are permitted whenever the governmental authorities (or their econometricians[37]) think conditions warrant a change. No discipline is imposed on the authorities to adopt policies either to control inflation differentials or otherwise to cushion the economy against real shocks. Instead the Williamson plan encourages politicians to take the easy way out by changing the target exchange rate. If they do so they may either unleash speculative excesses, and/or depress aggregate demand, and/or adopt beggaring-thy-neighbor policies because of their subjective judgments on the correct target.

In fact, in the Williamson plan, if a nation was to experience an acceleration in core inflation, it is not necessary to change the exchange rate. Instead it may be appropriate to increase the target rate of unemployment. If such policies are pursued simultaneously by several large trading partners, the result can be global depression.

Implicit in the FEER plan is the belief that any exogenous real shocks produce only short-run movements away from the immutable equilibrium position. The idea that authorities should develop real targets is based on a fundamental belief that either there exists an ahistoric, immutable steady-state macro equilibrium that assures stable (medium run? over the cycle?) normal capital flows, FEERs and NAIRUs for each country, independent of the policy decisions that the authorities take to converge to this long-run equilibrium. If this is true, then, in a free market environment, the system will always revert to this equilibrium. Williamson is merely impatient with the speed upon which the free market reaches the assumed-to-exist preprogrammed equilibrium. According to Williamson and Miller, the economy, prodded by intelligent authorities, will show a greater 'speed of convergence' than the 'automatic pilot' of a free [38] marketplace. It is not clear why Williamson and Miller believe that their authorities will establish the correct FEERs quicker than the free market can. Moreover, if the necessary immutable preprogrammed equilibrium does not exist, then both the free market and Williamson and Miller's intelligent authorities may be searching for a nonexistent Holy Grail, observed only in the daydreams of classical international macro economists.

Arrow and Hahn[39] have demonstrated that if contracts are made in terms of money, then there need *not exist* any set of prices and exchange rates that assures a general equilibrium which assures, in an open system, the exact balancing of exports, imports and international payment flows. In the context of Williamson's target proposal, This means that as long as international trade is conducted by the use of money contractual agreements, then it is not logically possible to prove that there will be any set of exchange rates that will assure a current account balance for all nations. Nor can it be proven that there exists a set of exchange rates that assures a natural rate of unemployment in all nations. It may be impossible for central banks to negotiate the FEER that achieves the simultaneous equilibrium targets that Williamson has set for them.

Williamson does not discuss this possibility. Williamson merely assumes that there exists an equilibrium set of interest rates, exchange rates and domestic prices in each country that can be found by negotiation of central banks to assure the achievement of simultaneous internal and external equilibrium.

Because he unquestionably accepts the neutral money axiom, McKinnon argues that there is never a need for the authority to change the initial PPP rate provided they follow the rules he suggests. In the McKinnon proposal, it is presumed that efficiency wages and real wealth transfers due to trade imbalances will adjust to the nominal anchor of fixed PPP rates.

In contrast to McKinnon's claim that a once-and-for-all fixing of exchange rates is all that is required, Williamson claims that the FEER target should be changed every time there is new data on differential inflation rates among nations or changed expectations by policy makers on net normal international capital flows. The Keynes–Post Keynesian architectural proposal, on the other hand, provides specific criteria to indicate when, and if, there should be a change in nominal exchange rates. These changes should primarily reflect relative changes in the real costs of production among trading partners and/or prevent domestic inflation in efficiency wages from spilling over to other nations. Under specific circumstances, exchange rate changes also will be made to alter the terms of trade against nations who are living beyond their *full employment level of real income*. Moreover, the analysis presumes than any 'natural rate of unemployment' which requires those who are willing, and competent, to work at the going wage to be unemployed in order to control inflation is neither natural nor a desirable target for policy.[40]

What about speculative pressures? Since a nation can exercise capital controls under the Keynes–Post Keynesian proposal, any speculative pressures can be shut down – as long as there is cooperation among trading partners and law-abiding residents in the various nations. Williamson's scheme, on the other hand, is vulnerable to speculative excesses that can defeat the whole purpose of his proposal. McKinnon assumes away speculative pressures by asserting that as long as market traders *believe* the authorities will keep the rates unchanged without imposing any regulations on international financial flows, there can be no reason to speculate. McKinnon does not deal with the case where traders begin to doubt either the authorities' ability or their will.

What about trade imbalances? In McKinnon's fixed exchange rate scheme, trade deficits or surpluses could continually develop 'depending on relative national imbalances between savings and investments'.[41] Those nations where *ex post* savings exceed domestic investment (assuming no government deficit) must, by definition, generate trade surpluses, and vice versa for nations with trade deficits. Nevertheless, according to McKinnon, there is no need for either trading partner to initiate an adjustment process to this trade imbalance. Adopting a variant of the classical specie-flow adjustment mechanism McKinnon claims that all that is required is a net transfer of real capital from the deficit to the surplus trading partner. This transfer is accomplished by normal market processes as the hypothesized relative expansion of bank money in the deficit nation results only in a price increase of nontradables (relative to tradables) in the trade-deficit nation. The oversaving (surplus) nation experiences 'a slower increase in . . . nontradables prices'.[42]

If money is presumed neutral, there can be no change in the level of employment in the deficit (or the surplus) nation due solely to the alleged greater expansion (contraction) of bank credit money supply. Since the price of tradables is, by hypothesis, kept in line in each nation through foreign competition and a PPP exchange rate, then the alleged relative rise in the money supply in the deficit nation can only induce a rise in the price of nontradables (and vice versa for the surplus nation). This differential sectoral inflation rate, within a coordinated common aggregate inflation rate among the trading partners, is the hypothesized McKinnon mechanism for transferring real wealth from the nation suffering from the deficit to the surplus nation.

McKinnon claims, but does not prove, that '[a]lthough these relative price movements within both countries would be modest, gradual, and need not be permanent, they would be sufficient to support the transfer of savings from one highly open economy to another'.[43]

This wealth transfer would continue until the rising real wealth of the surplus nation stimulates a sufficient increase in its demand for imports while the declining real wealth of the deficit nation induces a sufficient reduction in its demand for imports to bring about a trade balance. Although the surplus nation becomes richer and the deficit nation poorer because of this hypothesized wealth transfer induced by differential rates of money growth between the trading partners, global economic growth is unaffected as long as one accepts the neutral money axiom. By presumption, therefore, no aggregate real economic losses occur as nations adjust to trade imbalances in the McKinnon analysis.

In the absence of money neutrality, however, one cannot demonstrate that the McKinnon proposal will resolve the problem of payment imbalances without imposing *real* deflationary consequences on all trading partners – at least in the short run in which we live. To his credit, however, McKinnon does at least recognize that in his PPP system trade deficits can continually occur because of differential rates of savings, real income growth and so on. Most orthodox theorists claim that all trade imbalances will be completely extinguished by free market processes.

Williamson's scheme would permit continuous current account deficits that are consistent with the 'underlying capital flow over the cycle'. Although Williamson and Miller admit the difficulty in estimating, or even defining 'normal' net capital flows, they believe that ratios such as external debt to either GNP or exports puts 'a limit on the size of acceptable current account deficits in the medium term'. They conclude that 'admittedly there is no formula that permits translation of such [a ratio] criteria into an objective number for the flow of capital'; nevertheless they still encourage 'guesstimates' for possible target ratios, apparently hoping wide zones compensate for the possibility of wild guesstimates.[44]

14.6   WHAT IF?

If we presume the possibility of a nonneutral monetary system in any run, except the long run when we are all dead, then one can raise the following 'what if' queries. What if the only possible negotiated targets that can achieve a current account balance were to result in a global Great Depression? Would Williamson still recommend his target zone scheme? How much (medium-term) unemployment would Williamson find acceptable to achieve current account balance under his scheme? If Williamson insists on his plan, even if the 'lowest rate of unemployment' compatible with his proposal involves massive layoffs and a stagnating or declining world economy, why should the FEER proposal be accepted as an improvement over the current system? If his response is 'In our paradigm, the output and inflation paths are pinned down by the requirement for internal balance'[45] and this hypothetical path is secured by the assumption of a neutral money and a NAIRU which is 'natural', then Williamson has solved the problem by assumption and definition.

Both McKinnon and Williamson merely assume that their respective recommendations, in an otherwise *laissez-faire* system, will produce (almost) a natural rate of full employment growth without (significant) inflation. In Williamson's analysis, full employment without significant inflation translates into an achievable and acceptable (to whom?) level of unemployment or NAIRU which does not change as the authorities try to attain NAIRU. If inflation starts off above an acceptable level, unemployment must be pushed up to a NAIRU level sufficient to achieve a decline in the inflation rate.

McKinnon does not prove that his proposals will assure full employment without inflation any more than adopting Williamson's target zone proposals will achieve a NAIRU that does not imply either significant unemployment rates and/or high (but not accelerating) rates of inflation. The objectives of either the Williamson or McKinnon architectural proposals are achieved by the assumptions underlying their analytical models. Both McKinnon and Williamson merely assume that a global general equilibrium exists and is readily achievable. They do not, and logically cannot, demonstrate the existence of such an equilibrium.

The empirical evidence suggests that it is prudent to design an international payments system that if, or when, circumstances tend to cause global depressions and/or inflations, there is a stand-by institutional arrangement available to offset these depressing and/or inflating forces and possibly even prevent these forces from developing. The rules of the entrepreneurial system should encourage an environment conducive to global real economic growth no matter what the differences are in incomes and propensities to save and invest of the trading partners in an interdependent economic community.

McKinnon has argued that Williamson's claim that flexibility provides a facilitating payments adjustment function is 'a false economic doctrine' since trade balances are more a response to 'pervasive macroeconomic repercussions', that is, the export import balance depends primarily on income elasticities and income effects, than on price elasticities and substitution effects.[46] McKinnon argues that a trade imbalance can persist because of different income elasticities for imports and exports. Keynes and the Post Keynesians would agree with McKinnon in this contention. This Post Keynesian argument has been discussed in Chapter 9 under the label of Thirlwall's Law.[47] Nevertheless, McKinnon implicitly believes that persistent trade imbalances due to differences in income elasticities and so on will not create any global depressionary problem. McKinnon's neutrality of money presumption solves this Thirlwall's Law problem by assuming it away. Implicit in the McKinnon argument is the belief that

1. these income elasticity differentials among nations will always be harmonized to assure global real economic growth and fully employed resources, and
2. trade payment imbalances *per se* can never unleash global depressionary forces, at least as long as participants in a free market do not doubt that the exchange rates parities are fixed for the indefinite future. Neither empirical evidence nor theory applicable to an entrepreneurial

economy (that is, theory that does not require the neutrality of money) justifies McKinnon's sanguine approach.

What if the configuration of income elasticities for imports and exports is such as to condemn the poorest nations of the world to a continual lowering of their relative (and possibly their absolute) standard of living as the evidence since 1973 suggests? Would McKinnon continue to recommend his plan?

What if the global economy experiences concurrent trade imbalances and a severe recession at the same time. Should the world's economic fate be left to private market arbitrage to correct these real disturbances which can impose severe economic losses and distortions? Or should the architecture of the system have already built-in the best stand-by institutional mechanism human ingenuity can devise to alleviate the possible economic distress and to promote rapid economic recovery? If, one adopts the McKinnon view, then one must believe, as President Hoover did during the Great Depression that, even in the darkest of times, prosperity is just around the corner. If one adopts the Keynes–Post Keynesian view, on the other hand, depressions and/or inflationary episodes are not inevitable. The entrepreneurial system can be redesigned to avoid great depressions and inflations that inflict lasting economic woes on great segments of the population.

Finally, it should be noted that neither Williamson nor McKinnon has a plan to assure a long-run stable standard of international value. McKinnon argues that if foreign exchange traders believe that governments will fix nominal rates 'into the indefinite future' then commodity arbitrage plus mutual monetary adjustments assures conversion to 'the same rate of commodity'[47] price inflation. 'Although McKinnon indicates that the conversion inflation rate is preferably zero', there is nothing in his system that assures that the conversion inflation rate could not be significantly different from zero.[48] If the convergence rate of inflation exceeds zero, there will be no long-run stable international standard of value in the McKinnon system. Under provision #7 of the Keynes–Post Keynesian proposal, on the other hand, the IMCU would provide its holders with an invariant international standard no matter whether the domestic rates of inflation in the various nations converged (or did not converge).

By implicitly invoking the theoretical 'law of one price', McKinnon argues that private sector free market arbitrage involving standardized tradable commodities assure that the derived demand for labor and therefore money-wages 'would eventually reflect differentials in productivity growth',[49] so that relative efficiency wages would, in the long run, be fixed.

The Keynes–Post Keynesian proposal, on the other hand, does not rely on the definitionally true, but inane, 'law of one price'[50] to assure the long-run alignment of relative efficiency wages among trading partners. Instead our proposal builds such a requirement directly into its operation.

Unfortunately, McKinnon's plan, like Williamson's, does not explain how one would deal with potentially disruptive forces if they arise. Would McKinnon still advocate his plan if social and political actions caused wages to rise more rapidly than productivity even as the nation faced a trade deficit? Under McKinnon's proposal where all inflationary rates would tend to converge, if political and social powers forced wages to rise more rapidly than productivity in any major trading partner, the effect must be to force a convergence towards a common higher inflation rate, *unless* additional depressing pressures are applied to weaken workers' wage demands. And would not the resulting increase in unemployment lower import demands and therefore have spillover consequences to the trading partners?

Accordingly, would McKinnon advocate his proposal if severe and pro-longed unemployment and business losses were the necessary requirement for any nation (or group of nations, or even world economy) to make the necessary adjustments to bring about a current account balance and an approximate zero rate of inflation?

Finally, neither the Williamson nor the McKinnon proposal addresses the plight of the less-developed countries (LDCs) in recent decades. In fact, as we have already argued, trade imbalances due to differing income elasticities may push poor deficit LDCs into increasing poverty. The Keynes–Post Keynesian system is specifically designed to foster behavior by the richer members of the global community (a) to assure that poorer nations are provided with sufficient international effective demand to fully employ their labor force and facilities and (b) to encourage grants and direct foreign investment from the surplus nations of the world to facilitate more rapid economic growth in the LDCs.

14.7 CONCLUSION

Some, for example, Williamson,[51] think that the Post Keynesian specific clearing union plan, like Keynes's bancor plan a half century earlier, is Utopian. But no progress will be made unless we rethink and reform the entire international payments system. Global depression does not have to happen again if our policy makers have sufficient vision to develop this Post Keynesian approach. The health of the world's economic system will simply not permit us to muddle through.

NOTES

1. This does not deny that some groups of nations have created a supranational central bank and currency, for example, the euro. Under the plan suggested in this chapter, nations would be free to develop their own regional supranational bank and clearing mechanism that would operate as a single unit in the larger global clearing union proposed below.
2. Correspondent banking will have to operate through the International Clearing Agency, with each central bank regulating the international relations and operations of its domestic banking firms.

   Small-scale smuggling of currency across borders and so on, can never be completely eliminated. But such movements are merely a flea on a dog's back – a minor, but not debilitating, irritation. If, however, most of the residents of a nation hold and use (in violation of legal tender laws) a foreign currency for domestic transactions and as a store of value (for example, it is estimated that Argentineans hold close to US$5 billion), this is evidence of a lack of confidence in the government and its monetary authority. Unless confidence is restored, all attempts to restore economic prosperity will fail.
3. M. Mayer, 'The Asian disease: plausible diagnoses, possible remedies', Levy Institute Public Policy Brief No. 44, Annandale-on-Hudson 1998, pp. 29–30.
4. Ibid., p.31.
5. Some may fear that if a surplus nation is close to the trigger point it could short circuit the system by making loans to reduce its credit balance *prior* to setting off the trigger. Since preventing unreasonable debt service obligations is an important objective of this proposal, a mechanism which monitors and can restrict such pretrigger lending activities may be required.

   One possible way of eliminating this trigger avoidance lending loophole is as follows: an initial agreement as to what constitutes sensible and flexible criteria for judging when debt-servicing burdens become unreasonable is established. Given these criteria, the clearing union managers would have the responsibility for preventing additional loans which push debt burdens beyond reasonable servicing levels. In other words, loans that push debt burdens too far, could not be cleared though the clearing union, that is, the managers would refuse to release the IMCUs for loan purposes from the surplus country's account. (I am indebted to Robert Blecker for suggesting this point.)

   The managers would also be required to make periodic public reports on the level of credits being accumulated by surplus nations and to indicate how close these surpluses are to the trigger point. Such reports would provide an informational edge for debtor nations, permitting them to bargain more successively regarding the terms of refinancing existing loans and/or new loans. All loans would still have to meet the clearing union's guidelines for reasonableness.

   I do not discount the difficulties involved in setting up and getting agreement on criteria for establishing unreasonable debt-service burdens. (For some suggestions, however, see the second paragraph of provision No. 8.) In the absence of cooperation and a spirit of goodwill that is necessary for the clearing union to provide a mechanism assuring the economic prosperity of all members, however, no progress can ever be made.

   Moreover, as the current international debt problem of African and Latin American nations clearly demonstrates, creditors ultimately have to forgive some debt when they previously encouraged excessive debt burdens. Under the current system, however, debt forgiveness is a last-resort solution acceptable only after both debtor and creditor nations suffer from faltering economic growth. Surely a more intelligent option is to develop an institutional arrangement which prevents excessive debt-servicing burdens from ever occurring.
6. Oversaving is defined as a nation persistently spending less on imports plus direct equity foreign investment than the nation's export earnings plus net unilateral transfers.
7. Whatever 'excessive' credit balances that are redistributed will be apportioned among the debtor nations (perhaps based on a formula which is inversely related to each debtor's

per capita income and directly related to the size of its international debt) to be used to reduce debit balances at the clearing union.

8. The efficiency wage is related to the money-wage divided by the average product of labor; it is the unit labor cost modified by the profit mark-up in domestic money terms of domestically produced GDP. At the preliminary stage of this proposal, it would serve no useful purpose to decide whether the domestic market basket should include both tradable and nontradable goods and services. (With the growth of tourism more and more nontradable goods become potentially tradable.) I personally prefer the wider concept of the domestic market basket, but it is not obvious that any essential principle is lost if a tradable only concept is used, or if some nations use the wider concept while others the narrower one.

9. This is equivalent to a negative income tax for poor fully employed families within a nation. (See P. Davidson, 'A modest set of proposals for solving the international debt crisis', *Journal of Post Keynesian Economics*, **10**, 1987–88, pp. 323–38 for further development of this argument.)

10. The actual program adopted for debt-service reduction will depend on many parameters including: the relative income and wealth of the debtor *vis-à-vis* the creditor, the ability of the debtor to increase its per capita real income and so on.

11. For example see R.T. McKinnon, 'Monetary and exchange rate policies for international financial stability', *Journal of Economic Perspectives*, **2**, 1988, pp. 83–103; R.T. McKinnon, 'Interest rate volatility and exchange rate risk', *Contemporary Policy Studies*, **8**, April 1990, pp. 1–17; J. Williamson, 'Exchange rate management: the role of target zones', *American Economic Review Papers and Proceedings*, **77**, May 1987, pp. 202–204; J. Williamson and M.H. Miller, *Targets and Indicators: A Blueprint for International Coordination of Economic Policies*, Institute for International Economics, Washington, DC, 1987; J. Williamson, 'On designing an international monetary system', *Journal of Post Keynesian Economics*, **15**, Winter 1992–93, pp. 81–92.

12. McKinnon, 1988, p. 87.
13. Williamson, 1987, p. 202.
14. Ibid., p. 200.
15. Williamson and Miller, 1987, p. 9.
16. Williamson, 1987, p. 202.
17. Ibid., p. 202.
18. Williamson and Miller, 1987, p. 12.
19. McKinnon, 1988, p. 87.
20. Williamson, 1987, pp. 201–3.
21. Ibid., p. 201, italics added.
22. Ibid., pp. 201–2, italics added.
23. Ibid., p. 202.
24. Williamson and Miller, 1987, p. 12.
25. McKinnon, 1988, p. 100.
26. Ibid., p. 87.
27. M. Friedman, 'A theoretical framework for monetary analysis', in *Milton Friedman's Monetary Framework: A Debate With His Critics*, edited by R.J. Gordon, University of Chicago Press, Chicago, 1974, p. 27.
28. McKinnon, 1988, pp. 87–8.
29. Friedman, 1974, p. 27.
30. Williamson, 1987, p. 202.
31. Williamson and Miller, 1987, p. 10.
32. In fact, the FEER targets initially estimated by Williamson and Miller (1987, p. 73) 'were based on calculations with current account targets for the years 1976–1977 and . . . then [subjectively] updated in the light of major changes in the world economy'. They admit that 'no systematic effort' was made in their updating the calculated FEER for each nation. They promise a more systematic method of updating 'in subsequent work' but they have not provided one. If their method for initially estimating the FEER targets is illustrative of how FEERs that are compatible with normal capital flows over the cycle

should be done, then, apparently, an acceptable working hypothesis for empirically establishing the normal capital flow requires only a two-year history (1976–77) to establish a benchmark.

Moreover, what FEER should be calculated initially? Can one estimate a benchmark 'normal' capital flow from observations occurring during the current flexible rate regime which both Williamson and McKinnon argue are fundamentally flawed? If not, then the initial FEER target depends on what some bureaucrats, either without any data, or with flawed data from the current regime, assume is the correct FEER. If their initial target is in error, then they will have to make significant adjustments in future periods. If the public knows that adjustments will be made, then the FEER plan is subject to the possibility of excessive speculative movements.

33. Williamson and Miller, 1987, p. 19.
34. McKinnon, 1988, p. 93.
35. If significant change was not envisioned, this would imply that the existing system already had established the 'correct' exchange rate.
36. J. Williamson, 'Exchange rate management: the role of target zones', *American Economic Review Papers and Proceedings*, 77, May 1987, p. 202.
37. Williamson thinks it is merely a 'technical exercise' to determine the set of exchange rates which simultaneously produce internal and external equilibrium.
38. Williamson and Miller, 1987, p. 50.
39. K. Arrow and F.H. Hahn, *General Competitive Equilibrium*, Holden-Day, San Francisco, 1971, p. 361.
40. Those employed economists who advocate a natural rate of unemployment target should be required to give their weekly paycheck to one of the naturally unemployed in exchange for whatever compensation the latter receives while remaining unemployed.
41. McKinnon, 1988, p. 98.
42. Ibid., pp. 98–9.
43. Ibid., p. 99.
44. Williamson and Miller, 1987, pp. 58–9.
45. Ibid., p. 57.
46. McKinnon, 1988, p. 94.
47. R. McKinnon, 'Monetary and exchange rate policies for international financial stability: a proposal', *Journal of Economic Perspectives*, 2, 1988, p. 100.
48. For a further discussion, see A.P. Thirlwall, 'The balance of payments constraint as an explanation of international growth rate differentials', *Banco Nazionale del Lavoro Quarterly Review*, 129, 1979, pp. 45–73, and P. Davidson, Winter 1990–91.
49. McKinnon, 1988, p. 97.
50. This law lacks substance because if any two units of a commodity are associated with different prices, then, by definition, they are different commodities. Accordingly, relying on arbitrage to maintain purchasing power parity over time defines away the problem. If apples on Friday do not have the same price as they had on Monday, then, according to neoclassical economic theory, Friday's apples are a different commodity. There is no change in PPP when different commodities have different prices.
51. J. Williamson, 'On designing an international monetary system', *Journal of Post Keynesian Economics*, 15, pp. 88–9.

15. The economy and the twenty-first century

As this book is being written, the global economy is teetering on the worst global recession since the Great Depression of the 1930s. The terrorist attacks on the World Trade Center on September 11, 2001 were not only an attack on the American way of life, but were also a severe blow to the entire financial capitalist world. The only question that remains is will the major capitalist economies again try to muddle through with the hope that a *laissez-faire* market system is the best of all possible worlds in this worst of times or will we use this troubled time to rebuild and strengthen the financial capitalist system that is the best hope for a civilized global community that humankind has been able to devise.

15.1 THE POSITIVE ROLE OF GOVERNMENT

In Chapter 1, we listed five key points that can be extracted from Keynes's vision of the capitalist system. In the almost 70 years since Keynes wrote we still find that the outstanding faults of the economic system in which we live are its failure to provide a job for everyone willing and able to work and its arbitrary and very inequitable distribution of income and wealth both nationally and globally. Moreover in recent decades, the mainstream of the economics profession has promoted this persistent unemployment flaw to a positive virtue in its concept of a non-accelerating inflation rate of unemployment (NAIRU) instead of labeling unemployment for what it is – a social waste and public disgrace. Positive actions and innovative institutions can be developed to prevent any significant, persistent unemployment from occurring in an open multinational economic system.

Current mainstream economic analysis has supported policy decisions that pay homage to the need to maintain a 'natural rate of unemployment' that economically penalizes the less fortunate in our community. The purpose of this volume has been to encourage a movement in theory and policy toward an entrepreneurial, market-oriented economy where all who want to work can be gainfully employed. Providing a full employment society is also bound to improve the existing distribution of income and wealth. If, after assuring a perpetuating full employment economy, the resulting distribution of income is still found to be socially too inequitable, then there will be resources available to further modify the full employment distribution of income toward a more socially desirable equitable standard. Of course this does not mean that there must be a complete equality of income and wealth.

> There are valuable human activities which require the motive of money-making and the environment of private wealth ownership. Moreover, dangerous human proclivities can be canalised into comparatively harmless channels by the existence of opportunities for money-making and private wealth, which, if they cannot be satisfied in this way, may find their outlet in cruelty, the reckless pursuit of personal power and authority, and other forms of self-aggrandisement. It is better for a man to tyrannise over his bank balance than over his fellow-citizens; and whilst the former is sometimes denounced as being a means to the latter, sometimes at least it is an alternative. But it is not necessary for the stimulation of these activities and the satisfaction of these proclivities that the game be played for such high stakes as at present. Much lower stakes will serve the purpose equally well, as soon as the players are accustomed to them. The task of transmuting human nature must not be confused with the task of managing it.[1]

Just as there is a need for government to take a positive leadership role in defending the community against terrorist attacks that threaten the very foundation of the degree of civilization that we have already reached, so there is a need for government to defend the economy from fast exit liquidity attacks that threaten the viability of the entrepreneurial system. This will require central bankers to understand that their primary function is to provide all the liquidity that the community requires both for financing and funding investment projects and for providing a security blanket for savers under Keynes's banking principle. Just as war is too important to be left to the generals alone, so, in a civilized society, the fight against inflation cannot be left to independent central bankers.[2] Since domestic inflation is a symptom of a fight over the distribution of income, the government, in its role of the protector of the economic peace, will have to restrain the domestic combatants in this battle via an incomes policy that is compatible with the political and cultural ethics of the nation.[3]

After the central bank has provided all the liquidity that the community wants at a nominal interest rate that is as low as possible (close to zero), if there is still significant unemployment in the system, then the government should undertake running a capital account deficit to employ the otherwise idle resources to produce, with the cooperation of private entrepreneurial initiative where possible, productive facilities to provide additional economic comfort to the residents of the nation.

In an open economy context, the government of nations should join together in a clearing union, similar to the one advocated in Chapter 14 that resolved international liquidity problems in a manner that provides an expansionist bias to international transactions, rather than the contractionist bias of the current 'liberalized' international payments system.

A slight paraphrasing of Reinhold Neibuhr's famous 'serenity prayer' might well be the moral of this volume: God give us the grace to accept with serenity those things in an entrepreneurial economy that cannot be changed, courage to change the economic institutions which must be changed to promote possibilities for a civilized society, and the wisdom to distinguish the one from the other.

NOTES

1. J.M. Keynes, *The General Theory of Employment, Interest and Money*, Harcourt, Brace, New York, 1936, p. 374.
2. The call for an 'independent' central bank by proponents of the quantify theory of money is an implicit recognition that 'tight' money policies can be effective in constraining inflation only by inflicting politically (and socially) unacceptable severe economic damage to some workers and enterprises in a nation. For orthodox economists, 'independence' is merely a euphemism for permitting unnecessary and damaging economic costs to be inflicted on those with the least ability to defend themselves in order to enhance the economic condition of those who are likely to be the wealthiest in the community. (For a discussion of inflation and incomes policies, see P. Davidson, *Post Keynesian Macroeconomic Theory*, Edward Elgar, Cheltenham, 1994, Ch. 9.)
3. For a discussion of incomes policies, see ibid., Ch. 9 and G. Davidson and P. Davidson, *Economics For A Civilized Society*, 2nd edn, Macmillan, London, 1996, Ch. 9.

Index